PASSPORT TO MURDER

TRUE STORIES OF FOREIGNERS KILLED IN IRELAND

PASSPORT TO MURDER

TRUE STORIES OF
FOREIGNERS KILLED IN
IRELAND

ALI BRACKEN

Gill & Macmillan

Gill & Macmillan Ltd
Hume Avenue, Park West, Dublin 12
with associated companies throughout the world
www.gillmacmillan.ie

© Ali Bracken 2010
978 07171 4772 4

Typography design by Make Communication
Print origination by TypeIT, Dublin
Printed in the UK by JF Print Ltd, Somerset

This book is typeset in Minion 10pt on 12.5pt.

The paper used in this book comes from the wood pulp of
managed forests. For every tree felled, at least one tree is
planted, thereby renewing natural resources.

A CIP catalogue record for this book is available from the
British Library.

5 4 3 2 1

CONTENTS

ACKNOWLEDGMENTS

Firstly and most importantly, heartfelt thanks to all the families of foreigners whose deaths are detailed in this book who gave up their time to share their memories of their loved ones.

A special thanks to the many members of An Garda Síochána who spoke to me in detail about how they investigated the murders. This book would not have been possible without the co-operation of gardaí. Thanks also to the Police Service of Northern Ireland (PSNI) who gave up their time to meet with me on several occasions.

Thanks to all my friends and colleagues at the *Sunday Tribune*. In particular, the *Tribune*'s Security Editor, Mick McCaffrey, provided invaluable advice from his experience with writing true crime books. The *Tribune*'s picture editor, Maureen Gillespie, and photographer Mark Condren also kindly provided photos at short notice. An extra special thank you to *Irish Daily Star Sunday*'s Ken Foy, for his help when I was researching this book.

My friends and family have been very supportive. Thanks to my mother, father, brother and sister. My sister, Claire Bracken, proof-read every chapter and her feedback is deeply appreciated. Thanks to all the staff at Gill & Macmillan, particularly Publishing Director Fergal Tobin.

Finally, thanks to my boyfriend, Chris O'Driscoll, for all his love and support, and for making me endless cups of tea when I felt as though I would never finish writing this book.

Ali Bracken

INTRODUCTION

It is a fact that the Irish media does not show as much interest in the murder of a foreigner as it does in the murder of an Irish person. While there have been some high-profile killings of non-Irish nationals in Ireland, in the main the deaths of many foreigners who have been murdered here have passed under the radar. Indeed, many well-known killings of foreigners in Ireland have only achieved notoriety because of the involvement of an Irish person in their death. This book seeks to counter this by examining in depth the murders of 22 foreigners across the island of Ireland. With interviews of many of the families of the murdered men and women, as well as confidential information from An Garda Síochána and the Police Service of Northern Ireland (PSNI), this book attempts to tell the human stories behind the headlines in each tragic case.

The birth of the Celtic Tiger in the late 1990s changed the demographics of the country beyond recognition. Ireland's robust economy made headlines around the world and there was a massive surge in the number of asylum seekers arriving in Ireland. There was also a steady increase in the number of economic migrants, particularly after 2004, when Ireland opened its doors to ten new EU member states, resulting in a massive influx of job seekers.

To put the situation in context, in the first three years of the 1990s only 160 people applied to the Irish authorities for asylum. But in 2002, the average was almost 1,000 people per month. But as Ireland tightened its immigration policy, as well as the impact from the global recession, the numbers of people seeking asylum gradually went into steady decline. Just 2,689 people sought asylum here in 2009. Economic migrants also began to leave in their droves in 2009. The good times simply didn't last. Within the space of six months, hundreds of thousands of jobs were lost, especially in the construction sector, where many Eastern Europeans had secured employment.

Ireland transformed at the turn of the century from a country inhabited predominantly by an indigenous population to a multi-culturally diverse nation. This marked a difficult period of social change. Some Irish people struggled to cope with the many new communities establishing themselves all over the country. Misconceptions abounded because the government failed to put in place policies that would help garner mutual cultural understanding between the Irish population and the new communities. The non-Irish nationals attempting to settle into life in a new environment encountered a range of problems. Issues like racism, poverty, access to education and the development of ghettoised communities because of bad planning soon emerged. It didn't take long for some of these festering problems, particularly as a result of isolation and loneliness, to result in violence and death.

This book looks both at the murder of foreigners in Ireland by other non-Irish nationals as well as killings of foreigners by Irish people. For the families of those left behind, the nationality of the person who killed their loved ones is ultimately insignificant. Nothing can bring them back. But Irish societal issues have influenced many of the murders of foreigners here and shaped the development of the country's social fabric.

Media coverage of the murders of tourists to Ireland has been more extensive overall than immigrant killings. The most renowned murder of a foreigner in this country is of the visiting kind, that of the unsolved killing of French woman Sophie Toscan du Plantier (39) in west Cork in 1996. Gardaí have never had enough evidence to charge anyone in relation to her violent killing despite twice arresting the former chief suspect in the case, English journalist Ian Bailey. In 2008 the French authorities decided to launch its own investigation into her murder. The French inquiry into her killing is essentially a statement of criticism directed at the Irish criminal justice system—gardaí were unable to bring charges against anyone, so now it is the turn of the French to try to do so. Fundamentally, this goes against how justice should be administered. There is currently an attempt under way to extradite Ian Bailey to France to answer questions about the murder. In reality, it's unlikely the French investigation will result in anyone being charged with her murder. All it will do is raise Sophie's family's hopes. The inquiry into her death in France was initiated because of who Sophie was. Her late husband Daniel was relatively famous and had friends in high places, including former French president Jacques Chirac. Influential people in French society successfully lobbied the government until the inquiry was established. Undoubtedly the families of murder victims deserve answers about how their loved ones died. But who decides when one person's life is more valuable than the next?

In 2008 Justice Paul Carney made controversial comments in his courtroom about the number of cases he was dealing with, where immigrants were stabbing each other to death in drink-fuelled rows. He said some immigrants who have not integrated into Irish society "buy vodka or beer in the off-licence and are drinking in a flat when a row breaks out and one person reaches for a kitchen knife and stabs the other person". He painted a stark picture of immigrant life in Ireland. A flurry of criticism followed his remarks which were branded by some as racist and stereotypical.

By failing to acknowledge that many foreigners are stabbed by Irish people, Justice Carney left himself open to criticism. But he raised an important issue and one that is reinforced by statistics. In a five and a half year period between 2003 and 2008, over a quarter of fatal stabbings in Ireland claimed the lives of foreigners. In that time period 100 people were fatally stabbed and 26 of those victims were non-Irish nationals. In more than half the cases, other foreigners have been charged or are suspected of carrying out these killings.

Justice Carney was correct to a point. Many fatal stabbings of foreign men have been carried out by their fellow countrymen, often their friends, who were struggling to come to terms with life in Ireland. The most recent census found that foreign nationals accounted for more than 10 per cent of the population, so the number of immigrants stabbed to death in this time period was highly disproportionate.

The country's second most infamous murder of a foreigner— the killing of Kenyan Farah Swaleh Noor (38) in 2005—was a crime committed by two Irish women. Noor was brutally murdered at a house in Ballybough before his body was dismembered and dumped. Charlotte Mulhall was later convicted of his murder while her elder sister Linda was jailed for his manslaughter.

More recently, the murder of Polish men Mariusz Szwajkos (29) and Pawel Kalite (29) in 2008 in a vicious screwdriver attack carried out by David Curran who was just 17 years old sent shockwaves through Irish society. While racial taunts were an element in the build-up to the double murder, the killings were not considered racially motivated. But following this tragedy, many migrants living here expressed concern about an undercurrent of racism in some parts of the country, and gardaí have acknowledged that proving race-related crime is not a black and white issue. Racism in Ireland is alive and well. A report by the us State Department recently found that Ireland continues to have a significant problem with racism towards minorities and immigrants. The us State Department 2010 Human Rights Report on Ireland said discrimination and attacks against those newly arrived and certain ethnic groups were a growing issue. "Societal discrimination and violence against immigrants and racial and ethnic minorities, including Asians, Eastern and Baltic Europeans, and Africans, continued to be a problem", according to the report. "There were racially motivated incidents involving physical violence, intimidation, graffiti and verbal slurs."

In April 2010, Toyosi Shitta Bey (15), originally from Nigeria, was stabbed fatally outside his home in Tyrrelstown, west Dublin. An Irishman has been charged with his killing. Possible motives for his killing have been voiced among the African community here but cannot be explored in depth in this book as it is before the courts and cannot be discussed for legal reasons.

The housing estate where Toyosi lived has a sizeable African population. Indeed, west Dublin's immigrant population is disproportionately high. The Blanchardstown area has the fastest growing population in the country, but more significantly, 22 per cent of its population, or double the national average, are non-Irish nationals. This has given rise to concerns over the possible ghettoisation of immigrant communities around the country. Ireland does not yet have—and may never have—deprived immigrant ghettos, as has happened in France and the UK. But it isn't just in west Dublin that immigrant communities are becoming concentrated. Part of a housing estate in Athlone, Thornbury Drive in Willow Park, has been christened 'Little Lagos' because of its African population. And this development is by no means unique. All around the country, large groups of immigrants are forging communities. There are large groupings of Burmese in Castlebar in Mayo, Kurds in Mullingar, Brazilians in Gort and Kenyans in Dundalk. They are living together both by choice and necessity.

In 2007, 16 foreigners were the victims of murder or manslaughter in Ireland. In 2008, eight foreigners were killed here. In 2009, nine non-Irish nationals were the victims of killings, according to the latest statistics from the Central Statistics Office (CSO). Investigating the murders of foreigners in Ireland is something An Garda Síochána has adapted to. But it has presented many challenges for gardaí. In some countries such as parts of Russia, China and Africa a deep mistrust of the police exists and people are fearful of co-operating with the authorities in any way. Gardaí have done significant work with new communities here to try and earn their trust. The Garda Racial and Intercultural Unit, established in 2001, has helped ease this transition. Gardaí have also come across many cultural nuances when investigating the murders of foreigners. For example, Chinese people will often not provide information that might be useful if being questioned or assisting gardaí with their enquiries unless they are asked specifically about the issue. When detectives were investigating the murder of Romanian Adrian Bestea (21) in 2001, they learned that a Ukrainian man who played a key role in his killing did not expect gardaí to thoroughly investigate his death. In some countries the scope of a police investigation can vary depending on how 'important' the person who lost their life is considered to be. Although the Irish media become fixated about some murders, while almost completely ignoring others for a range of different reasons, every murder investigation launched in Ireland is thoroughly probed by gardaí and the PSNI, regardless of the race, age or class of the victim.

This book tells the stories behind the murders of 22 foreigners in Ireland. Some were economic migrants; others were immigrants, while some were tourists. Coping with the murder of a loved one is life changing for any family. But to try and come to terms with the violent death of a relative who has lost their life far from home, in a country with different laws and customs, compounds the tragedy. This book is dedicated to all the victims and families of foreigners who have been murdered in Ireland.

01 | INGA-MARIA HAUSER

Photographs taken on her daughter's last holiday are all Almut Hauser has left—images of an attractive blond-haired, blue-eyed teenager posing at various tourist attractions and beauty spots. But no pictures of Inga-Maria Hauser in Northern Ireland exist. She was murdered shortly after she set foot on soil in County Antrim 22 years ago. The belongings from her rucksack were strewn around her semi-naked body when it was discovered. Among them her camera, eight rolls of film and her diary. All are now cherished possessions at her mother's home in Munich. These items are all that returned from her teenage daughter's ill-fated travels.

At just 18, Inga-Maria was anxious to travel and see the world. With her parents' blessing, the German teenager was independent enough to embark on a backpacking holiday around Europe alone, with her journey due to end in Cardiff, Wales, where she had arranged to stay with a friend. From her native Munich, she travelled to Holland and then over to the UK. Using an inter-rail ticket, she travelled around cities in England and then up to Scotland before deciding to journey to Northern Ireland. She arrived by ferry in Larne, Co. Antrim, on the evening of 6 April 1988, with plans to catch a train to Belfast and then travel on to

Dublin. But she never made it that far. She was murdered shortly after she disembarked from the ferry in a ruthless attack at the height of the Troubles in the North, appalling in equal measure the local community and police, who have so far been unable to catch her murderer.

Evening was setting in two weeks after she arrived by ferry when a local sheep farmer found her body. She had been dumped in an isolated part of Ballypatrick forest, just outside Ballycastle in north Antrim. The 18-year old was partially clothed and had suffered a violent sexual attack before her neck was broken in the vicious assault that ended her life. The callous murder of an unsuspecting young tourist horrified communities north and south of the border. And 22 years on, police are getting as close as they have ever been to catching her killer, thanks to developments in forensic science.

"It was the last thing this farmer expected to find when he was doing his evening rounds," says Detective Superintendent Raymond Murray, the officer in charge of the investigation for the Police Service of Northern Ireland (PSNI). The teenager's rucksack and its belongings lay strewn around her body, which had been left exposed on open ground. "She was not buried or covered up in any way. She was not in a shallow grave, as the media have repeatedly reported. The way she was left tells us that the person responsible didn't want to hang about. If she had been carried 50 yards, her remains could have been left deep in the forest. If that had happened, she may never have been found. There are a few possibilities as to why her body was left out in the open this way. Her killer, or killers, could have been shocked by what they did. Or the person responsible could also have been in a rush. Or perhaps whoever was responsible was concerned their vehicle would be spotted in the area so they left quickly to save time. It is more common for people to be abandoned in this way after they have been murdered than for their killer to try and conceal the crime. Because of the evidence of a sexual attack, police believe a man was responsible for her murder but cannot rule out that more than one person was involved."

When news began to trickle out that the body of a young

woman had been found in Ballypatrick forest, there was a huge amount of public and media interest. It remains one of Northern Ireland's most notorious murders, still making headlines more than two decades on. "The local community were deeply affected by what happened. This killing was different from the daily diet of bombs and bullets. What happened to her was the crossing of a last bastion for the community," adds Murray. "It upset everyone deeply. People just felt that this was not the Northern Ireland they knew. That a young girl from a foreign country could come as a tourist and end up sexually assaulted and murdered in north Antrim, it did not sit easy with the general public, then or now."

The severity of the injuries the teenager sustained was also of concern both for police and the local community as people soon began to speculate that a sex attacker and murderer may be prowling around north Antrim waiting to strike again. Police believe it is likely that she was murdered in Ballypatrick forest, not killed elsewhere and then dumped at the isolated spot. "She died of a broken neck. In terms of how her neck got broken, it was most likely a manual attack rather than an implement used. There were other injuries present, particularly trauma to the face. She was beaten around the head, essentially. It hasn't been ruled out that there could have been more than one killer," says Murray. "We don't know if the sexual assault and the murder were carried out in one seamless attack, but we are satisfied it was a sexually motivated attack. But aside from this, this murder is a true mystery."

It didn't take long for police to piece together who Inga-Maria was. Her camera and diary, as well as other personal belongings, helped them verify her identity. But determining how she ended up being murdered and discarded deep in a north Antrim forest has never been established. Soon detectives were able to piece together the teenager's last movements. On the evening of 6 April Inga-Maria boarded the *Galloway Princess* as a foot passenger. The Stranraer ferry from Scotland was bound for Larne. There were two definite sightings of Inga-Maria on the boat. Two individuals who were travelling together were able to describe the dress Inga-Maria was wearing, the badges she had on her rucksack, and both recalled that she had two white shoes tied to her rucksack. Another passenger subsequently told police that she saw a young woman fitting Inga-Maria's broad description getting into a lorry with a man as the boat was docking. This sighting was extensively investigated but has never been substantiated as a positive identification. It is not that police believe this person is telling them anything other than the truth. But as she was unable to provide specific details of Inga-Maria's appearance, police have never been able to ascertain if Inga-Maria was in fact the passenger observed getting into the lorry with a man.

"Went from Glasgow to Ayr and from there to Stranraer to get over to Ireland. Saw the sea, beautiful and mysterious, wonder where I stay tonight, need more money," was the last entry Inga-Maria wrote in her diary on 6 April 1988 before she boarded the Stranraer ferry bound for Larne. "She did have some money and an inter-rail ticket. It is our hypothesis that she had to get in a vehicle as she left the ferry or shortly after she got off the ferry. But we have never identified that vehicle despite extensive efforts," says Murray. "That is what we do know. Everything else is speculation." And, as is always the case with an unsolved murder, speculation and theories have abounded. The ferry was regularly used by British soldiers returning to duty in the North, as well as by lorry drivers. Some have speculated that she was killed by a soldier. But there has never been any tangible evidence to point police in this direction.

An even more far-fetched theory has been that the 18-year old was killed by a female police officer. Rumour has it that Inga-Maria met the police officer and her father on the ferry. The young backpacker was then left alone with the woman's father and they got along so well that when the police officer returned, she flew into a rage when she saw them together as she feared her father was cheating on her mother. The story goes that the woman delivered the fatal blow to the back of Inga-Maria's neck. Shocked and shaken by the killing, the woman and her father supposedly then took the body to a remote spot in the forest which was where she was found, several miles from their own home.

The most persistent rumour concerns a local lorry driver. While police acknowledge that Inga-Maria must have boarded a vehicle as she got off the boat or soon after it docked, some locals have developed a scenario about how this came to pass. The rumour—dismissed by police as unhelpful, idle speculation—has it that Inga-Maria met a young man and fellow traveller on the ferry, and they struck up a flirtatious rapport. A lorry driver began to watch them and became sexually attracted to the young German. When the ferry docked, Inga-Maria and her friend went their separate ways, but the lorry driver sought her out and offered her a lift to Belfast after striking up a conversation. She agreed. But instead of taking her to Belfast, he drove instead to Ballypatrick forest, an area he knew well, and raped her. The local theory has it that this man didn't mean to kill her but broke her neck accidentally as she struggled to get free from his grasp. "There have been theories, but that really is all that they are. There is no substance to any of them," says Murray. "We only deal with the facts."

It had been Inga-Maria's intention to travel from Larne to Belfast and from there on to Dublin. She had arranged to meet a friend in Cardiff in Wales on 9 April and was due to get the ferry from Dublin. The station where she could have caught a train to Belfast was right opposite where the *Galloway Princess* docked. No one knows why she didn't stick to her travelling plans. Inga-Maria was not known to have hitch-hiked, so it has baffled police and her family as to why she would get into a vehicle with a stranger. But because she was low on money, it is possible that someone may have offered her a place for the night after befriending her on the ferry. "She didn't hitch-hike. She didn't need to when she arrived in Larne anyway. That's why it is such a mystery to us as to why she would get into a vehicle with someone she didn't know. Her body was found two weeks later, but we believe she was killed shortly after she got off the boat," says Murray.

Pathology has developed significantly in the past 22 years.

Initially, the pathology advice to investigating police was that the teenager had died in and around the time her body was found. This led the police investigation to probe where Inga-Maria had spent the last two weeks of her life. The possibilities were endless. She could willingly have gone with someone she met on the ferry who had befriended her but later murdered her. Or perhaps she was kidnapped, held captive for two weeks before she was sexually assaulted and killed. If she was alive for two weeks after she arrived in Northern Ireland, it was also quite possible that the person she got a lift with on the ferry was not the same person who killed her. Police spent considerable time trying to trace her movements over a period when she was already dead. There were numerous 'sightings' of her, including in the seaside village of Newcastle and in Belfast's Botanic Gardens.

But in 2004 the pathology tests were reviewed and police were informed that Inga-Maria died much sooner than previously believed and probably on or near the same day she arrived in Northern Ireland. "Initially, the pathology results indicated her time of death was around the time her body was found. But pathology has advanced a lot since then. But that information had a major impact on the original police investigation. Police in 1988 were working on the hypothesis that Inga-Maria got off the ferry with someone she met in a car or lorry and left with them. But as the pathology report suggested she did not die for two weeks, police investigated every possible scenario of what could have happened to her in that time. The places she potentially could have gone to and who she could have come into contact with in those weeks were mind boggling," says Murray. "To make things even more difficult, there was a young German backpacker with a similar name travelling around north Antrim at the same time. This created a lot of well intended but erroneous sightings and confusion for the original murder investigation team."

It was a major police priority to locate the more than 300 passengers on the *Galloway Princess* that day. "We can't say we spoke to every single passenger on the boat, but we have done our absolute best to reach them all. There was particular focus on tracking down everyone who was in a car or lorry. That has always been a major focus of this investigation," adds the detective. Some of those on the ferry were lorry drivers and were tracked down and questioned by RUC detectives. Another ferry was docking at the same time in Larne and police also spoke to a significant number of those passengers.

When the revised pathology found that Inga-Maria died soon after she arrived in Larne, it immediately made sense to investigating police almost two decades later. The teenager was an avid postcard sender to her family and friends back home and her correspondence stopped just before she arrived in Larne. The last entry in her diary was on 6 April. The eight rolls of film found among her belongings were developed and returned to her parents, but not one photo showed that she had spent any time in Northern Ireland.

Inga-Maria was a confident and self-sufficient young woman. At just 18, she went travelling around Europe alone, befriending other young travellers along the way. "She seems to have been a lovely young woman, quite trusting and willing to see the good in everyone. She met a lot of different people who were also inter-railing as she was travelling around. She was interested in culture and seeing the sights in the United Kingdom. She had been looking forward to doing the same in Northern Ireland and the Republic of Ireland. She was a sociable and outgoing person. She spoke English well," says Murray. "While she does seem to have been a trusting type of person, she was not believed to have been overly naive."

The initial murder investigation was extensive. Considerable police resources were made available to try and catch her killer. The local community also helped the police in any way it could. The year after her body was found, forensic experts found DNA that may belong to Inga-Maria's murderer in Ballypatrick forest. "There was DNA then too. Seventy local people were ruled out as owners of the DNA early on as a result of this science, but there have been significant developments in the field since then," adds Murray. "The amount of co-operation the police got at the time and up to the present day has been unbelievable. The police have put hundreds and thousands of hours into solving this case."

Inga-Maria's murder was the first case from Northern Ireland to feature on *Crimewatch* UK and unlike many murders in the North, it has consistently made headlines in the south. A reconstruction of her last known movements was shown on BBC's *Crimewatch* in June 1988. Police leading the hunt for the killer at the time were pleased by the response to the programme; it was estimated that more than 100 calls came into the Ballycastle incident room and the London studio at the time. A reconstruction of the events that led up to her killing has been broadcast many times since. When detectives made an appeal for information on *Crimewatch* in 2005, a new witness came forward saying she saw the young German getting into a lorry and noted the registration number. Unfortunately, this information led to a dead end. In the same *Crimewatch* broadcast, Detective Superintendent Pat Steele, who was then leading the investigation, appealed to a person who anonymously telephoned police in 2002 and provided vital information about the case to again make contact. "It is my personal belief that the person who made that call knows who killed Inga-Maria. I would ask that person to call back," Steele said during the broadcast. In April 2002, Ballycastle police station received an anonymous phone call. The caller relayed information about Inga-Maria's killer that police at the time believed was genuine. But further extensive enquiries by detectives were able to identify an individual who was subsequently eliminated.

In this decade, one person has been spoken to under caution in relation to her murder. In 1988, shortly after her killing, a man was arrested and questioned but was later released without charge. "Do we have a prime or chief suspect? They are not words I'd use. I can say that the person spoken to in the past decade is not the same person who was arrested shortly after her body was found. But I will only rule people out after we find out what happened to her. Until we know what happened, the enquiry will continue as far as we can go with it," explains Detective Murray. "The people of north-east Antrim are resolute in getting some kind of answer. There is still deep shock over her killing, especially among those of an age who remember it. It's a very emotive issue." Detective Inspector Tom McClure, assisting with the renewed investigation into Inga-Maria's case, says her killing has shown no sign of fading from locals' memories. "What happened to Inga-Maria is seen as a stain on the character of this area. It's unresolved and people want answers," he says.

Inga-Maria's parents Almut and Josef have travelled to Ireland twice since their daughter's murder. They journeyed to the North to identify her body in 1988 and then the following year when both came to see the murder scene Almut made a rare, impassioned appeal for information: "It was unspeakable sadness just to stand there in that meadow where my child had lain. When a mother loses a daughter people forget very quickly but the mother left on her own never forgets. I hope the people of Northern Ireland never forget Inga-Maria." Before they got that fateful phone call in 1988, her parents were already anxious about their daughter's well-being as she had failed to contact them for two weeks. Inga-Maria had a close relationship with her parents and had remained in constant touch with them during her travels.

Inga-Maria's father Josef died four years ago. Her mother Almut still lives in Munich and has never given up hope that her daughter's killer will be brought to justice. In 1991 the couple offered a reward of £3,000, their life savings, to catch the killer, but no valuable information was proffered. Now aged 67, Almut is encouraged by the extent of the ongoing efforts by police to find Inga-Maria's murderer. Inga-Maria was due to turn 19 one month before she was killed and had initially planned on travelling straight from her home in Munich to visit her friend in Wales during the Easter holidays. But when her friend said she had to change the date when Inga-Maria could arrive, the 18-year old decided to still leave on the date she had planned but instead travel around the UK and Ireland as she had already paid for her train ticket. Since her death, her parents have never been inclined to speak publicly about the tragedy that befell the family, preferring to grieve privately. But her mother has spoken about how her daughter was pleased when her travel plans changed as it gave her a chance to travel more around Europe. She was particularly curious about Ireland. Twenty-two years have now passed and Almut, more than anything, wants answers about her daughter's final movements so that she can finally stop pondering the possibilities. Because her murderer has never been caught, she also harbours fears that her daughter's killer may have struck again.

RUC officers travelled to Germany and interviewed all of Inga-Maria's friends after her death. It has been the support of her daughter's close friends over the past two decades that has helped Almut deal with her loss. To mark what would have been her 21st birthday, her parents invited all of her friends over to celebrate her memory in their flat. After Josef's death in April 2006 from cancer, Almut moved to a smaller apartment on the same street. He died almost 18 years to the day when their daughter's body was discovered. Almut keeps her daughter and husband's memories very much alive. Photographs of Inga-Maria's travels on her final holiday take pride of place in her home. Every few days, she travels to the nearby cemetery to light candles for her daughter and her husband.

Police also actively pursued the theory that Inga-Maria's killer may have struck elsewhere. In 1995, the battered body of French student Celine Figard was found in Worcester, UK. She had hitched a lift with a lorry driver and her body was found in a lay-by, 70 miles from the point where she had disappeared ten days before. Senior RUC officers investigating the unsolved killing of the German teenager contacted police in West Mercia to try and establish if there was a connection due to the similarities between the killings. But police soon tracked down lorry driver Stuart Morgan for the murder and rape of the French student and it was confirmed he had no DNA link to Inga-Maria. He was later found guilty and sentenced to life in prison for his crime.

While unsolved murder investigations never close, Inga-Maria Hauser's brutal attack and killing has been re-examined every few years since her death. Developments in DNA and social science have meant that these reviews are not merely a re-examination of the evidence, but have led to significant advances in solving the case. In 2003, police hired a behavioural profiler and later a geographic profiler. The behavioural expert developed a profile of the characteristics of Inga-Maria's murderer. This is based on what is known about the killing and sexual attack as well as evidence left behind at the crime scene. This expert gave police his view on the man's age, ethnicity, personality, previous behaviour and possible criminal background. "We get this information updated all the time. However, the experts advising us are always pointing out that it's just guidance and not a definitive profile of the person or persons that killed her," adds Murray. The two profilers were brought to the scene in Ballypatrick forest where the teenager's body was discovered. The report furnished by the geographic profiler has been pivotal to the police investigation. He reported back to police that the person who killed the 18-year old seemed to have extensive knowledge of Ballypatrick forest, much more so than a casual visitor. Her killer deliberately chose a secluded area of the forest to murder her and then dump her body, knowing that most people who visit the forest would never venture that far, ensuring her body would not be easily found. The forest is known to have been used at the time by people who rented forestry plots, Forestry Service employees, subcontract labourers and turf cutters who had turbary rights. Ruling these people out of their enquiries has been a priority for police.

When Inga-Maria was murdered in 1988, DNA technology was in its early stages. There have been ground-breaking advancements in the 22 years since then. Most developed counties now have DNA databases. These store forensics of people that have been previously arrested or convicted of another crime. The databases are routinely screened when forensics are recovered from crime scenes. In early 1989, the original police investigation successfully used emerging forensic technology to recover a DNA profile from the place where Inga was murdered. Police then obtained voluntary DNA samples from 70 local men and compared this against the crime scene sample. None was a match and all these men were eliminated as suspects.

The science used to obtain the DNA profile in 1989 is now obsolete in most laboratories throughout the world. It has been updated several times with modern systems which are much more powerful and discriminating. Today, when a DNA profile is recovered from a crime scene, police have the advantage of being able to search the DNA database for a matching profile. The original DNA profile obtained in 1989 is not compatible with modern DNA systems and therefore cannot be compared against the DNA database. This presented a considerable problem for any subsequent reinvestigations into the murder of Inga-Maria Hauser.

In 2005, Detective Inspector Tom McClure commenced a review of all forensic aspects of the initial investigation and made an exciting discovery. Despite the fact that 17 years had passed since the murder, the detective recognised something unusual where her murderer may have left behind vital evidence at the crime scene. With the help of scientists, a male DNA profile was obtained from the remaining crime scene material. Police will not say exactly where this DNA profile was recovered from as it is the basis of the PSNI's current investigation. This DNA is far more discriminating than the original forensics discovered in 1989 and, most importantly, can be compared against profiles held on modern DNA databases. Detectives had high hopes when the forensic sample was sent for comparison against the Northern Ireland and UK DNA databases for the first time. Unfortunately there were no matches. The DNA profile was also forwarded to numerous countries across Europe and beyond for comparison against their databases, again without a match. It may simply be the case that the man whose DNA was found at the crime scene has not been detected for any offence since the introduction of DNA databases in the late 1990s. The next natural step in the murder investigation was to commence a voluntary DNA screening.

Police studied all the information provided by the behavioural and geographic profilers and developed a potential profile of the person responsible for Inga-Maria's murder. This profile was then used to prioritise a list of approximately 1,800 men who had come into the enquiry for any reason. Part of the rationale for this was that expert analysis of similar cases throughout the UK has concluded that the person responsible is often someone who has already been spoken to by police or was "in the system" for some other reason. Out of this number, the top scoring 1,000 men, most of whom worked and lived in the area or were on the *Galloway Princess*, were then invited to provide a voluntary DNA swab to eliminate them from the enquiry. Several retired detectives were hired to assist with the DNA screening. Police gave an assurance that the samples provided would not be compared against any other crime or loaded on to the DNA database and would be destroyed when the investigation concluded. This strategy gained the trust and confidence of many of the men. The plan was also well received in the local community where there remains a strong desire to see the killer brought to justice. But despite high hopes, none was a match. "Out of the 1,000 people only a handful refused," says Murray. "We were able to rule out those that did refuse as suspects in the end anyway."

But thanks to continuous advances in forensics, police were also able to embark upon a new avenue of investigation. Although the male suspect who left forensics at the crime scene is not on the DNA database, it is now possible to identify him if a close relative is on the database. The "familial DNA process" is used as a method of trying to find a close relative of an offender whose DNA sample has already been stored on a database. The UK's Forensic Science Service got involved to assist police with this. "There are two ways of doing it. One is searching for the DNA of an offender's parents and the other is looking for a match to their siblings," explains Murray. "Research has shown that people who have committed serious crimes often have family members who are also involved in crime. That's why this familial DNA screening can be so successful."

These forensic advances enabled police to carry out a DNA trawl of the Northern Ireland and UK DNA databases searching for potential family members of the owner of the crime scene DNA profile. Some 3,000 possible matches came back. This was then narrowed down considerably to a list of 500 males. Using a new type of DNA analysis, those 500 potential relatives of Inga-Maria's killer have now been ruled out as family members of the owner

of the suspect DNA profile. Yet again police had hit another brick
wall.

But in February 2009 a new breakthrough in the investigation
brought a ray of hope. DNA profiles belonging to women who are
on the National UK DNA database were found to have similar
characteristics and a possible familial link to the male suspect's
forensics collected from the crime scene. Officers have since
talked to some of these women, who are from various locations
across the UK including Northern Ireland, and have been able to
eliminate their male relatives from their enquiries.

There remain a number of female profiles on the UK DNA
database which contain similar characteristics to the forensics
from the crime scene. "DNA science is developing all the time. We
can infer from the way that DNA characteristics are inherited that
there is a possibility—and no more than that—that in this small
female group there is a male relative's DNA profile which could
match the DNA profile from the crime scene," says Murray. "It is
important that we locate the male relatives of this limited
number of women so that a sample can be taken from them and
they can be eliminated from this investigation."

The probe into Inga-Maria's murder shows no sign of abating.
Detectives are constantly reviewing and updating the forensic
strategy which is focused on using the latest advances in science
to solve this notorious murder. The latest strategy involves the
familial analysis of a list of more than 600 DNA profiles obtained
previously from a prioritised list of males in Northern Ireland.
The objective of this analysis is to find the owner of the crime
scene DNA profile from a family member who may be on the DNA
database. Hundreds of these will soon be ruled out and police will
then pursue any of the matches that are flagged as having enough
similarities to warrant further investigation.

Inga-Maria's murder investigation remains very active,
particularly for a 22-year-old case. But trying to a find her killer
is a time-consuming and expensive process. If police have no
major breakthrough in the next two batches of possible DNA
matches, they have no more immediate plans to conduct more.
"Murder enquiries can go quiet for periods, but they never close.

If we have a breakthrough, then we'll keep people on the investigation team. But we cannot reasonably be expected to continue indefinitely with the resources attached at the moment to this case. But the new DNA that Tom and the scientists found, that will always be there. No one can imagine where DNA is going. All we do know for sure is that it will continue to advance. We have other families, other victims and other cases. All of them have to receive a good quality investigation also."

Because Inga-Maria was murdered so long ago, the police investigation has had to adapt. Mulling over forensics, weighing up risk factors and the possible character traits of her killer in a bid to rule out hundreds of potential DNA matches is not the traditional type of police investigation people imagine in a murder hunt. "There has been a phenomenal amount of work done on this case. It's not edge-of-your-seat police work; it's people working themselves to the edge of their intellectual ability. We sit in rooms for hours on end pouring over figures and forensics. That is the only way we can solve this," explains Murray.

Despite optimism over advances in DNA, catching Inga-Maria's killer is by no means a foregone conclusion. "I'm confident that I'll do my damnedest to solve it. But any detective who says they can definitely solve a crime is writing cheques they cannot cash. The amount of resources put into this enquiry has been huge. We have gone the extra ten miles," adds Murray. "Inga-Maria was a young woman with her whole life in front of her who met a terrible death in Northern Ireland. We owe it to her memory and to her family in Germany to bring her killer to justice. I believe a specific group of people with knowledge of Ballypatrick forest can help us. I would ask them to do the right thing."

02 | SOPHIE TOSCAN DU PLANTIER

Some murders simply refuse to be forgotten. It has been 14 years since filmmaker Sophie Toscan du Plantier was beaten to death outside her holiday home near the sleepy village of Goleen in west Cork. Her unsolved killing still makes headlines today, both in Ireland and France. That Sophie was stunningly beautiful, middle class and married into an influential family has ensured her death received continued media attention. No one has ever been brought to justice for her murder. A new inquiry into her death is ongoing in France, guaranteeing that her killing will continue to be newsworthy. Add to the mix of this enthralling case a former chief suspect, English journalist Ian Bailey, who wrote about her murder for several newspapers and has a criminal history of violence against his partner. But it is what has happened behind the scenes that truly makes this story even more fascinating. Gardaí have never had enough evidence to charge anyone with her murder. Investigating detectives even suffered the embarrassment of their key witness withdrawing her statement and accusing gardaí of putting pressure on her to falsely state that she saw Ian Bailey on the night of the murder.

Sophie Toscan du Plantier (39) arrived at Cork Airport on the morning of Friday 20 December 1996. She travelled to her five-bedroom holiday home overlooking Dunmanus Bay a few miles from Schull in a hired Ford Fiesta. On the way she called to a Texaco filling station at Ballydehob and bought kindling to make a fire. Later that day she visited the Courtyard Bar and Restaurant in Schull before driving home, about three miles outside the town. That evening she spoke briefly on the phone to Josie Helen, the caretaker of the house. The secluded holiday home was a place Sophie loved to visit. It was also the ideal place for her to try and get some work done, as it was so remote. She worked for the film production company, Les Champs Blancs, producing TV documentaries. "She used to get there as often as possible to work on her film work or write scenarios. She was totally dedicated to her work," says Jean Antoine Bloc, vice-president of the Association for the Truth about the Murder of Sophie Toscan du Plantier. The group was established in December 2007 to campaign for an investigation by French authorities into the murder of the mother-of-one in west Cork. "Ireland was to Sophie a second native land. The west Cork region and the hills reminded her of that area in France where she spent most of her vacations as a child." But the very isolation that Sophie craved has also been one of the main impediments to solving her murder.

On her second day at her holiday home, Sophie went shopping locally for groceries and withdrew money from a cash point. At 4.30 pm that afternoon she was seen outside her house by a local, and that evening she telephoned her husband Daniel Toscan du Plantier in France. He wasn't home but returned her call at 11 pm. The next day, 22 December, Sophie was seen walking at the nearby Three Castle Head. She loved to walk and be out in the fresh air. She also visited friends in the neighbourhood. She had bought the holiday home five years earlier and had got to know some people in the locality.

The next morning at 10 am, her battered body was found lying in a laneway not far from the house. She had been murdered the night before. Inside her house there was no sign of a struggle. It appears she answered the door to her killer and was fleeing her attacker when she was murdered. The person responsible for her death possibly called to her home and then a row ensued between them.

Her injuries were horrific. The terror she must have endured during the frenzied, sustained assault is unimaginable. Sophie put up a strong resistance, fighting hard to stay alive. Fragments of hair were found beneath her fingernails, possibly belonging to her killer. Sophie suffered severe injuries to her head, neck, chest, arms and legs. At least two different weapons, a concrete block and a smaller stone found at the scene, were used by her murderer. Dr John Harbison carried out the post-mortem and wrote a grim account of visiting the scene on the morning the French woman's body was discovered. "In the approach to these cottages, I observed the dead body of a female lying on the grass verge of the roadway. The principal feature of the body was that the head, shoulders and both arms were heavily blood-stained," he wrote in his confidential report.

The cause of death was laceration and swelling of the brain, fracture of the skull and multiple blunt head injuries. "The dead woman had long hair which had become entangled in vegetation. It was obvious that she had severe head injuries because there were gaping wounds on the right side of the forehead and the right ear was severely lacerated at its lower edge. Beneath the lacerations on the right side of the forehead I could see tissue and noted that there was depression of the skull extending from the right eyebrow back as far as the temporal bone," according to the post-mortem.

The autopsy report details a long list of injuries she suffered during the attack. Her eyes had haemorrhaged and her nose had superficial injuries. Her upper lip had been torn away from the gum and there was a "depression" on her right cheek showing clear evidence of a fracture. The French woman had three long lacerations to her face, the largest of which was about one and three-quarter inches in length. She had a row of dark abrasions along her right eyebrow and scratches all over her face. There were wounds on her chest, a series of cuts and abrasions almost too numerous to list. "There were gross injuries of the head and neck, arms and hands. These hand injuries, including fractures, constituted defensive wounds, indicating that she put up a considerable fight with severe defensive injuries to both hands," wrote Harbison.

She was discovered by her German friend and neighbour, Shirley Foster. Sophie was wearing a pair of cotton long johns and a cotton top with socks and heavy shoes. The long johns had been ripped on a nearby barbed wire fence, but there was no evidence of any sexual assault. It was the view of the then state pathologist that a cavity block at the scene and a large stone could have been used during the attack. The cavity block rested on the dead woman's blue dressing gown. She did not appear to have been dragged over the ground. The most likely scenario is that her killer pursued her as she ran down the hill, possibly towards a neighbour's house, as she tried to raise the alarm.

It was 23 December. Sophie had been due to go home and celebrate Christmas in France with her family the next day, Christmas Eve. As news of the murder spread, it quickly became a story of major interest to the media. Journalists descended upon west Cork to report on the horrific killing of the French woman, whose husband was relatively well known in France. West Cork was renowned as one of the country's foremost beauty spots and was a major tourist attraction. Murders were virtually unheard of. That a tourist could be so brutally killed at Christmastime outside her holiday home was particularly shocking for the community.

When the story broke, local freelance journalist Ian Bailey had a major advantage over all the national press—local knowledge. He immediately became involved in reporting on the murder. He wrote numerous reports about the killing. The first was published on 28 December and the last on 10 February, the day he was arrested in relation to her murder. He wrote for the *Star*, *Paris Match* and the *Sunday Tribune*. He has denied allegations that he reported things only the killer would have known. In the *Sunday Tribune* on 29 December 1996, Bailey wrote: "The evidence indicates that she was pursued down the rocky track from her home and killed by repeated blows to the back of the head."

Within 24 hours of her murder, west Cork was full of rumour

and speculation about why anyone would want the young filmmaker dead. Some of these rumours were printed in the press. Bailey himself incorrectly reported in the same article in the *Sunday Tribune*: "Ms du Plantier . . . had recently informed [her husband Daniel] she intended to remarry her first husband . . . on several occasions she had visited west Cork with different companions."

Daniel du Plantier, who died in 2003 after remarrying, maintained that he and his wife were not estranged at the time of her murder. He utterly rejected the slur on his wife's character suggesting she visited her holiday home in Cork with other men. Her late husband even had his own theory about the circumstances that led to her murder. "I can imagine it well. She could be extremely cutting. She faced someone who was probably drunk, and he made a pass at her and she rejected him in an insulting way and he went crazy. It was like her to go outside to talk to him; she wasn't afraid of anything."

Ian Bailey soon emerged as the chief suspect in the murder investigation, which was led by Superintendent Liam Horgan. In the days and weeks following the murder, Bailey told several people that he had become a suspect. A member of the public also told gardaí she saw Bailey near the murder scene but later withdrew this statement. He also had a history of violence against his partner, artist Jules Thomas, and around the time of the murder had scratches on his hands and forehead. Bailey said he sustained the scratches while killing three turkeys and cutting down a Christmas tree on the afternoon of 22 December. Forensics have never linked Ian Bailey to Sophie's death. He gave gardaí a sample of his DNA in January 1997.

No conclusive DNA profile of Sophie's killer was found at the murder scene. DNA analysis of the hair found under her fingernails has been inconclusive. At least three sets of DNA tests have been conducted since her death; as technology advances, more forensic analysis can be carried out.

On the morning of 10 February 1997, Ian Bailey was arrested and brought to Bandon garda station. His partner Jules Thomas was also arrested on suspicion of withholding information. Both were later released without charge and Bailey denied any involvement in the murder of the French woman. The main basis for his arrest was a witness statement gardaí received from shopkeeper Marie Farrell. She told gardaí in January 1997 that she saw Bailey at a bridge close to Sophie's home on the night of the killing. It was first alleged that Bailey tried to intimidate her to withdraw this statement. Then in 2005 she withdrew her statement to the effect that she had seen the English journalist on the night of the murder, saying she had been put under pressure by gardaí to make a statement against Bailey.

Following his release from custody, the Manchester-born journalist was photographed and named in the press. He even did an interview with Pat Kenny on RTÉ 1 after his release from Bandon garda station. Over the next year the garda investigation continued. Detectives spoke to several people who claimed the journalist had told them he was responsible for the killing. This has always been strongly refuted by Bailey, who says he told people that others were saying he was responsible. Eleven months later, in January 1998, Bailey was arrested for a second time as part of the murder probe. Again he was released without charge.

The garda investigation continued for the next few years without any major breakthrough. Plain and simple, without any witnesses to the killing or forensics linking anyone to the murder, there was insufficient evidence. Bailey had become the self-confessed chief suspect for her murder, which was widely reported. This essentially ended his career as a journalist. He has since gone on to study law. In December 2003, Bailey began a two week libel hearing against eight Irish and British newspapers who he said defamed him. He claimed his life, career and reputation had been destroyed after he was branded Sophie's killer. But this move backfired spectacularly both in financial terms as well as the damage it did to Bailey's reputation. In fact, some of the evidence heard at the libel trial is the basis for the attempt in France to extradite him.

Six of the eight newspapers Bailey attempted to sue were cleared of defaming him. In his judgement, Judge Patrick Moran described the former journalist as a violent man who sought out the limelight and enjoyed notoriety. Judge Moran found that the articles, which had said that Bailey was the chief suspect for the murder of Sophie Toscan du Plantier, were justified. He found in favour of Bailey in relation to one allegation contained in articles published in the *Sun* and the *Irish Mirror*, which claimed he had been violent towards his ex-wife Sarah Limbrick. Judge Moran found that no evidence was brought to support this contention in articles in the *Sun* and the *Irish Mirror*, and he awarded Mr Bailey damages of €8,000 in total.

"The allegation of libel means that a person's standing has been reduced in the eyes of an ordinary person. . . . Mr Bailey was in the witness box for three and a half days. He was a very cool witness . . . He told us about how he was treated by gardaí, and being hounded by the media," said Judge Moran. "He allowed himself to be interviewed by the media. He was interviewed by the Pat Kenny programme, first by researchers, then he spoke to Pat Kenny. This to me is quite unusual for someone who has been arrested on suspicion of a charge of murder. Normally a person would withdraw into the background. One can only draw from this that Mr Bailey likes the limelight, that he enjoys attention and notoriety."

The judge said that his partner, artist Jules Thomas, was also a calm witness giving evidence during the libel trial. In his action, Bailey complained that he was branded a violent man towards women and a murderer. But the judge took the view that since Bailey had been criminally convicted of assaulting Jules Thomas, the newspapers were justified in describing him as violent towards women. "Unpleasant things were put to her [Jules Thomas] relating to violence. She tended to put this under the carpet, say it was due to drink, it was nothing at all. The question of violence towards women is a question of fact. What came across as a result of questions from Mr Gallagher [legal representative for several of the newspapers] is that Ms [Jules] Thomas had suffered three nasty assaults. Mr Bailey appeared in the District Court on one of those and received a suspended sentence. Mr Bailey said when he was violent it takes place domestically and is a domestic problem. I deal with a lot of family law in this court. One rarely comes across instances of beatings. In this case we have three. Violence once would be unusual. Violence twice would be very unusual. Three times is exceptional. The District Court gave a six-month suspended sentence, because his partner [Jules Thomas] said she forgave him. Otherwise, the district justice would have had no hesitation in imposing a custodial sentence. I certainly would have no hesitation in describing Mr Bailey as a violent man." While there was evidence he had assaulted his partner Jules Thomas, there was none to suggest he had ever been physically violent towards his ex-wife. "I found he was a violent man, but there is no evidence he was violent towards his ex-wife. He has been defamed in relation to that," said the judge.

Under cross-examination, Bailey denied that he left his house on the night of the murder or that he had burned a mattress and other material in a bonfire three days later. When it was put to him that his partner Jules Thomas had said that he had left the bed and arrived the next morning with a mark on his forehead, he described this as "absolute nonsense". He said that he had got out of bed to do some writing but did not leave the house, and the mark on his forehead came later in the morning while cutting down a Christmas tree. In another line of questioning he denied that he had conducted a campaign of "intimidation and harassment" against local shopkeeper Marie Farrell.

Judge Moran also said he did not believe Ian Bailey's evidence that he did not know the French woman. Instead, the judge accepted the testimony of a local man Alfie Lyons, whom Ian Bailey had done some work for. "Mr Lyons gave evidence that he was 80 to 90 per cent sure he had introduced Ms du Plantier to Mr Bailey. On the balance of probabilities, I accept his evidence." But the judge did otherwise accept Bailey's evidence that he did not know Sophie, go to visit her, or go out with her for a drink.

During the libel action, landscape gardener Bill Fuller testified that Bailey, speaking of himself in the second person, told him: "You did it. You saw her in Spar on Saturday. You saw her walking up the aisle with her tight arse. You fancied her. You went up there to see what you could get. She ran off screaming. You chased her to calm her down. You stirred something in the back of your head. You went too far. You had to finish her off."

Bailey was also accused of telling or strongly implying to at least seven other people that he killed Sophie Toscan du Plantier. He said that people had simply misunderstood him—that he was either joking or recounting what other people said about him.

Three witnesses—Ritchie and Rosie Shelly and Malachi Reed—testified that Bailey admitted the murder to them. Mr and Mrs Shelley had spent New Year's Eve 1998 with Ian Bailey and Jules Thomas at their home in The Prairie in Schull, Co. Cork. Over the course of the night they discussed poetry and the French woman's murder two years earlier. "Mr Shelley wandered into your bedroom looking for a phone and you said to him, 'I did it, I did it, I went too far.' And you broke down and sobbed," said Paul Gallagher, senior counsel for the newspapers.

Mr Bailey responded that he was simply repeating what everyone was accusing him of. "I said it was being said that I did it. That is a mantra I kept hearing. At Christmastime, it all comes back. It is quite dreadful. I have lived with it for seven years. Unless something is done it will keep coming back."

The libel action also heard that Bailey told then *Sunday Tribune* news editor Helen Callanan that he had killed Sophie Toscan du Plantier. "It was being said that I was the killer. I said to her in jest, 'That's right, yes,'" said Bailey. "It is hard to take a false allegation seriously." He made these comments to the news editor before his first arrest in relation to her murder.

The libel trial also heard about Bailey's conversations with a teenage boy. In early 1997 Bailey gave 14-year-old Malachi Reed a lift home. According to the teenager, the former journalist told him he "bashed her brains in" with a rock. Again, Bailey said he was only repeating what people were saying about him. Shopkeeper Marie Farrell also gave evidence at the libel action. She said she saw Bailey on a bridge near the murder scene in the early hours of the morning following the murder. At first she did not know him, but later when she saw him in Schull, she recognised him as the man on the bridge. "She said she came here reluctantly. On the balance of probabilities, I accept what Mrs Farrell told me," said Judge Moran, "that the man she saw at the bridge was, in her view, Ian Bailey."

Bailey's attempt to sue the newspapers was, overall, an abject failure. Not only did he receive only €8,000 in damages, the two-week hearing was akin to a mini-trial with several witnesses telling of how Bailey had linked himself to the crime. His propensity for violence towards women was also revealed and the judge did not mince his words about the type of man he believed Ian Bailey was.

Things improved somewhat for the unemployable journalist in October 2005. Shopkeeper Marie Farrell claimed that a statement she had made to gardaí saying she saw Bailey at Kealfadda bridge in the early hours of the morning following the murder of the French woman was false and that she had been coerced into making it by investigating officers. When this emerged, Bailey's solicitor Frank Buttimer wrote to the then Garda Commissioner Noel Conroy expressing concern that his client had been arrested on foot of a statement made by the shopkeeper, which she later withdrew. An internal garda inquiry was launched into the handling of the murder investigation. But the Director of Public Prosecutions (DPP) directed that no officers should be prosecuted following a review of the garda handling of the case.

Ian Bailey decided to appeal his libel case against the newspapers to the High Court. But the case ended unexpectedly in February 2007 when he suddenly withdrew all of his claims. After beginning his legal battle against the newspapers four years previously, Bailey left the High Court in Cork without winning any damages and with the central allegation made by the five newspaper groups still standing: that he was a reasonable suspect in the Sophie Toscan du Plantier murder. The newspapers restated their position that they never said he was the murderer. The papers also agreed to contribute €70,000 towards Bailey's costs, but not to pay any damages to him, and waived costs awarded to them in his original failed action. Bailey's solicitor Frank Buttimer described the striking-out of the case as an "honourable compromise". The newspapers took a different view, essentially accusing Bailey of an admission of defeat by withdrawing his case.

In 2008 Bailey's legal team launched a High Court action against the garda and the State seeking damages for wrongful arrest, assault and "terrorising and oppressive behaviour". He claimed he suffered severe personal injuries and is seeking damages, including aggravated and punitive damages, for unlawful arrest, false imprisonment, malicious prosecution, assault, battery and trespass to the person. He also alleges intentional infliction of emotional and psychological harm, harassment, intimidation and terrorising and oppressive behaviour. It is Ian Bailey's position that gardaí tried to frame him for the murder of Sophie Toscan du Plantier.

But the journalist-turned-law-student wasn't the only one still legally preoccupied with the fall-out from the murder of Sophie. The French-led investigation into Sophie's death got a major boost in 2008. While the garda investigation remained technically open, the DPP directed in July 2008 that no one was to face charges following an internal garda review into its investigation of the murder. Because the garda investigation was no longer advancing, the Irish authorities finally agreed to hand over the extensive garda murder file to French magistrate Patrick Gachon. Judge Gachon, assisted by Judge Nathalie Dutartre, was appointed to investigate the murder in France. This decision to hold an inquiry in France did not come about overnight. The French-led investigation was prompted by intense lobbying by her relatives and friends since her death. In 2007, Sophie's uncle, scientist Jean-Pierre Gazeau and her cousin, Francis Lefevre, set up the Association for the Truth about the Murder of Sophie Toscan du Plantier, which is also lobbying for the harmonisation of EU laws to allow victims' families abroad greater access to information.

It has attracted the support of prominent figures in French politics and entertainment including a former justice minister and the president of the Cannes Film Festival. Sophie's late husband Daniel was a close personal friend of former French

President Jacques Chirac, who took an interest in the case. As far back as 1997, Paris magistrate Brigitte Pellegrini was assigned to investigate the death of the French mother-of-one following an action brought by Sophie's husband Daniel and her parents against "persons unknown".

But Pellegrini's enquiries went nowhere after several applications to the Irish authorities seeking information on the case were unsuccessful. But just as the Irish authorities essentially admitted their investigation had stalled, things began to gather pace across the water. As well as receiving the garda file in 2008, Sophie's remains were exhumed from a graveyard in the south of France earlier the month before. New DNA tests were conducted, but nothing of significance has yet been found.

Judges Gachon and Dutartre spent three days in Cork in July 2009 carrying out enquiries about the murder before returning to Paris. They were familiarising themselves with a number of locations associated with the 39-year old's killing, as well as speaking to serving and retired gardaí involved in the investigation. In October 2009, Supt Liam Horgan of Bantry garda station and Det. Garda Jim Fitzgerald of Bandon garda station travelled to Paris and testified at the private hearing before the two magistrates for three days. The judges then considered the garda evidence in consultation with the French state prosecutor (equivalent to the DPP in Ireland). It didn't take long for the French to make their next move.

Late on Friday 23 April 2010, Ian Bailey was arrested on foot of a European arrest warrant in relation to the French woman's murder. "That's a load of bollocks. This is an illegal arrest based on false information," he told Sgt Jim Kirwin as he was taken into custody. The French authorities are now seeking the extradition of Ian Bailey to France in connection with the killing. The next day at the High Court, the former journalist was granted bail. His barrister called into question the motive of the State acting on the arrest, given that the DPP had already decided that Bailey has no question to answer.

The decision by magistrate Judge Gachon to issue a European arrest warrant followed a close examination of the garda file on the killing and affidavits sworn by the two gardaí who gave evidence at private hearings before his inquiry. It is Judge Gachon's view that Bailey knew certain details about Sophie's murder before these details were confirmed by gardaí. While her body was discovered just after 10 am on 23 December, Sophie was not identified until 12.30 pm. During his libel action against newspapers in 2003, Bailey testified that the first he knew of the killing was when he received a phone call from Eddie Cassidy, west Cork reporter for the then *Cork Examiner*, sometime after 1.30 pm on 23 December.

In his evidence, Cassidy confirmed that he rang Bailey at 1.40 pm and told him that the body of a foreign woman had been found somewhere in Toormore. But he denied that he had ever said she was French or that she had been murdered. But two witnesses called by the newspapers—gardener Caroline Leftwick and musician Paul O'Colmain—testified that they received phone calls from Bailey on the morning of 23 December during which he mentioned the murder of a French woman.

The judge also has some queries about the scratches the former journalist had on his face and in the aftermath of the murder. He said he suffered the scratches while killing turkeys and cutting down a Christmas tree the day before Sophie was killed. But in a statement given to gardaí in 1997, a witness has told how they saw Bailey in the Galley bar on the night of 22 December. They were sitting quite close to him and did not see scratches of any kind on his face.

It remains to be seen if Ian Bailey will be extradited to France. The French authorities have said he is wanted for the alleged "wilful homicide and serious assault and battery" of Sophie Toscan du Plantier. His legal team will fully contest the warrant in the High Court and are prepared to appeal the ruling to the Supreme Court if they lose. His solicitor Frank Buttimer believes the attempted extradition raises broader constitutional issues.

In France, Sophie's family finally feel as if they are on the brink of finding out the truth about what happened to her on that cold night at Christmastime 14 years ago. Her parents Georges and Marguerite Bouniol are elderly, but still regularly travel to her west Cork holiday home to mark the anniversary of her death. Her brother Bertrand explained once why the family feel the need to visit west Cork: "We keep going back to Ireland to Sophie's house to find her spirit." Sophie's son Pierre Louis was 15 when his mother has murdered. He has rarely spoken publicly about her death but did break his silence in 2004 when he voiced his frustrations. "I was 15 years old when this happened. I have tried to stay away from this story when, in the meantime, my grandmother and my family were struggling to find the secret behind this mystery," he told a French television programme. "Now, I am keen to speak, to tell of my bitterness with Irish justice, which is going round in circles . . . Policemen did not perform their task correctly."

The Association for the Truth about the Murder of Sophie Toscan du Plantier believe that the justice they seek will not happen overnight. "Years are in front of us to bring justice and equity to our case," says Jean Antoine Bloc, vice-president of the association and close family friend. "Following the arrest warrant against Ian Bailey, we have the feeling that for the first time in years we are heading somewhere. If Mr Bailey has nothing to hide and is completely innocent as he has always said, then it should not be difficult for him to come to France and explain everything to the magistrate. Marie Farrell would be the best witness to listen to about the reasons and circumstances that drove her to withdraw her testimony."

Sophie's friends and relatives believe they know who murdered the filmmaker. "If someone is convicted, we would have reached our goal," adds Jean Antoine Bloc. "We would get justice, and we would experience finally relief and peace."

03 | BELINDA PEREIRA

While most people were still celebrating Christmas with their families, the young English-born woman travelled from London to Dublin on Christmas Eve to work as a prostitute. It would be the last journey she would ever make. Within five days her lifeless body, strewn naked on the bed where she had sex with several men, would be discovered by her pimp. Perhaps in a last act of humanity, incompatible with the cold-blooded murder just a moment earlier, her killer covered her body with a blanket. Twenty-six-year-old Belinda Pereira was dead, having suffered multiple blows to the head with a blunt instrument. It was 29 December 1996.

Her pimp, a man from Monaghan, arrived at the brothel on Mellor Court, Lower Liffey Street, Dublin, in the afternoon of 29 December to collect money Belinda had taken from clients and check up on how business was going. She was one of his most popular girls. She was of Sri Lankan heritage and her dark skin gave her an exotic look that Irish men were slowly becoming more accustomed to as the first major influx of immigrants from various cultures had begun to trickle into the country.

Belinda had been working alone out of the two-bedroom upmarket apartment on Lower Liffey Street in the city centre.

Her pimp, who now lives and works in the UK, told gardaí he entered the apartment with his own key and found Belinda naked on the bed in a pool of blood, covered by a blanket. She was clearly dead, he told gardaí later, and he phoned the authorities who found him at the scene minutes later in a shocked state. A murder investigation was launched that would eventually lead detectives to question a Catholic priest and two members of An Garda Síochána—all of whom had contacted the young prostitute enquiring about sex in the days before her killing.

It wasn't Belinda's first visit to Dublin. Two months earlier she had travelled over to work as a prostitute for ten days. She told her parents she was visiting a friend in Dublin. They had no reason not to believe her. Belinda had only been on the game for a year when her life was cut short and she had managed to keep her secret safe. She sold her body in Norwich working out of an apartment with other women, but she wasn't hardened to the life of prostitution. Belinda never sold herself on the street, preferring the security of working within four walls where punters had to make an appointment. It was safer that way, she reasoned, and you were far less likely to get caught by the police. Unlike many women on the game, she was not a drug addict. She was on the game to make money and, like most prostitutes, saw it as a short-term means to an end. No little girl ever dreams of growing up to be a prostitute. Her parents knew nothing of the double life their young daughter was leading. They thought she was employed doing secretarial work for various employers, which she had been, until the work dried up. A senior garda who investigated the unsolved murder recalls that her parents were understandably shocked when told that Belinda had been found dead. First, they had to try and absorb the fact that their daughter had been murdered. But the second piece of information truly left them reeling: she had been killed while working as a prostitute in a Dublin brothel.

The Pereiras moved to London in 1966. They were hard-working people who relocated to the UK so the children they planned to have would have plenty of opportunities. Two years after they arrived, Belinda was born, followed a few years later by her brother. She grew up in Wimbledon and attended the Ursuline convent in the area. Her father worked at Harrod's for several years before securing a job at Lufthansa Airlines at Heathrow Airport, while her mother worked as a typist. The couple had split up at the time of their daughter's murder. Her father was only a couple of years off retirement when Belinda lost her life. It shocked both her parents to the core. They both left England and went back to Sri Lanka shortly after her murder. Gardaí got the distinct impression her parents blamed themselves and wished they had never left Sri Lanka. If they had only stayed in their homeland, they told themselves, their beautiful daughter would never have met such a tragic end.

Life seemed to treat Belinda well in her early years. Her parents worked hard to provide a middle-class lifestyle for their children, and Belinda was a bright student at the convent school she attended. She was also a beautiful young woman. Her family have no idea how their daughter got involved in the murky world of prostitution, which made the garda investigation into Belinda's background all the more difficult to unravel.

Within minutes of Belinda's pimp telephoning the emergency services, gardaí arrived on the scene. Immediately, this man became the chief suspect. He was a married man in his 30s who had originally worked in the sausage industry in Co. Monaghan. He was small fry, not a major pimp at all, according to the senior garda involved in the murder probe. He had about eight women working for him and had been making a lot of money up until Belinda was killed. He was a dapper type of man and Belinda never even knew his real name. Gardaí put him under surveillance after the murder, which impacted negatively on his business interests. Eventually, he left Ireland and separated from his wife. He now lives in the UK and gardaí know where to find him if the need arises. The Monaghan man is involved in letting property in the UK, which is essentially a front for running brothels. While he was initially a suspect, gardaí are now reasonably satisfied that Belinda Pereira's pimp did not murder her.

The post-mortem found that Belinda had been dead for several hours when her pimp phoned gardaí. There are several reasons detectives now believe he was not involved in her murder. The post-mortem found that she was killed late on the night of the 28th and the Co. Monaghan man had an alibi for the night—he was drinking in a local pub in Crumlin where he lived and was captured on CCTV footage outside the pub at 11 pm, which was around the time she was killed. This man had no history of violence. Gardaí interviewed extensively all the women who worked for him, as well as several madams who ran brothels in Dublin, and all maintained he was entirely a non-violent type. No one ever seemed to have had a run-in with him, but this alone wasn't enough to clear him as a suspect. Because of his line of work, it was never in this man's interest to contact gardaí when he came across Belinda's dead body. If he had murdered her, detectives reasoned, he would have been more likely to flee the scene or try and dispose of the body. But, as the man who found the body was heavily involved in the underworld of sex-for-sale, suspicion was naturally going to hang over him. It's a suspicion that will remain until gardaí catch her killer. And this 14-year-old murder investigation has not been forgotten about: the Serious Crime Review Team, commonly known as the cold-case unit, has been urged to re-examine the case. Led by Detective Superintendent Christy Mangan—who is familiar with the case as he was previously based at Store Street garda station where the investigation was led—is understood to be open to the idea of re-examining the murder that continues to perplex gardaí despite exhaustive enquiries.

Because of his line of work, Belinda's pimp was cagey with gardaí from the beginning. He didn't reveal everything he knew at first about the young English prostitute because he feared he'd face charges relating to his own illegal activities. He was very evasive with gardaí. One of the main reasons he remained a suspect for so long was because he initially held back information from the detectives. But gardaí desperately needed the Monaghan man's help, particularly during the early stages of the investigation. He was the only person who knew Belinda was here and the reason for her trip to Dublin. His co-operation was vital.

The murder investigation was led by detectives at Store Street garda station and extensive resources were deployed to catch her murderer. The brutality of the killing over the Christmas period captivated the general public's attention. It also sent shockwaves through the underworld as prostitutes feared a 'Jack the Ripper' may be on the loose, while pimps came under pressure to protect their business interests as gardaí visited brothels as part of their enquiries.

Within days, gardaí established some vital facts about the young woman's last movements and background. She had worked as a call girl in Norwich for about 12 months working from an apartment with other women. Then she saw an advert in an English magazine looking for prostitutes to come to Ireland to work, one week at a time. She jumped at the chance. It was a change of scenery from Norwich and the money offered was better. Belinda called the number on the advert and this is how she first came into contact with the pimp from Monaghan.

He was more than happy to give her a trial—many of the women working for him were English prostitutes who worked week-on/week-off—and invited her over to Dublin. She came to Dublin in October 1996 to work as a prostitute for the man who would later discover her dead body. Gardaí have never been able to establish for certain if this was her only trip to Dublin working as a prostitute before her murder two months later. Her pimp insisted to gardaí that he only arranged for her to come to Dublin on two occasions, but everything he told detectives was always queried, as self-preservation was never far from this man's mind. Officers could also not rule out that Belinda may have travelled to Ireland previously to work for someone else, but they have no evidence to suggest she did.

Belinda's week-long trip over in October proved a success. With her dark skin and model-like figure, she was a hit with the punters. Naturally, her pimp was happy and encouraged her to come back soon. Eventually, she agreed to come back over Christmas. On Christmas Eve she flew into Dublin Airport and made her way to the up-market flat where she would be available to receive male callers from Christmas Eve until New Year's Eve, as she was due to fly back to London on New Year's Day. It certainly wasn't a conventional way to spend Christmas. Normally, the Monaghan man would have had two women operating out of the Liffey Court brothel. But because it was Christmas, no one but Belinda was willing to work.

Because of her looks, age and demeanour (the fact that she was not a heroin addict) meant her pimp could charge top dollar for her. Belinda was a high-end prostitute; an hour with her cost £120. This is how it worked: her pimp put an advert in *In Dublin* magazine, which at that stage still carried several ads offering prostitution services. Within two years of Belinda's death, gardaí began a major crackdown on the vice industry and *In Dublin* magazine publisher Mike Hogan was fined €62,700 because his magazine allowed advertising offering sex for sale. The magazine closed not long afterwards. Belinda's murder was one reason this garda clampdown was initiated. Belinda's pimp advertised a mobile phone number in *In Dublin* magazine under the heading, "Swedish, Brazilian, Italian and black beauties".

From the moment Belinda arrived at the brothel on Lower Liffey Street, she was inundated with calls on the mobile phone that had been left for her at the premises. On Christmas Day, more than 35 men called enquiring about her services. On St Stephen's Day, over 40 calls were made to her mobile. Business picked up on the 27th; almost 50 calls were logged to her phone. And on the day of her murder, between 70 and 80 punters telephoned the young prostitute. Gardaí established through telephone records that Belinda was alive up until 10 pm on the 28th. It is believed that soon after that, she let someone into the apartment, presumably after the buzzer was sounded. Only two people know exactly what unfolded next that led to her brutal murder. One of them is dead and the other killed her. Did he— and gardaí do believe it was a he—go to the apartment with murder on his mind? Or was there a row and did he kill her on the spur of the moment in anger?

Belinda's killer struck her once on the head with a heavy object, possibly a hammer, which stunned her. He then struck her several more times and she fell backwards on to the bed. She was naked but was not sexually assaulted by her attacker. He turned the apartment upside down before fleeing into the night. Nothing was stolen. There were no signs of defensive marks on Belinda's body. The fact that she was naked suggested to gardaí that whoever killed her had been a potential customer. She seemed to be taken off-guard by the killer, possibly because of a sudden row between them, and she didn't seem to have the chance to put up much of a struggle. The murder weapon has never been recovered, despite a massive search of the nearby River Liffey.

State pathologist Professor John Harbison would later tell an inquest into her death that she died of lacerations and contusions of the brain, subdural haemorrhage and fracturing of the skull caused by multiple blows with a blunt instrument.

As the door was not forced and there was a buzzer to allow visitors in, it is believed Belinda allowed the murderer into the apartment. It appears she thought this man was a punter—her nakedness when killed suggests they had agreed upon having sex. The most important piece of evidence gardaí found at the scene was the mobile phone. What began next was the time-consuming task for gardaí to try and get in touch with everyone who called the young woman in the five days since she arrived in Dublin. They needed to find out the identity of all the men who had contacted her enquiring about sex, which they hoped would lead them to her killer. Just over 200 men had telephoned the young prostitute.

Gardaí got the full list of phone numbers that had contacted the mobile phone left for Belinda during her stay. Mobile phones were still a recent phenomenon, but the vast majority of calls Belinda received were from mobile phone numbers, not landlines. Gardaí then went to the various mobile phone operators and asked for the names and addresses of anyone who had called Belinda. The phone companies co-operated with the garda investigation and within a couple of weeks of her killing, detectives had the names and addresses of every last person who had called her. Detectives had cause to raise their eyebrows at some of the men who had contacted the prostitute. A Catholic priest had phoned Belinda enquiring about sex. So had two members of An Garda Síochána, a number of barristers and solicitors and a well-known journalist. Detectives were lucky that since mobile phones were in their infancy, everyone who had called her had registered their phone. Nowadays, criminals change their phones on a regular basis, never register them, and some will only use a phone once before discarding it.

Armed with the full list of names, gardaí then began the task of contacting all the men who rang Belinda. There were garda appeals in the weeks following her murder and some men had got in touch with gardaí voluntarily to tell them they had visited her for sex. It was an embarrassing situation for all the men involved. Detectives felt particularly uneasy having to get in touch with the priest to interview him about the matter, but he co-operated fully. Detectives are confident they tracked down every last person who telephoned Belinda. Some had visited the young woman for sex; others had made appointments to see her later on, while a few just phoned for fun but had no intention of visiting the brothel.

Many of the men were married and the detectives were discreet about how they went about their enquiries. Gardaí did not knock on people's front doors asking questions in front of their families. None of the wives of the men involved found out about their husband's indiscretions. Naturally, many of the men were absolutely terrified they would face criminal charges for visiting or even contacting the young prostitute, or worse still, become a suspect in the murder. For many of them, it was the first time they had had any kind of brush with the law and they were petrified about the consequences. But the detectives were not interested in charging these individuals with soliciting sex. The only thing they were interested in was catching the killer. Gardaí simply wanted as much information from these men as they could provide about Belinda. As is always the case, the men who had visited the young prostitute were from all walks of life. But there were a couple that gardaí regarded as somewhat strange. The men that caused alarm bells to sound with the detectives were investigated thoroughly but were all eventually ruled out of garda enquiries as they had alibis.

In the months that followed, gardaí established the exact order of those who had visited the 26-year old over the Christmas period leading up to her death. All the men who had slept with her gave blood and DNA samples. None matched DNA found at the scene believed to be that of the killer. The last person to have visited Belinda for sex was obviously of great interest to gardaí. He was a man in his 40s who co-operated fully. He freely admitted making regular visits to prostitutes all over the city. He readily gave fingerprints and a blood sample and was ruled out as a suspect.

The investigation into the murder of Belinda Pereira was one of the most extensive ever launched at that time. Over 400 statements were taken. Almost a full room at Store Street station remains packed full of the hundreds of garda files relating to the case. The initial investigation went on for 16 months, with several gardaí working full-time on the investigation.

But as the weeks turned into months, no breakthrough in the case emerged, despite exhaustive enquiries and resources. Gardaí were unlucky that the vicinity around Lower Liffey Street where the brothel was located was not well covered by CCTV. While some gardaí were painstakingly taking hundreds of statements from men who had contacted Belinda, others were interviewing prostitutes, pimps and madams all over the capital. But this was tricky. These people all made their living working outside the law, therefore most were wary of speaking to gardaí. Of paramount concern to them was whether gardaí were trying to put them out of business. But in the aftermath of Belinda's death, all detectives were interested in was catching her killer. This took quite a lot of convincing, but word eventually spread among those involved in the vice industry that gardaí weren't trying to jail them. They were on the hunt for a murderer. Eventually, the women in particular began to come around. Following the young prostitute's murder, rumour and fear were rampant that this man would strike again and prostitutes were his prey. Some of these prostitutes believed that a 'Jack the Ripper' was on the loose in Dublin, and going to work was putting your life at risk. Fears of a serial killer targeting prostitutes turned out to be unfounded. But the level of concern was understandable. There is always a real element of risk for women on the game, but when another prostitute is murdered in their midst, that fear crashes into their reality and became a physical entity, a constant threat. So while some prostitutes were at first apprehensive about speaking to gardaí, they soon realised it would be to everyone's benefit to have this man taken off the streets. The madams and pimps were not quite as forthcoming. They were acutely aware that should gardaí target them, they could face charges of organising prostitution, which can carry lengthy prison terms. A spotlight was being shone into their murky world and they didn't like the attention. As well as visiting the city centre brothels, gardaí also spoke to women involved in on-street prostitution.

Some of the prostitutes interviewed remembered Belinda. Some complained that she acted as if she was above the others, possibly because she shunned drugs. Eventually a trust emerged between the women and investigating officers and, to a lesser extent, some of the pimps and madams. The other prostitutes that worked for Belinda's Irish pimp, the man from Monaghan, hadn't a bad word to say about him. He was never violent and never ripped off the women, always splitting the money 50:50. Some of the other pimps were less scrupulous and were violent. After getting tip-offs from prostitutes, gardaí extensively questioned and investigated other pimps considered particularly dangerous, but none emerged as a suspect.

Detectives were keen to discover if Belinda's killer might have previously attacked other prostitutes and followed up every lead the women gave them. What had happened really scared them and put a lot of pressure on the pimps. Those heavily involved in organising prostitution allowed gardaí to install cameras in all the hallways into the brothels in case another woman was targeted. Gardaí began to get regular calls from prostitutes if they had a customer that frightened them. They would even take down the man's car registration and pass it on to gardaí if they thought a client seemed in any way suspicious. Detectives chased up every piece of information, but none of it led to anything significant. In total, more than 100 prostitutes were questioned about violent clients. Less than a month after Belinda's murder, a prostitute told gardaí about a severe beating she received at the hands of a violent pimp. This woman was also from the UK but regularly travelled to Dublin to work as a call girl. The attack took place a few months before Belinda's killing and the woman hadn't gone to gardaí because she was on the game. This man, a pimp in his 30s, was later questioned, but he had an alibi for the night of the murder. Detectives were told this man was known to demand sexual favours from prostitutes.

The investigation also brought the detectives over to Belinda's hometown, London. It was explored, and later ruled out, whether someone could have followed her over from the UK to kill her. About four or five other English women were working for the same pimp in Dublin as Belinda and all were extensively interviewed. Belinda didn't have a boyfriend at the time of her killing. But she did have a close male friend whom gardaí questioned in the UK and were satisfied he had nothing to do with her killing.

Gardaí never learned how Belinda ended up getting involved in prostitution, but found out she had saved much of the money she earned on the game. This was possibly an indication that she planned not to work in the sex industry long-term. Her family's sense of shock over the circumstances of her death seemed impossible for them to shake. Their grief became almost unbearable when the garda investigation began stretching into months and still her killer hadn't been caught. Within 18 months of her death, both had separately returned to live in their native Sri Lanka.

Detectives visited them in London and they also travelled to Dublin to formally identify her body. Belinda lived with her mother who was in Sri Lanka celebrating Christmas at the time of her daughter's murder. Belinda worked hard to keep her profession a secret from her family and many of her friends.

Travelling to Dublin to earn money selling her body was the perfect way for her to remain anonymous and not risk her family finding out.

Back in Dublin, the investigation continued. While the pimp from Monaghan was initially the chief suspect, as the investigation progressed gardaí began to move away from this theory. The full-time investigation into her death ended after 16 months. Gardaí continued to follow up any leads, such as calls from prostitutes about violent clients. Twelve months after her murder, there was a major review of all the evidence. And as recently as three years ago, detectives once more meticulously went through every aspect of a murder that has puzzled some of Dublin's most seasoned murder detectives, most of whom have now retired.

In more recent years, detectives have considered whether Belinda's killer had been a previous visitor to the brothel and called in unannounced and then killed her. It is possible that Belinda had been expecting someone else and buzzed the murderer in. It is a theory that is given considerable credence, mainly because detectives believe they have ruled out all the men who telephoned Belinda for sex.

There have been countless appeals from gardaí over the past 14 years for information that could help solve the case. At an inquest into her death 19 months after her killing, Dublin city coroner Dr Brian Farrell appealed for anyone with information to come forward. The inquest was told that some 700 specific jobs in relation to the case had been completed. While the murder investigation remained open, the coroner was told by detectives that the inquest could conclude as there were no imminent plans to charge anyone in relation to her murder. The jury returned a verdict of death by unlawful killing, giving her family a small sense of finality, detectives hoped, but certainly not closure. "We have taken this investigation as far as we can. The fact that it has never been solved has been of major disappointment to myself and several others because of the huge effort put into it," says the senior garda, who spoke on condition of anonymity as the case remains unsolved. "We've gone as far as we can with it. All that's left in a last effort to try and solve it is if the cold-case team has a look at it. It was a sad and lonely way for Belinda to die. It's certainly one of the most tragic cases I've ever investigated."

04 | SUKHDEV SINGH

In a chance meeting that would determine the rest of their lives, Sukhdev Singh bumped into his old acquaintance Ram Pal while on a trip home to India in the summer of 2000. The two men had much in common and plenty to talk about. Sukhdev had been living with his family in Ireland for 30 years, where he owned and ran a successful takeaway and restaurant in Dublin city centre. Ram was a chef and, like his friend, spent much of his adult life living abroad. His wife and children lived in the village of Mukandpur, in the state of Punjab, and ran a bakery while Ram worked abroad. Over a 20 year period he lived and worked in Saudi Arabia, Pakistan and Afghanistan to provide for his family. Both were well-respected and dedicated family men. Everything they did was done to help better the lives of their wives and children. Sukhdev came from the village of Talwandi Phattu, half a mile from Mukandpur, and the pair knew each other since their youth. After chatting a while, they soon felt it was destiny that determined their chance meeting. Ram Pal told his friend he had always dreamed of following in his footsteps and bringing his family to live in the western world. Sukhdev said he was looking for someone to help him run and invest in his restaurant in Dublin. Why didn't he come back to Ireland with him?

It seemed like a perfect opportunity for both men. Fifty-nine-year-old Sukhdev was looking for a business partner and someone to help with the day-to-day running of his demanding business, Dave's Restaurant and Takeaway, at 67 Dorset Street. Ram (49), a talented chef, was looking for a business opportunity that could help him relocate his family to the west, considered by many people in the eastern world as the land of opportunity and possibility. The men agreed to go into business together and within a couple of months, Ram Pal secured a working visa to travel to Ireland. He arrived in Dublin filled with enthusiasm about the new venture, and Sukhdev was equally excited about having a new business partner, someone to help shoulder his business burdens. No one could have anticipated that both men would end up dead by the beginning of the next year. One would die from stab wounds, the other from a broken heart. The story of how Ram Pal killed his friend Sukhdev Singh, which in turn led to his own death, has never been told before.

Sukhdev invited his friend to live at his home in Ryevale Lawn in Leixlip, Co. Kildare. He soon became part of the Singh family. At first everything went very well. Ram Pal got along with all of the family, but soon cracks began to show in his relationship with Sukhdev as they disagreed on how the business should be run. The pair would often sleep overnight at Dave's Restaurant and Takeaway, as they often had to work late. Everyone in the area knew and liked Sukhdev, who was affectionately known as Dave Gill by the locals. He had owned and run the restaurant for several years and everyone knew him as a hard-working, gentle family man. The Indian restaurant was successful and had many regular customers. Locals who got to know Ram Pal in the months he lived in Ireland before his death described him in similar terms—an industrious family man who spoke all the time of how his wife Vena Kumari and his three sons and daughter would soon join him in Ireland.

But adjusting to life in Ireland without the love and support of his family proved a stressful time for Ram Pal. He was almost 50 years old and had invested both money and time in Dave's Restaurant. The success of this partnership was necessary to secure his family's future. Deep down, he probably felt that if this venture failed, he would have few more opportunities to achieve the life he desired for his family. Sukhdev, on the other hand, felt that he knew best how the business should be run, having owned and operated it for several years. He also had the experience of living and working in Ireland for 30 years and had proven himself a success. Ram was of the Hindu faith while Sukhdev was a Sikh although religion had no bearing on what happened between the two men in the early hours of 12 January 2001. After a long night's work they decided to sleep overnight at their workplace, but an argument broke out between them over how the restaurant was being run. In a moment of madness in the heat of the row, Ram picked up a knife and stabbed his friend several times in the upper body until he fell to the ground dead. After realising what he had done, Ram Pal lay on the ground inside the front door of the restaurant and tried to cut his own throat. Doctors would later tell detectives there were six hesitation cuts on the Indian man's throat, as well as a deep gash he inflicted on himself during his suicide attempt. He did enough damage to render himself unconscious but not to take his own life.

When morning broke, Sukhdev's wife Swarn became concerned when she didn't hear from her husband. She tried repeatedly to phone the restaurant, but there was no answer. By mid-afternoon she was worried enough to drive from their home in Leixlip with her son to their restaurant on Dorset Street.

When she opened the restaurant's front door, Swarn Singh was greeted with a scene that will be forever engrained in her memory. Ram Pal's bleeding and unconscious body was immediately visible as it was blocking the doorway. Not far from him lay her dead husband. Within minutes gardaí from Fitzgibbon Street and the emergency services arrived at the scene after being contacted by a shocked and distraught Swarn. It was quickly established that one man was dead and the other was seriously injured. Ram Pal was rushed to the Mater Hospital while the scene was sealed off. At first detectives explored whether both men may have been victims of a racist attack by someone who broke into the restaurant. But this was quickly ruled out as there was no evidence of forced entry, and Ram Pal became the focus of the investigation.

Chief Superintendent Al McHugh (now retired) and Detective Superintendent Cormac Gordan (now retired) at Store Street garda station oversaw the murder probe. Detective Inspector Hubert Collins (now retired) and Detective Sergeant Walter O'Sullivan (now detective superintendent) from Fitzgibbon Street station led the investigation.

Doctors at the Mater informed the detectives that the hesitation wounds on Ram Pal's neck were a clear indication that they were self-inflicted. It is extremely difficult to cut your own throat; few people take their own lives using this method. Medics also told gardaí that Ram had no defensive wounds on his body that pointed to a struggle between the two men before the fatal stabbing. Ram was ten years younger than Sukhdev and was physically much bigger and stronger. Before interviewing Ram, gardaí speculated whether he might have stabbed his friend because he assaulted him, but the medical evidence suggested this was not the case.

He remained at the hospital for 18 nights until he was in a fit enough condition to be arrested and taken to Mountjoy garda station to be questioned in relation to the death of Sukhdev Singh. Immediately, he admitted stabbing him. "He was profoundly remorseful, one of the most remorseful people I've ever had in custody," according to a senior garda involved in the investigation, who spoke on condition of anonymity. "He'd never been in any trouble with the police before. He told us he became enraged during a row and stabbed him. He was extremely upset." Two days later on 1 February 2001, he appeared at Dublin District Court and was charged with assault causing serious harm to Sukhdev Singh at Dorset Street on 12 January. He was remanded in custody. "He couldn't believe what he had done. That's why he tried to cut his own throat. He was in a state of shock and remorseful and distraught beyond belief. He couldn't believe what had happened; he felt he was in a bad dream. He said it was self-defence but he didn't have any defensive marks," adds the senior garda.

Within three months, having reviewed all the evidence against him, the Director of Public Prosecutions (DPP) directed that Ram Pal be charged with his friend's murder. It is not unusual for the DPP to increase the charges against someone after considering the evidence in detail. But it was a shock for Ram Pal. On 16 May the 49-year old appeared again at the Dublin District Court and was charged with murder. After he was charged, Ram Pal told gardaí: "I did not realise it happened, it was in self-defence. I am sorry and I want to go back to India. Sukhdev also took a knife to me. If possible, send me back to my kids. I am not well here." He was again remanded in custody by Judge David Anderson and sent back to Cloverhill Prison. He was due to stand trial for Sukhdev Singh's murder in May 2002.

Ram Pal was speaking the truth when he told detectives he was unwell. As a result of killing his friend, the middle-aged man fell into a deep depression. Languishing in Cloverhill Prison, he had a lot of time to contemplate his actions. He knew that Sukhdev was dead because he took a knife to him. He knew that his friend's family, who had become an extension of his own family, were now without a husband and father. He knew that his own family were in India, unable to visit him and were now without his financial support for the foreseeable future. He felt he had let everyone down. Ram Pal's life had changed beyond all recognition because of the violence he inflicted on his friend during a heated row. He wanted to serve his sentence for his crime in India, but he knew that the judicial system did not operate that way, that he must serve whatever prison sentence was handed down by the courts in Ireland. While he told gardaí that he had acted in self-defence and that Sukhdev took a knife to him, there was no evidence to support this. Detectives have since speculated that maybe this was something he tried to convince himself of in order to justify his actions.

Physically and psychologically, Ram Pal could not cope with what he had done. On the morning of 28 March 2002, prison officers found his dead body in his cell. He had suffered a heart attack. In less than two months' time he was due to stand trial for his friend's murder. "He was an overweight man and Indian people can be prone to heart disease. But his heart attack was really stress-related because of what had happened," adds the senior garda. "Essentially, his body could not cope with what he had done. He had fallen into a deep depression at the time of his death. Really, he died of a broken heart."

The prison chaplain at Cloverhill accompanied his body back to India and met with his distraught wife and children. Vena Kumari found it hard to reconcile how her loving husband, who had left his family to become involved in a new business enterprise with his friend, now lay dead before her in a wooden box. Accepting that he had also admitted stabbing Sukhdev Singh proved even harder.

The tragedy that befell Sukhdev Singh because of the actions of Ram Pal left two families fatherless and husbandless. Detectives involved in the investigation were stuck by how everyone they interviewed described the two men in such similar terms— honest, hard-working, family-orientated men who had never been in trouble with the law. While Sukhdev was the victim, it was obvious to gardaí that Ram Pal could not cope with life in Ireland and the extreme violence he displayed was at least partly driven by the pressure he had placed himself under. His responsibilities weighed heavily on his shoulders and eventually he snapped.

The killing of Sukhdev Singh did not attract the glare of media attention and Ram Pal's subsequent death in custody meant there would be no trial. Therefore the background to this tragic tale has never emerged until now. "People are judged by their actions, not their past history or their intentions and that is correct. To stab someone to death is a terrible thing," adds the garda. "There was substantial evidence against Ram Pal. But it is important to remember that he died an innocent man in the eyes of the law. That has to be respected. It is not for us to judge him."

05 | YUE FENG AND LIU QING

He was their best friend. Their older, wiser companion the two 19-year-old Chinese students thought they could turn to for counsel when they ran into difficulties living so far from home. But 23-year-old Yu Jie was harbouring a deep resentment. His young friends were wealthy and Yu was not. This jealousy spurred him to carry out a premeditated act of double murder, killing the teenage couple separately and then setting fire to their bodies in their Dublin city centre apartment in 2001.

The double murder sent shockwaves through the Chinese community in Ireland, ultimately leading to the issuing of a death threat to Yu Jie from his fellow countrymen during his trial.

The 23-year old murdered Yue Feng and his girlfriend Liu Qing in March 2001 and was convicted of their killings two years later following the longest jury trial in Irish legal history. His total detachment to his horrific crime unsettled some of Dublin's most seasoned murder detectives. He cut the figure of an unlikely killer. Initially, he was a prize witness for gardaí, assisting them extensively with their enquiries and was not under any suspicion whatsoever. "He never once showed any remorse," recalls Detective Superintendent John McMahon, who investigated the case as a detective inspector at the Bridewell station. "He only cried for himself."

Yu Jie had been living in Ireland for almost three years when he committed his crime. The young man knew Liu Qing and Yue Feng from home and when they moved to Dublin in 2000, he took them under his wing. All three came from Shenyang in the province of Liaoning in north-east China, a city of seven million people which was very different to the Irish capital at the time. Dublin had developed into a prosperous European city, while Shenyang was a grey metropolis experiencing severe economic problems. The city's youth were eager to travel.

The Chinese community in Dublin at the start of the century were a close-knit community. Yu Jie, who was also known as Jack, was working at McDonald's in Phibsboro, as well as holding down another job as a dishwasher at a restaurant in Temple Bar. Like many Chinese students, he was here on a visa and was supposed to be attending an English language school. But many of these so-called schools were then operating as money-making rackets. Yu was paying one of the visa-scam institutions a fee to ensure they provided him with letters stating he was attending classes so he was permitted to stay in Ireland. A crackdown of operations at these institutions would soon follow and minimum attendance and registration was introduced. But Yue Feng and his girlfriend Liu Qing were genuinely studying in Dublin. Yue Feng had considerable financial support from his family, unlike Yu Jie, so he did not need to work and could concentrate on his studies. His girlfriend was studying English at the Swan Training Centre on Grafton Street and worked part-time in a Chinese restaurant in Malahide. Yu Jie resented that he had to work two jobs to pay his rent, as well as the visa scam school, while his young friends had little financial worries in comparison. The 23-year old also had a burgeoning gambling problem to support. His begrudgery began to grow and culminated in a row with Yue Feng in July 2000. The teenager had travelled back to China to visit his family as his grandmother was sick. During the trip his father Lian Sheng Yue, a millionaire company manager in the oil business, told his staff to give his son $30,000 (€28,400) cash. This was to cover tuition fees for Yue and his cousin, who was also living in Ireland, as well as living expenses and medical and life insurance.

The teenager returned to Dublin and told his older friend about the money he now had. Astonished by the sum, Yu Jie asked his friend for a loan. But he refused. The cash was not his to lend; it had to last a long time and support his cousin also, he explained. The teenager thought that was the end of it, that his older friend accepted his refusal. "We believe he asked him for money after his first trip home but when he refused, a lot of resentment built up in Yu Jie," says McMahon. When Yue Feng and his girlfriend returned from another visit to China to celebrate the Chinese New Year in early March 2001, Yu Jie believed the teenager would again bring back a similar amount of cash. With murder on his mind, Yu plotted in detail how he would get away with killing his friends and steal the vast sums of money he assumed would be in their apartment.

On the afternoon of 12 March 2001, Yu Jie arranged to meet Yue Feng at his apartment on Blackhall Square, off North King St, Dublin 7, after he finished English classes. He knew that his girlfriend had lectures that afternoon and wouldn't be home until after 5 pm. Since he never admitted to the murder, gardaí do not know exactly what happened between the two men that led the older but much smaller man to kill his teenage friend. It is possible there was another row after he asked for money, but detectives are satisfied that the double killing was planned because of its meticulous execution. The two friends were having tea together in the sitting room of the apartment when Yu Jie caught Yue Feng unawares and strangled him from behind as he sat on the sofa. This would have been no simple task. Yue Feng was six foot tall and the diminutive killer was about seven inches smaller. At the post-mortem marks were found on both wrists of the teenager's charred body, suggesting he had been restrained. A piece of pink cotton cord, most likely belonging to a camera or a pair of glasses, was later found under the sofa by Detective Frank Tracey, which would later prove instrumental in the trial as the pattern from the cord was imprinted on his friend's neck. Yu Jie strangled his friend from behind until his body stopped struggling. "Possibly in a rush of blood to the head, he strangled him. There could have been another row over money, but we don't know because he never admitted to any of it," says McMahon. "About 15 seconds is all it would have taken using the cord to kill him. He went into that apartment with the idea of doing it. He knew Yue Feng was back from his morning class and his girlfriend had an afternoon class."

He had a four hour wait until Liu Qing was due home. Yu Jie stole his dead friend's keys and bankcard and let himself out of the apartment. He went to a nearby ATM machine and took €10 out of his friend's account. He did this so he could get a receipt to check how much was in the account. He would have been disappointed to learn there wasn't anything close to the thousands he had just killed for. He then went back to the apartment, calmly waiting for Liu Qing to return home. He also searched the apartment for the cash he had been so sure his friend's wealthy father would have given him. But there were no vast sums of money to be found. Yue Feng hadn't needed to ask his father for more money as he still had enough for the time being from the original $30,000 he had given him eight months earlier. When he was arrested eight days after the discovery of his two friends' bodies, he had only €600 on him and had withdrawn small amounts of cash from Yue Feng's bank account. It is also believed he stole cartons of cigarettes from the apartment the couple had brought back from China. Gardaí believe the double killer also paid off a couple of small debts in the following days, but all in all he got little financial gain for taking two young lives.

After 5 pm Liu Qing came home and was captured on CCTV entering the Blackhall Square apartment complex and checking her mail box, blissfully unaware her boyfriend lay dead upstairs. Moments later she too would join him in death, murdered by one of her closest friends. Moments after she let herself into apartment 2A, gardaí believe Yu Jie attacked the young student. Armed with the same pink cord that had already proven an able murder weapon, he strangled her to death with greater ease than it had taken to kill her boyfriend. No marks were found on her wrists at the post-mortem to suggest she was restrained.

He then dragged both bodies into their bedroom. He placed them lying side by side on the double bed they shared. He then let himself out of the apartment, making sure the alarm was switched off. Yu Jie wore a baseball cap at all times when entering and exiting their apartment block, although he was unaware there was a hidden CCTV camera in the dome of the complex. The callous, unprovoked double murder did not seem to trouble the 23-year old's conscience as later that night he went gambling with two of his housemates. He returned to the apartment the next day, most likely just to check the bodies had not been discovered. The young couple shared their apartment with another couple, but they were away at the time. In the early hours of the next morning, Yu Jie again returned to the apartment on his bicycle after his shift finished at McDonald's in Phibsboro. He was armed with petrol hidden under his jacket and let himself in. He doused the bodies of his two young friends with petrol and set them alight in a crude attempt to conceal the double murder. But he used much more petrol than was necessary and was lucky to escape from the room without suffering burns himself when the petrol caused an explosion. The force of the blast sent a chair in the room through the double glazed bedroom window.

He hastily made his exit from the apartment. But as he emerged, a neighbour who had come to her door after she heard the explosion spotted him. But she didn't pay too much attention to the young Chinese man, as she thought he was just taking out the rubbish.

Worried that he had been seen, Yu quickly left the building and cycled to the house he rented in Finglas with several other Chinese students. Liu Sha Sha, one of his roommates who had worked with him in McDonald's earlier that night, found him "the same as usual". The next day, all hell broke loose. Liu Sha Sha went to her language college and saw a notice in the school informing students of the fire at the young couple's apartment and asking anyone with information to come forward. She immediately rang Yu Jie. She told him of the fire and he seemed shocked. He told her he was still sleeping, but promised to go over to their apartment as soon as he got up.

He arrived outside the Blackhall Square complex in the late morning with three other Chinese friends. He was one of the first of the couple's friends to approach gardaí offering to assist in any way. "He couldn't have been more helpful. He gave us an extremely detailed statement over four days. He told us all about his two friends and how they had just returned from China and they'd gone home to celebrate the Chinese New Year," says McMahon. "He spent several hours with us and was extremely useful to us in terms of finding out the background of these two students. If we didn't know as much as we do now, he really was the perfect witness."

While Yu Jie was assisting detectives with their enquiries in the four days following the discovery of the students' strangled and charred bodies, he was not under any suspicion. He was perfectly relaxed in all his dealings with gardaí; he was so at ease that he even asked the Chinese interpreter hired to assist gardaí with their enquiries out on a date. She agreed and the pair went out once together before he was arrested on suspicion of double murder eight days after the young couple's bodies were found. Only once did Yu Jie betray any emotion. The day after the fire, gardaí asked him to identify his two friends. He was taken to the city morgue in Marino. "After he identified the two bodies, he was sick," says Detective Sergeant Alan Bailey, who investigated the killings as a sergeant at the Bridewell. "It was the only time I saw him show any emotion whatsoever."

Philip Hickey, who was a member of a host family that provided accommodation and support for Yue Feng in his first month in Ireland, also identified the bodies. When he attended the city morgue that same day, he saw Yu Jie coming out after the first identification in a very distressed state. It seemed the partially charred bodies were a difficult sight for any eyes to absorb, even the killer's.

The fire brigade knew almost immediately when called to the scene in the early hours of 14 March that they weren't dealing with a normal, domestic fire. They were called to the Blackhall

Square apartment complex to extinguish the fire by residents who heard the explosion. Firefighters John Chubb and Graham Parkes had some difficulty gaining access to the bedroom and Phibsboro fire station officer Eugene Duignan was about to call for a sledgehammer when one of them shouldered the door in.

The firefighters first noticed an elevated fire in the bedroom, concentrated around the bed. The fire was small and it was put out quickly. When the smoke cleared, the firemen became suspicious. The bottom of the bed was severely burnt and a partition wall beside it had shifted some eight inches from the skirting board. "I assumed it was some pressure blast—explosion in other words," Eugene Duignan told the murder trial. He noticed that Yue Feng's body on the bed had a small amount of blood at the end of his nostril and his tongue was protruding. He formed the view that the death was suspicious and told all personnel to withdraw from the scene. District fire officer Jim Murphy shared his concerns. On viewing the bodies, he too became convinced it wasn't a natural fire death. He noted that the bedroom window had been blown out and there was broken glass outside. This suggested a small, localised fire, or flash-over, where an accelerant such as petrol could have caused it. Gardaí were immediately notified and they sealed off the scene. None of the fire brigade smelt any petrol or other such fumes when they removed their breathing masks outside the apartment. But forensic examiners later found partially evaporated petrol on the remains of the couple. In her post-mortem examinations, state pathologist Dr Marie Cassidy said the couple were dead at least 20 hours before the discovery of their bodies.

In the meantime, gardaí were questioning as many neighbours and friends of the young couple as they could find to try and establish their last movements. They were also studying footage from a ceiling-mounted glass dome on the inside of the apartment block at Blackhall Square that concealed a CCTV security camera. Everyone the detectives interviewed had to provide them with details of their movements over the days when the couple were murdered and later set alight. Suddenly, holes began to appear in Yu Jie's story. Gardaí routinely checked out what Yu had told them about visiting USIT the morning after the murders took place. They discovered he went in the afternoon, not the morning, and that he was wearing the same clothes as the man in the CCTV footage seen entering his friends' apartment block on three occasions between 12 March and the early hours of 14 March. He had told the detectives he hadn't seen his friends since they returned from their trip to China. Yu's roommate Liu Sha Sha was also able to identify him as the person on the security videos entering the couple's apartment complex despite the fact that a cap was concealing his face. Gardaí's star witness suddenly became their chief suspect. Eight days after their bodies were discovered, the 23-year old was arrested on suspicion of the murder of his two teenage friends.

Yu was arrested in his rented accommodation at McKee Avenue in Finglas. In the days before detectives called to his home, there was a discussion at senior garda level about who should be hired as an interpreter during his detention. Obviously the previous interpreter with whom Yu Jie had gone out on a date could not be called upon because of their personal relationship. It became an issue that many of the Chinese interpreters could know, or know of, Yu Jie because of the close-knit nature of the Chinese community in Dublin. It was also of concern for gardaí that after his arrest, the suspect could only be held for 12 hours without charge. This meant it would be crucial that the interpreter spoke the same dialect of Mandarin as Yu Jie and that the interpretation of the suspect's replies could not be queried in court. With all of this in mind, gardaí liaised with Interpol looking for a police officer who could speak Mandarin Chinese and translate their interrogation of the 23-year old. Gardaí were in luck. Zhijin Zuo, a third assistant commissioner of the Chinese police and a qualified medical doctor and forensic pathologist, had been seconded to Interpol working as a disaster victim identification expert in Lyon, France, at the time. He flew to Dublin immediately.

Once under arrest, Yu Jie changed his story dramatically. He had initially told gardaí that he hadn't seen his friends at all since they had come back from China a couple of days previously. But in custody, he identified himself on CCTV footage entering their apartment complex on three occasions between 12 and 14 March and also confirmed his identification on more security footage taken at the USIT office on Aston Quay on 13 March wearing the same clothes he had worn the day before when he killed the two teenagers. But he still denied responsibility for the double murder. His explanation for returning to their apartment just before 1 am on 14 March when the fire was started was because he was worried for his friends. He said the explosion occurred when he got to the door and he then ran away in fear.

Despite the seriousness of the accusations against him, Yu Jie remained relaxed while under arrest. As well as CCTV footage—some of which depicted Yu Jie entering the apartment complex's main entrance with Yue Feng shortly before he strangled him to death—gardaí had also obtained his fingerprints from the couple's apartment. But the 12 hour arrest period was running out for detectives before all the necessary questions were put to Yu Jie as the translation and interpretation of his responses under questioning was proving a time-consuming process. He was asked if he would agree to continue being questioned voluntarily. He declined. Detectives were in touch with the DPP's office and just as his period of detention was about to run out, the DPP directed gardaí to charge the 23-year old with the double murder.

All the evidence linking him to the killings was circumstantial, but gardaí were satisfied the case against him was strong enough to secure a conviction. As well as CCTV, Yu Jie's fingerprints were found on one of two mugs on the sitting room table in the apartment. He had been drinking tea with Yue Feng before he strangled him. His fingerprints were also found on Yue Feng's glasses, which were found at the apartment. Gardaí had also recovered the piece of pink cord used as the murder weapon. The 23-year old was denied bail.

His trial began on 13 January 2003 and lasted 60 days, making it the longest jury trial in Irish legal history. It began in dramatic fashion. Gardaí were informed of a death threat issued to Yu Jie from within the Chinese community as the trial got under way. It was taken seriously, and he was provided with an armed guard for the duration of his court case. "It was a threat of sorts but it wasn't from a triad or underworld gang or anything like that. It was a general threat really. It might not have been serious but of course we have to treat anything like that extremely seriously. The double murder had caused a huge amount of upset within the Chinese community here," explains McMahon. "There was a lot of anger over what had happened. The two families were obviously distraught and the wider community felt that Yu Jie had let the community down in a major way and tarnished them all. This was a young man with no criminal record and he was very well known and well liked here by other Chinese people. They were shocked and appalled by this and found it hard to come to terms with."

Gardaí felt that a far more realistic danger Yu Jie faced was a possible attack by other Chinese inmates in prison during the 22 months he spent on remand awaiting trial. But he remained unscathed over this period. When he emerged from prison for his trial, the young murderer remained upbeat until the very end.

Over 200 witnesses were listed to give evidence during the trial at the Central Criminal Court. Several of them were former friends of the accused. The prosecution case was that Yu Jie acted alone.

One of the first to give evidence was Yue Feng's father, Lian Sheng Yue. Still displaying raw emotion but refusing to look at his son's killer while giving evidence, he spoke about how he planned to move his son away from Ireland as he believed it was an unsuitable environment. Following his divorce in 1992, Lian Sheng Yue became responsible for the financial support of his son. In October 1999, his son told him he wanted to go to Ireland to study, but his father disagreed with his plans. But as his girlfriend had decided she was going, Yue Feng applied for a Chinese passport to go with her. His son had his mind made up and when he left for Ireland in February 2000, Lian Sheng Yue transferred $5,000 in tuition fees for him. In June 2000, he returned home for a visit and his father arranged for company staff to hand his son $30,000. He did not want his son to have to work, but to focus on his studies instead. But not long after that,

Lian Sheng Yue decided he wanted his son to leave Ireland. "I learned through other sources that the environment for study was not suitable for my son," he said. "I wanted to transfer him from Ireland to Australia, and I went to Australia myself to see what the environment there was like."

Five relatives of the two students came to Dublin a couple of weeks after their murder. Both of the teenagers' mothers were hospitalised separately after receiving the devastating news. Liu Qing's family were not as wealthy as Yue Feng's. Her extended family dug deep to raise the thousands necessary to send her to study English in Ireland. Her uncle Song Shoutian said the 19-year-old student last spoke with her family five weeks before she was found dead. "She rang about once a month and wrote often. She really liked her life in Ireland and was getting on well. When she last called there was no indication that anything was wrong. She seemed happy as usual," Song Shoutian said shortly after her death. Her parents were divorced and her mother, Song Xiu Li, became ill and was rushed to hospital in Jiamusi city in Heilongjiang province after being told of the murder. Qing's father also went into deep shock after hearing the news. "We only have enough money to send one person to Ireland to identify the body and to bring her home," her uncle added.

Yue Feng's mother was also taken to hospital and received medical treatment when she arrived in Dublin because she was suffering from deep grief and fatigue. The families were briefed by gardaí during their trip to Dublin and informed that Yu Jie had been charged with the double murder.

Much of the subsequent double murder trial focused on CCTV footage, as well as interviews with Yu Jie in custody. He made a remarkable attempt to change his story about why he was seen entering his friends' apartment on Blackhall Square over the period when they were murdered, as well as leaving the apartment after the fire broke out. Before his arrest he told gardaí the last time he was in the Blackhall Square apartment was before his two friends left for a visit to China in early 2001. But when under arrest, he told gardaí that before he went to China, Yue Feng gave him a set of keys to his apartment. Asked did he still have the keys, Yu Jie told gardaí: "No, I have thrown out the keys. In the Liffey. I threw the keys into the river. I was afraid." He then told gardaí he wanted an opportunity to tell everything from the beginning. At this point gardaí hoped they might get a full confession out of Yu Jie. But instead, he concocted a far-fetched story that the jury ultimately did not accept. He said that Yue Feng asked him to visit him in Blackhall Square on the day he was killed because he was in some kind of trouble. His young friend had planned to buy Chinese ink paintings during his trip home but he hadn't managed to, according to Yu Jie. This had angered Chinese people in Ireland who had given him money to buy these paintings as he had spent all the cash. Yu Jie told gardaí the 19-year old asked him would he lend him £10,000, but he didn't have the money. He told gardaí that he stayed at the apartment talking to Yue Feng and his girlfriend when she got home about their concerns. They were fearful over possible repercussions over spending other people's money, he said. When he left their apartment on 12 March, he insisted they were both still alive. He said he returned to the apartment the next day and again, later that night, because he was worried about Yue Feng. When he visited the apartment on the morning of 13 March, he found the bedroom door locked, he said. Later that night, he went there again, but as he got to the apartment door, he heard an explosion. Yu Jie told gardaí that when he heard the explosion, he got a shock and ran out. Then a neighbour came to the door and he thought he would get into trouble, so he left. Not for a moment did gardaí believe this version of events. The CCTV footage spoke for itself—Yu Jie was the only person to enter and exit his friends' apartment over the period when they were murdered and later set alight.

The neighbour of the student couple who saw Yu outside their apartment moments after it exploded into flames could not be 100 per cent sure that it was Yu Jie that she saw. She picked Yu and another man out at a garda identity parade while he was under arrest. Una Murphy heard an explosion at around 12.55 am on the morning of 14 March in one of the other apartments and she opened her door and looked out. She saw a man standing outside apartment 2, about ten feet from her. He looked straight down at her and there was a rubbish bag beside him. She went back inside her apartment and told her friends it was just someone putting out rubbish. She thought she had seen this man before among Chinese people who would come and go on the corridor from apartment 2. She admitted in court that she found it difficult to distinguish between Chinese people sometimes and between Chinese and Japanese people. At the identity parade, she picked out No. 1 and No. 9. "When I looked at everyone and then looked at No. 9, I just froze. I had a gut feeling it was him," she said. Number 9 was Yu Jie.

Detectives believe they tracked down the garage in Finglas where Yu Jie bought the petrol he later doused his friends with. Gardaí trawled all the petrol stations in the city centre, Finglas and surrounding areas to try and establish where he bought the accelerant. Gardaí thought they had struck gold when an employee recalled selling petrol to a young Chinese man on 13 March. But this individual was not considered a reliable witness and was not called to give evidence.

Yu Jie convinced his friend and flatmate to provide him with an alibi of sorts on the night of the fire. She later admitted to gardaí that she hadn't been entirely truthful with them as Yu Jie asked her to lie for him. Liu Sha Sha slept in the sitting room in the house in Finglas with Yu Jie and another Chinese man, Liu Pin. She identified her former friend on a photograph taken from CCTV footage of the entrance hall to the young couple's apartment. On the night of 13 March, she and Yu Jie finished work in McDonald's of Phibsboro at around 12.30 am. She shared a taxi home with the manager of the restaurant, while Yu Jie said he would get home on his bicycle. He returned home at around 1.30 am after he went to the apartment at Blackhall Square to set the bodies alight.

When she first spoke to gardaí after the young couple were discovered murdered, she told them she did not know if Yu Jie had a bicycle or not. Asked why she had not told them that in fact he had a bike, she replied, "Yu Jie said don't mention anything in relation to the bike." He was concerned witnesses saw him cycling to and from the murder scene. Liu Sha Sha met Yu Jie when she moved into the house he was living in in Finglas a week after coming to Ireland in November 2000. They became close but were just friends. He had a bad temper, as did she, and they sometimes had loud arguments. But he never displayed violence towards her. All in all she had grown fond of him and they had got to know one another very well as they both slept in the same sitting room for four months until his arrest for murder. "I think he's not a bad person," she said. "But sometimes he's acting like a child. He's got a bad temper; he has a good heart." He was a smiley person, she explained, and told bad jokes that only he thought were funny. Over the three days he carried out and tried to conceal the double murder, she noticed no change in his demeanour or behaviour.

When Yu Jie wasn't working one of his two jobs, he spent a lot of his time gambling. It was a problem that seemed to be spiralling out of control at the time he carried out his crime. Arunee Hennessy, the owner of the Bangkok café on Parnell Street where Yu had worked at one stage, told the trial that Yu once told her that he sometimes played blackjack on the machines in Dr Quirkey's Emporium in O'Connell Street and that he had lost £1,000 playing it. Appalled, she told him he was crazy for throwing that much money away.

The night the 23-year old strangled his two friends to death, he didn't show up at 5 pm to take over as a dishwasher in Wollensky's restaurant in Temple Bar, where he held down a second job. At 5 pm he would have been lying in wait for Liu Qing to arrive home so he could strangle her. He telephoned his housemate Liu Pin, who also worked as a dishwasher at the same restaurant, and said he couldn't make it to work because of traffic. By 8 pm, after murdering his friends and laying their dead bodies side by side on their bed, he decided to go gambling. His housemates Liu Sha Sha and Liu Pin went with him to an amusement arcade near Phibsboro. Liu said it was normal practice for him and Yu to go gambling about three times a week. They usually played poker machines, costing one pound a game. Why did they gamble so much each week? "Entertainment," Liu Pin told the trial.

Gardaí established that Yu Jie had a few debts but nothing substantial, and he was sometimes late paying his rent. It seemed he wasted a lot of money gambling in amusement arcades and he wasn't particularly good at managing his wages. But he didn't appear to have got himself into serious debt. While robbery was the main motive for his crime, jealousy and resentment over his young friends' lifestyle seemed to spur him on to carry out his cold-blooded killings.

For three weeks over the course of his trial, the jury were not present as legal argument was heard and Chinese policeman Zhijin Zuo—who acted as an interpreter for gardaí while Yu Jie was in custody—gave evidence. Detectives say the policeman's contribution was invaluable. "There was a trial within a trial for three weeks. Yu Jie said he was ill while in custody, that he had a severe headache. But the Chinese policeman was a qualified medical doctor and it was clear from the tapes that he was not unwell," says McMahon. "Much was made of the fact that this policeman was sent over from China to intimidate him. That couldn't have been further from the truth. It was clear on the taped interviews that Yu Jie was very relaxed and was smoking cigarettes and not intimidated in any way. It was extremely useful for us to have such a professional policeman of the same nationality assisting our investigation. When a Chinese person replies yes to a question, this sounds very much like a no. Understanding small things like that can be very important. There were also cultural differences he assisted us with. Unless you ask a Chinese person a direct question, they won't offer the information. A lot of the Chinese community were initially reluctant to talk to us, but eventually they co-operated fully."

As well as Yu Jie's fingerprints, what was believed to be his ear print was also found at the couple's apartment. It was sent to a specialist in Holland for analysis and Justice Henry Abbot indicated that he would accept it as evidence. But at the last moment, prosecuting counsel Denis Vaughan Buckley withdrew it. Detectives were unhappy at the time but soon learned that a murder trial in the UK was thrown into disarray over the use of this evidence and it could have jeopardised the entire court case. "There could have been a call for a retrial if it had been used," says McMahon. "It was a great call by Denis Vaughan Buckley not to use it."

One of the original 12 members of the jury passed away from natural causes during the 60 day trial and another was injured in a road traffic accident. "We had all become like a family, we were in that courtroom for so long," recalls McMahon. "They deliberated for two days and then came back with a unanimous guilty verdict."

When they emerged from the jury room, one member was crying and the remainder looked drained and exhausted. Their verdicts were announced in the absence of any friends or relatives of either of the victims. No family ever turned up to support the diminutive murderer. "No one from his family ever contacted us about him or came over to support him that we were aware of," adds McMahon.

After the verdict, Yu Jie remained impassive, but within minutes he was smiling and laughing with his lawyers and translators. Justice Abbott praised gardaí for their extensive investigation. As he was led away in handcuffs, Yu Jie shook hands with some of the gardaí. "Good game," he told one. "Go to the gym," he joked to another. "He never had any animosity towards us at all," says McMahon. "But he did finally break down as he was being led away. But his tears were for himself, not for the two friends he killed." The Chinese policeman also made a point of shaking hands with everyone involved in the case, but walked straight past Yu Jie without giving him a second glance before leaving the courtroom when he concluded his evidence.

Yu Jie has since been refused leave to appeal to the Supreme Court. He is serving his life sentence at Dublin's Wheatfield Prison and works in the laundry, which is considered a plum job. If he is released from prison in the future, he will be deported back to China. If he had carried out his crime in his homeland, he would most likely have faced a firing squad. "In China, when you kill someone, you are in a way killing the rest of that family's future because most couples only have one child. Liu Qing was an only child," says McMahon. "There was a lot of anger felt over what he did. His life could be in danger if he returned to China. He is ten times better off in Ireland than he would be in China."

06 | ADRIAN BESTEA

They were young and in love. But the romance between the 21-year-old Romanian and his 31-year-old Russian girlfriend was never destined to become the stuff of fairytales. Adrian Bestea met and fell in love with Marina Sourovtseva in 1999 when fate threw them together by housing the two asylum seekers at Santa Maria hostel on Dublin's Charlemont Street.

Adrian was young, handsome and carefree. He had finished the Irish equivalent of secondary school in Romania and worked a variety of jobs before he decided to travel as there was still considerable unrest and political instability in his homeland following the fall of Communism. He chose Ireland when a friend told him of the great social life in Dublin and the booming construction industry where it was easy to find work. Marina was older, wiser and more ambitious. But she fell for Adrian's charms and within days of meeting him, they embarked on a tumultuous relationship that came to an abrupt end in 2001 when Adrian was brutally murdered, his body stuffed in a suitcase and dumped in the Royal Canal. While their relationship had always been turbulent, neither could have predicted it would end in death or that Marina would be convicted of involvement in her lover's murder. "It's a tragic tale of young love," says retired Detective Superintendent Hubert Collins, who investigated the 2001 murder as a detective inspector based at Fitzgibbon Street station, "and how the romance between these two young people went completely sour."

Marina had been living in Dublin for several months when she met Adrian. She had a 5-year-old son from a previous marriage who was being cared for by her family in Russia. Highly educated, Marina was an English literature college graduate. Like many people living in Russia at that time, she wanted to get out of that repressive country and to travel the world. She was bright, attractive and full of plans for the future. She planned for her son to eventually join her in Ireland. She applied to study English at Dublin's Portobello College and was granted a three month study visa. When this expired, she didn't want to go home. She wanted to travel and her long-term goal was to move to the US. Instead of leaving Ireland in April 1999, she claimed political asylum and was housed by the State at Santa Maria on Charlemont Street, which was then state-run housing for asylum seekers.

The path that led Adrian to Dublin was rockier. A few months before he was finally permitted entry to Ireland, he was turned away at Dublin Airport and sent back to Brussels. He remained in Belgium for a few months working for a local farmer. But he was determined to make it to Dublin, believing that was where his future lay. So a few months later he tried again, this time arriving into Rosslare in Wexford by ferry from France. He produced a Czech forged passport and when the authorities realised it was a falsified document, he claimed asylum and was sent to the Santa Maria hostel. The two young adults' lives collided and they quickly became a couple after hitting it off. "He met Marina at the hostel and that's where the love story began," explains Collins.

Marina soon decided to move out of the asylum accommodation. She rented flat No. 5, 137 Strand Road, Sandymount in south Co. Dublin. Despite the fact that asylum seekers weren't supposed to work, she held down three jobs. "She was a woman who was very independent. She liked to pay her bills and take care of herself," says Collins. Not long after she moved in, the flat next door became available. Adrian rented it, then sublet it and moved into his girlfriend's flat. But the couple were fast discovering they were very different people. "When times were good, he lived there with Marina. But when times were bad, he moved out. This happened on several occasions," says Collins. "They had a very tempestuous relationship. Marina was a hard-working woman. She was earning and saving her money. She was also faithful to him. But he wasn't that interested in working. He was out on the town the whole time enjoying himself and meeting other women. Times were good in Ireland then; there were plenty of jobs. He'd have a job for a while before he'd lose it or quit. He wouldn't roll up his sleeves and work whereas she would. He was very possessive of her too. Their relationship was always on and off. He also became violent towards her." They were polar opposites, it seemed. All their friends could see it, but the couple remained blind. Marina was looking towards the future, saving money to move to the us for a better life. Adrian, on the other hand, was a man about town, who spent most of his time socialising and was quite happy to allow his girlfriend to support him financially. The ten year age gap also meant they were at different points in their lives emotionally and explains why Adrian, at just 21, was more interested in enjoying himself than planning for his future.

Marina would later tell gardaí that her boyfriend physically assaulted her on several occasions as their relationship began to deteriorate. But on the night of Sunday 8 July 2001, the beating was worse than usual. The fight started when she told him she was going into town to meet some friends. He didn't want her going out and tried to keep her at home. "They had a row. He beat her badly; he beat her black and blue. He tried to lock her in, but she got out of the apartment. Still in her nightdress, she came into town to meet her friends," says Collins.

She jumped into a taxi and met her friends as arranged at Sinnott's pub on St Stephen's Green. She was hurt, bleeding and embarrassed. Her two friends, a Ukrainian and a Russian woman, knew all about her problems with Adrian. "They had been telling her to get rid of him. It was a case of 'I told you so.' At this stage, Marina decided she'd had enough of Adrian and wanted to end the relationship for good. She also wanted to get back into her apartment. One of her friends said, 'I know someone who will get him out,'" adds Collins. Marina's friend took out her phone and called Igore Derjhack, a 28-year-old Ukrainian who was living in Mountjoy Square. She asked him if he would help a friend of hers by getting her violent Romanian boyfriend out of her apartment. He agreed he would, for a small fee, and the three women arranged to meet Igore on O'Connell Street. Without realising it, Marina had set in motion an incident that would change the course of her life and extinguish Adrian's altogether.

The group met up as arranged. Igore was with another man, a Latvian Russian man who has never been identified. Gardaí believe this man played a crucial role in Adrian's murder. As they stood around discussing plans about how they would force her Romanian boyfriend out of the flat, they bumped into another man whom some of the group knew, Latvian Dimitro Vasilibech (26). He decided to share a taxi with the group as he also lived in Sandymount. Marina parted company with her two female friends and hailed a taxi to take the three men to her apartment in Sandymount to evict Adrian. While Dimitro had initially planned on just getting a lift, he too decided to join the group who were planning on having a few drinks at Marina's flat.

It was around 7.30 pm when they arrived at 137 Strand Road. Marina rang the doorbell while the three men hid behind a wall and then followed her upstairs. Adrian barely had time to register his surprise at the sight of three men barging into his home. They pinned him on the bed while they punched him in the face, head and body. The assault lasted for about 15 minutes and he was then put sitting in an armchair. He wasn't badly injured but was stunned and bleeding. The group then began drinking vodka and wine. Gardaí don't know why the men didn't just throw Adrian out on the street as planned at that point but believe alcohol was a factor. Instead, Dimitro was given Adrian's bankcard and he went to a nearby shop to buy more vodka. But Adrian's account was empty so he bought the vodka with money Marina had given him. As he lived near by, Dimitro called home to his girlfriend who decided to go back with him to the flat and join the rest of the group. Armed with more booze, the perverse party continued. Dimitro and his girlfriend only stayed another half an hour at the apartment, until about 10 pm, but it was enough time for Adrian to again be assaulted as he sat in the armchair in the sitting room. Every time Adrian moved or spoke he was beaten, and as the night continued, the violence became more savage and sadistic. "These men were all ethnic Russians and had no respect for Romanians. They couldn't believe that Marina was actually going out with a Romanian. She had lost control of the situation. If Adrian said anything or moved, he got a slap. They treated him like an animal, like a dog. They beat him so hard that two crowns from his teeth came out," says Collins. "It was never Marina's intention to have him killed. It probably wasn't even the men's intention to kill him. They just wanted to put manners on him, but it got completely out of control."

Between 10 pm and midnight, the two remaining men continued to beat Adrian senseless without provocation. Gardaí are satisfied that it wasn't Marina's intention to have her boyfriend murdered because when she got back to her flat she telephoned some Romanian gypsies, friends of her boyfriend, and asked them to come and collect him as she was throwing him out. But as the beating took a violent twist, she fobbed his friends off when they arrived up from Sherrard Street to collect him.

Just after midnight, and at this stage very drunk, the two men told Marina to go to the nearby 24 hour garage and buy cigarettes. Obediently, she left them—and was later captured on CCTV at the garage—before returning home minutes later. In her absence, Adrian had been killed. He had been beaten around the back of his head with a tyre iron. "Most likely they realised they had gone too far and decided to finish him off because he was in such a bad way," adds Collins.

As morning crept in and the seriousness of what had happened began to sink in, Marina and the two men began to talk about what they should do next. "Marina's Russian. In Russia you don't contact the police when certain things happen. There's no trust in the police. It would have been the same with the other two men.

A lot of drink had been taken and they decided that going to police was definitely not an option," says Collins.

Igore, who would later claim to be a former policeman in the Ukraine, suggested they should take the body up the mountains and burn the remains. But their lack of transport proved a major obstacle for that course of action. Then the other man, the unidentified Latvian Russian, had an idea—why not put his body in a suitcase and throw it into the Royal Canal? Since no one had any better suggestions, that's what the group decided to do. But they needed a suitcase big enough to fit a body, so as morning crept in, the two men left the flat to buy a suitcase to conceal their crime from a shop in Dublin city centre's Talbot Street. "At this stage, Marina was terrified. She had only wanted them to evict Adrian. But she felt she didn't have any other choice but to go along with getting rid of the body. She said she was very afraid of the two men," says Collins.

The men soon arrived back with a large Elite black suitcase, which was just big enough to fit a human body. They managed to fold Adrian's remains in the foetal position, squeezed him into the suitcase and zipped it shut. The three of them then left the apartment and caught the No. 3 bus near the flat. They hopped off at Drumcondra Road and the two men wheeled the heavy suitcase along the Royal Canal bank about 50 yards from Binn's Bridge. Standing on the bank and presumably out of sight, they allowed the suitcase to slip down into the water. It was midday on 9 July 2001. Adrian's remains would lie undetected and decomposing in the water for the next 11 days. With the body disposed of, Marina parted company with the two men and in the coming days tried to put the horror of what had happened out of her mind by fleeing to London.

In the afternoon of 20 July, two young boys were playing down by the canal when they noticed the large black suitcase at the water's edge. "They were 12 or 13, a couple of local boys playing down there during the summer, throwing stones into the water. They saw the suitcase and were curious. They noticed the zip and opened it. A putrid smell emerged," continues Collins. "The boys didn't really know what they'd found but knew something wasn't right. They ran off and found two uniformed gardaí near by on the beat on Dorset Street. Gardaí went down and immediately recognised what was in the suitcase."

The fire brigade and more gardaí were alerted. The suitcase was half submerged in the water and the fire brigade winched it out. It was then tipped over and Adrian Bestea's remains fell out. A murder investigation was launched and a forensic tent was erected on the canal bank to preserve the scene. Within a day, the discovery of the unidentified remains became known as the 'Body in the Suitcase' murder. The media and the general public were intrigued by the callous manner by which the victim's killers had disposed of the body. Then state pathologist Professor John Harbison was contacted and he carried out a post-mortem on the remains. "The body had been stripped of all identification. He had no wallet or jewellery. All we had to go on was a brown leather jacket, which buttoned to the front. He was also wearing a black V-neck T-shirt with white stripes on the neck and jeans which had a 32 inch waist. He was a very slim man. He was also wearing blue boxers and socks and had been lying in the foetal position. The consensus between us was that he looked Eastern European, but we had nothing to confirm this. Two of his crowns were missing. They'd been knocked out of his mouth because of the severity of the beating. What was of paramount importance was to try and identify him," adds Collins.

Without being able to identify the victim, the murder investigation stalled. Thirteen days after the grim discovery, gardaí took the unusual step of releasing a photo of the dead man's face. But before this could be done, it had to be partially reconstructed by a specialist hired to make his face more presentable. Photos of his brown leather jacket were also released to the media. This practice has been used since in other murder investigations, most recently Kenyan Farah Swaleh Noor—whose murder in 2005 drew parallels with Adrian Bestea's because his body (minus his head) was also dumped in a suitcase in the Royal Canal—as well as the 2009 killing of Romanian woman Eugenia Bratis, whose unidentified body was discovered in the Phoenix Park.

It was the photo of the brown leather jacket that led to the first major breakthrough in the case. A group of Romanian gypsies that were friendly with Adrian recognised the jacket when they saw a picture of it on *Sky News*. They bought the *Evening Herald* later that day to examine the photos more closely and soon became convinced it belonged to their friend. None of them had been able to get in touch with Adrian for the past few weeks and were becoming increasingly worried. The group, which included Calin Voda and Constantine Salop, met up beside Mountjoy Square garda station and tried to decide what to do next. After procrastinating for several hours, Calin and Constantine went into the station. "They wanted to help but were afraid of the police. But thankfully, two of them decided to come in and talk to us. A lot of the immigrant community didn't think we'd have any interest in solving the case because it didn't involve an Irish person. The people involved in the killing believed that too, that we wouldn't care. In Ireland, all murder investigations are thoroughly investigated, regardless of what nationality the victim may be. But it's different in some of their home countries where it seems to matter who you are," according to Collins.

The two Romanians were able to give gardaí detailed statements with the help of an interpreter. They also took gardaí to where Adrian had lived with Marina at their flat on Strand Road. It was immediately obvious to gardaí that they had found the murder scene. While there had been a crude attempt to clean up the apartment, splatters of blood were still visible to the naked eye. The apartment had been abandoned, but the tyre iron used as the murder weapon remained at the scene. Detectives interviewed the neighbours who confirmed they had heard a serious disturbance a few weeks previously and a few days after that no one was seen coming or going from the apartment. Three weeks on from Adrian's brutal murder, and the garda investigation was gathering pace. Detectives believed they now knew the identity of the victim and had located the murder scene. The Romanian police were contacted as gardaí attempted to track down Adrian's family. Adrian's mother, Mariana Moraru, was a nurse and lived in Timisoara in Romania. She was separated from

Adrian's father, Marin Bestea, had remarried but was on good terms with her ex-husband. She immediately came to Ireland when she was told it was suspected that her son had been murdered. Her travelling companion who journeyed with her to Ireland was a close friend, Adina Duta, a medical doctor. Adina took a blood sample from Mariana, which was confirmed within a couple of days at the forensic state laboratory in Dublin as matching her son's. "She was a lovely, gentle woman. Adrian came from a very good background," recalls Collins. "His family was very surprised to hear he had become friendly with Romanian gypsies." Adrian had been raised in the repressive Communist regime in Romania, which fell in 1989. His family's fortune suffered as a result. Adrian's stepfather was demoted from being a judge to driving a lorry after the fall of Ceauçescu's Communist regime. Romania struggled to come to terms with its identity post-communism and it was not a prosperous country in the 1990s. Mariana, wanting the best opportunities for her son, went to work in the US to raise money so that Adrian could leave Romania and build a new life.

During her trip to Ireland, detectives brought Mariana to the spot on the canal bank where Adrian's body was found. Her grief brought some of the most senior officers investigating his murder to tears. "When you work with a family in these circumstances, you share in their pain," says Collins. "You see her grieve for the loss of her son and it's upsetting. She was distraught." Gardaí made an appeal to the Irish public during Adrian's mother's visit to help towards the repatriation of the 21-year old's body, which cost £4,000. The public responded well and the money was raised.

A service was also held at the Orthodox church on Dublin's Arbour Hill in Adrian's memory during his mother's visit. In Romania, a young man who dies before marrying is dressed as a groom for his burial. Somehow, in the midst of hasty arrangements to come to Ireland, Mariana had insisted on buying new clothes for her son to honour the tradition. Adrian had told her he wanted to get married and this was the closest she would come to imagining him on that happy occasion. She picked out a smart grey suit and crisp white shirt for him and had them laid carefully over a chair at the altar where his coffin should have been in the church. A pair of polished black shoes were also placed on the floor; a grey tie with a silver pattern completed the outfit. As Adrian's body was too damaged to be brought to the church, the clothes his mother carefully chose symbolised his presence.

Local Romanian priest Fr Ireneu Craciun conducted the service and Mariana was inconsolable throughout, often having to be physically supported as she fell to the floor sobbing, her heart broken. Eighteen different nationalities were packed into the small church, all united by faith. "Many are refugees with sufferings of their own, so they feel the grief and pain inflicted on the family by this brutal murder," the priest told the congregation. Mariana's friend Adina Duta spoke of the agony her friend was feeling at the loss of her only child and how she intuitively became worried about him when she didn't hear from him for several weeks. "He used to telephone her all the time and then he stopped. You know a mother's feelings. She was worried. I was with her when she got the fax from the police. She just laid down and pulled at her hair and cried. She was in despair." The doctor, who worked with Mariana at a hospital in Timisoara, had known Adrian since he was a small child. "He was a cheerful boy. He liked to sing, like his mother, and he liked flowers, especially the fragrance of carnations. He had plans. He wanted to get married and to raise money to buy a car so he could come back to visit his mother and take her to see Ireland. She is blaming herself for not keeping him in Romania. She says she should have put chains on his legs to keep him at home."

Adrian's father Marin was unable to make the trip to Ireland. He began to dig his son's grave while his ex-wife journeyed to Dublin. The parents later shared their grief at their son's funeral in Romania. Mariana was touched by the sympathy of the Irish public during her visit. "There were cards, money, flowers, telephone calls. One card said on the envelope: From an Irish mother to a Romanian mother. I didn't need to open it. I knew the feelings expressed inside," Rev. Craciun told the congregation.

Before she returned home, Mariana also heaped praise on gardaí for their support and dedication to catching her son's killers.

The murder investigation was building momentum. Detectives had learned the identity of Adrian's Russian girlfriend, Marina Sourovtseva, who had abandoned her apartment in the aftermath of his killing. Finding her became the focus of the investigation. Gardaí were knocking on every door trying to find out where she had gone. It was felt she would be the key to unlocking this case. Soon gardaí received information through intelligence that the Russian woman was living in an apartment in Kensington, London.

Gardaí accompanied by English police tracked down Marina early one Sunday morning in Kensington and knocked on the door of her apartment. "She was and wasn't surprised to see us, I suppose," recalls Collins, one of the senior officers sent to interview her in London. "She agreed to come to Kensington police station to talk to us. This was a woman who had never had any contact with police and wouldn't have had great faith in police in Russia. But she opened up to us. We knocked on her door at 8 am and by 1.30 pm that afternoon, she'd given us an outline about what had happened to Adrian Bestea in the last hours of his life. She told us the whole story. She agreed to come back and assist us with the investigation. She was relieved in a way to get it all off her chest. She hadn't been able to eat or sleep since it happened. She gave us what we needed. Within a day or two of her coming back with us, we had identified one of the main suspects."

Back in Dublin, Marina helped gardaí with their enquiries. She was informed she would likely face charges in relation to her boyfriend's killing, but for the time being gardaí needed her help identifying the men responsible for the fatal assault. She knew the first names of two of the three men in her house that night, Igore and Dimitro, but not the third man. The information she gave gardaí was instrumental in tracking them down. On 6 September 2001—less than two months after Adrian's killing—the net closed on Igore and he was arrested at his flat in Dublin's Mountjoy Square and later charged under section 3 of the Non-Fatal

Offences against the Person Act. He immediately admitted his part, to a degree, in the fatal assault. Gardaí soon learned that he was also an alcoholic. He was denied bail and was initially charged with murder, assault causing harm and the false imprisonment of Adrian Bestea. "He was a big, tall stocky man, a bear of a man," says Collins. "He didn't like getting caught. He told us he was a policeman in the Ukraine, but we never established this as the truth. We do know that at one stage his mother worked in a police station."

Four days later, Dimitro Vasilibech—who played a relatively minor role in the killing—was arrested at his home on Tritonville Road, Sandymount, and charged with assault causing harm to Adrian. Gardaí also treated him as a potential witness. He had shared a taxi ride with the group back to Sandymount and had been involved in the initial assault on Adrian but was not believed by gardaí to be one of the main aggressors. He also left the murder scene at 10 pm and did not witness Adrian's murder at around midnight. But, crucially, he tried to use Adrian's bank card on the night and that linked him to what happened. He also failed to alert gardaí when he left the apartment about the violence that was unfolding on Strand Road. His girlfriend, who went back to the flat with him on Strand Road for about half an hour, did not face charges as she did not partake in the assault.

With these two men charged and denied bail, detectives continued their search for the third man who took part in the violent assault against Adrian, a Latvian Russian national. Detectives believe that this man may have struck the fatal blow with the tyre iron. Investigating officers were developing links with the Russian and Eastern European communities in Ireland and, through intelligence, established that this man left Ireland two days after the murder. He most likely returned to Latvia or Russia. He used several different names, which was a common practice among ethnic Russians at the time, and he has never been tracked down. Adrian, Marina and Dimitro also used different identities in Ireland.

Only three men were present when Adrian Bestea was murdered. Since one was dead, the second had fled the country and the third—Igore—denied that he killed the young Romanian, it was decided the evidence to charge him with murder was not substantial enough and the charge was withdrawn. As Marina had left the flat to buy cigarettes when her boyfriend lost his fight for life, the truth about who killed the 21-year old could not be established.

After gardaí had charged Igore and Dimitro, their focus turned to Marina. On 19 July 2002, she was jailed for two years after pleading guilty to false imprisonment and assault causing harm to her 21-year-old boyfriend. The Dublin Circuit Criminal Court was told that she was terrified of Adrian, who beat her on countless occasions, and wanted the three men she hired to "teach him a lesson", but not kill him. The reason she never reported the domestic violence was because she was an asylum seeker, the court heard. Judge Yvonne Murphy said the circumstances leading to the murder of Adrian Bestea had been fully outlined to her, but she accepted that Marina never meant to have him killed. "The accused felt powerless to stop the situation getting out of control and I am fully satisfied that it was never her intention to have Mr Bestea killed," she said. "After her visa ran out she aligned herself with some undesirable people who would go out of their way to remain in the country illegally . . . Nevertheless the crime of false imprisonment is a very serious one and I feel that the most appropriate sentence would be one of three years, but I will take into account that she will have to serve the sentence outside of her native country and impose a term of two years."

Investigating detectives felt that Marina accepted her two-year sentence and, in some way, welcomed the punishment for her role in her boyfriend's killing. It was she, after all, who brought the three men to her flat where Adrian was killed. She was extremely remorseful and particularly distraught over the callous way her lover's body was discarded.

Dimitro Vasilibech was the second of the three to learn his fate after being charged in connection with the killing. On 20 March 2003, a shocked Dimitro was jailed for three years at Dublin Circuit Criminal Court for his role in the 'Body in the Suitcase' murder. He pleaded guilty to falsely imprisoning Adrian Bestea and assault causing him harm. Judge Murphy said while he did not participate in the events which led to the "sad and brutal" death of the young Romanian, he had joined in an earlier assault and did not seek help for Adrian after he had left the flat. Dimitro did not know either Adrian or Marina. He got a lift in a taxi with the group going "to teach Adrian Bestea a lesson" simply because he lived in the same area. But instead of going home, he went to Adrian's flat and participated in the assault on him. Judge Murphy noted that Dimitro had no previous criminal record, had worked hard and paid his taxes while in Ireland and would have to serve his sentence in a foreign jurisdiction with the ensuing language difficulties. She backdated his sentence to September 2001 when he was taken into custody for this offence. His defence counsel said it was a particularly difficult situation for Dimitro due to language barriers and that a lot of the prisoners were unsettled and had drug problems. Investigating Detective Walter O'Sullivan told the court that Adrian was not hit with any weapon while Dimitro was there, just fists. He added that Dimitro's girlfriend said that when they left, Adrian was asleep in the armchair but was still alive. Detectives have some degree of sympathy for Dimitro. He seemed to have got caught up in what happened by accident rather than as a willing participant. For ethnic Russians, it would be normal to help out a fellow countryman if they needed help with something, such as doling out a punishment beating. The young petrol pump attendant was shocked to be jailed for what he saw as his insignificant role in the murder.

Igore was the last to face the music over Adrian Bestea's murder. On 8 October 2003, he was jailed for three years for the assault and false imprisonment of the young Romanian. Igore was also jailed for an additional year for being an accessory after the fact to the murder by helping dispose of his body. He had been on trial for murder at the Central Criminal Court. But the State was forced to accept that there wasn't enough evidence to convict him of the murder as there were no witnesses to who struck the final fatal blow. As a result, Igore was rearraigned and pleaded guilty to the lesser charges which were accepted by the

State. Imposing concurrent sentences, Justice Iarfhlaith O'Neill said Adrian Bestea had been the victim of a "tragic tale" of "appalling violence". Adrian's mother came back to Ireland for Igore's sentencing and thanked gardaí for the painstaking work undertaken during the investigation into her son's killing. Investigating gardaí never saw Igore show any remorse for his actions, but say he clearly regretted getting caught. He had few redeeming characteristics, unlike Marina and Dimitro, who genuinely wished Adrian Bestea had not lost his life. Detectives learned that Igore was loosely involved with the Russian mafia and was considered a dangerous criminal in his homeland.

Igore was sentenced exactly 27 months to the day of Adrian Bestea's brutal murder. Had the other main suspect been present when the young Romanian was beaten to death not fled the country two days later, a murder conviction could potentially have been secured. But, given the circumstances, gardaí were pleased to have secured three convictions in relation to the killing. Igore and Dimitro were deported from Ireland upon their release from prison. Marina was granted a temporary visa to remain in Ireland after she was set free.

The wide-spanning investigation into Adrian Bestea's murder was one of the most extensive ever launched in Dublin at the time and several experienced gardaí were involved. As well as Walter O'Sullivan and Hubert Collins, other senior officers probing the killing included then Detective Superintendent Cormac Gordon (now retired), then Chief Superintendent Al McHugh (also retired) and then Assistant Commissioner Tony Hickey (also retired).

One of the biggest obstacles that gardaí overcame was convincing ethnic Russians and Eastern Europeans they had nothing to fear by co-operating with gardaí. It was one of the first experiences seasoned Dublin murder detectives had in dealing with these new communities. The knowledge and understanding garnered by detectives about how to interact with these nationalities would prove invaluable in several other murders and criminal investigations involving these communities that would take place in the not-so-distant future.

Adrian Bestea could easily have remained an unidentified corpse. It was the identification of his brown leather jacket by his Romanian gypsy friends that provided detectives with their first lead. Without that, the Body in the Suitcase murder would have remained unsolved. While his murder was undoubtedly alcohol fuelled, it was also a killing spurred by passion. A tragic love story with few redeeming characters.

07 | BETTINA POESCHEL

A curiosity in Irish culture drew Bettina Poeschel to visit the ancient Stone Age passage tomb at Newgrange. But an act of appalling savagery ended her life before she made it that far. A cruel twist of fate cast the unsuspecting young German tourist in the path of Michael Murphy, a predatory killer who had struck before. Bettina (28) would not have been walking along the Donore Road in Drogheda that rainy morning except that she had missed the bus to Newgrange. Equally, Murphy should not have been sitting in a construction hut at the side of the road as the German tourist walked by—he should have been working ten miles away in Gormanston, Co. Meath. But in the split second their lives collided, 40-year-old Murphy could not control his urge to rape and kill. The German tourist fell victim to a random act of murder by a man who was free to roam the streets, free to kill.

On the morning of 25 September 2001, Bettina arrived at the Bus Éireann station in Drogheda, having arrived by train from Dublin, where she was staying with a friend. It was the last morning of her six-day holiday to Ireland before she was due to return to Munich. "She was told she'd just missed the bus to Newgrange and the next one would be in an hour's time. It was

Adrian Bestea, the original 'body in the suitcase' killing. His battered body was found in a suitcase in Dublin's Royal Canal in 2001. (*Photocall Ireland*)

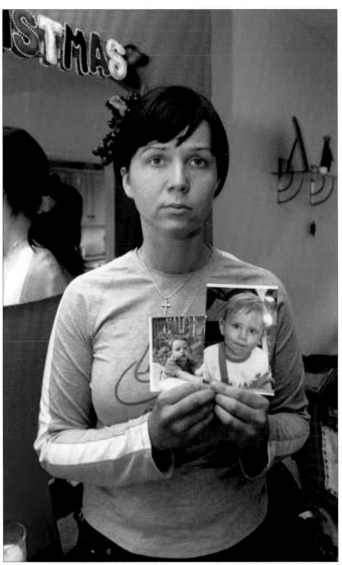

Murder victim Baiba Saulite holding a photograph of her two sons, Ali and Mohammed Rami. The two boys were kidnapped by her estranged husband but were later returned shortly before she was shot dead. (*Collins Agency*)

Hassan Hassan, estranged husband of Latvian Baiba Saulite. Detectives believe he ordered his wife's 2006 murder. He has since left the country with the couple's two sons. (*Courtpix*)

Bettina Poeschel, a German student, was raped and murdered by
Michael Murray in a random attack as she travelled to visit the ancient
Stone-Age passage tomb at Newgrange in 2001.

Eugenia Bratis, the Romanian mother of two found stabbed to death in the Phoenix Park in 2009, in an unsolved murder.

Nigerian Goodwill Udechuckwu bludgeoned his wife, Natasha Gray, to death with a lump hammer in 2003, before leaving her body upside down in the cot of their 5-month-old baby. (*Courtpix*)

Hua Yu Feng stabbed Linda Wang to death in 2003. He later attempted to take his own life. (*Courtpix*)

Twenty-one-year-old Chinese student Linda Wang, a talented musician, was stabbed to death by her friend Hua Yu Feng.

Englishman Ian Bailey is the self-confessed former chief suspect in the murder of filmmaker Sophie Toscan du Plantier. He is currently fighting an attempt to extradite him to France to answer questions about the 1996 murder. (*Mark Condren*)

Sophie Toscan du Plantier and her son Pierre Louis. (*Rex Features*)

about an eight mile walk. 'I'll walk. I like walking,' she told the man working at the bus station," recalls retired Chief Superintendent Mick Finnegan, who was in charge of the Louth-Meath garda division at the time of her murder. "He told her to keep an eye out for the next bus, as she could flag it down along the way." Her decision to set out on foot that morning cost the young woman her life. She set off up Watery Hill and along Donore Road. She walked past Michael Murphy in the pouring rain as he sat in a construction hut on the M1 bypass at the side of the road. He couldn't keep his eyes off her. Murphy and his three Latvian co-workers were waiting on the delivery of a generator and were then due to go to Gormanston. She noticed the men, but probably didn't pay them much attention. But Michael Murphy undoubtedly noticed her. "The Latvian men told us later that he paid particular attention to her as she walked past. He stared at her until she went out of sight. The other men recalled that she looked like a foreigner, but that was about all. About five minutes after she'd gone out of view, Murphy left the hut, gave the other workmen an excuse about why he had to leave for a few minutes, and sped off in his car in the direction Bettina had walked," says Finnegan. "His was an opportunistic and spur of the moment crime. He seemed to decide what he would do in a fleeting moment."

When Bettina came into his view a couple of minutes later, Murphy parked his car and began to pursue her on foot. "He followed her for about 300 metres on foot. He would have been gaining on her," says the retired garda. "He then jumped on her at a point in the road where there were no houses. He struggled with her until he got her into the bushes. Then he raped her and murdered her, most likely by strangulation, but his method of killing could never be definitively determined." Michael Murphy was no stranger to attacking unsuspecting women. He had already proven himself a violent, dangerous killer. After he was handed down a life sentence in 2004 for the German tourist's murder, the jury would learn that he had killed before and had several other serious convictions. In 1983, he strangled 64-year-old widow Catherine Carroll to death. He was found guilty of her manslaughter and was sentenced to 12 years in prison in 1984. He was released in 1992 after serving almost nine years. He did not emerge from prison a reformed character. He soon accrued a string of other convictions including armed robbery and, notably, a six-month sentence for the assault of two girls as they walked home from a disco in Drogheda. Murphy had grabbed the two girls by the neck and tried to pull them to the ground before they escaped.

Michael Murphy was no fool. He returned to the construction hut after raping and murdering Bettina and tried to continue his day as normal. But his co-workers noticed he seemed agitated. On a few occasions later that day and in the coming days, he would return to the murder scene to hide Bettina's body deep in the undergrowth and discard some of her clothing. He also brought some disinfectant he took from the construction site and doused her body with it in an unsuccessful attempt to remove his semen from her body, should she be found.

The young tourist's body would eventually be found, but not for several days. Bettina had decided to visit the megalithic passage tomb at Newgrange on her last day in Ireland. She went alone because her old school friend that she was visiting, Holger Sirtl, was working that day. She had a huge interest in culture, history and travelling. It was more than a passing interest—in Munich she worked as a journalist for the evening newspaper *Münchner Abendzeitung* as an arts, music and cultural writer. "She reviewed concerts, interviewed artists and loved offering a platform to relatively unknown artists," says her younger sister and only sibling Cornelia, speaking for the first time in several years about her sister's murder. "She preferred independent music to the mainstream. In the last 18 months before her death, Bettina and I shared a flat together. We were very close. She was not only my older sister but also my best friend."

Bettina had been planning her short break to Ireland for months. "She wanted to visit her very good old school friend Holger in Dublin. Holger was living there and was working as a management consultant. It was her first trip to Ireland. My sister loved to read. She read everything she could get her hands on, but was most interested in literature. When she was in Ireland, she was reading James Joyce's *Ulysses*. She could also paint very well. She could have pursued it professionally but in the end she loved writing more."

When Holger got home from work that day, he saw Bettina's suitcase by the door and wondered why she wasn't back yet. He immediately raised the alarm. He knew his friend had a flight to catch and that something was wrong when she did not return and he couldn't get through to her on her phone. A major garda search was launched after it was established she had taken the train from Dublin to Drogheda and was last seen walking up the Donore Road at about 11.30 am. But false sightings of the 28-year old led detectives to initially search the wrong area. Bettina never made it as far as Donore village. But on the day she was killed, a Dublin woman who bore a striking resemblance to her was seen by several people. "This woman was even wearing red shoes, as was Bettina. Witnesses saw her outside the post office and thumbing a lift towards the N2. This led us to extensively search the forests in the area, as well as the canals and the River Boyne," says retired Chief Superintendent Finnegan.

Bettina's father Jürgen and her younger sister Cornelia travelled to Ireland soon after being informed that she was missing. "I knew immediately that something awful had to have happened. Bettina was not the type to simply disappear off somewhere without telling anyone. I felt helpless," recalls her sister. "We felt unconscious. We functioned, but our environment was only shadowy. We tried to show strength, we wanted to hold the interest of the media in the disappearance of my sister. That's why we came to Ireland. We were able to begin our grieving immediately. We knew. And gradually no one else believed we would find Bettina alive as the days went on."

Gardaí had a wide area to search—it was eight miles from Drogheda's bus station to Newgrange. Before her body was found, gardaí considered that she could have been hit by a car and knocked deep into the undergrowth. Finally, 22 days after she disappeared, garda Pat Kelly assisted by Detective Inspector Brendan McArdle made a grim discovery. On their hands and knees, officers had crawled deep into a fox and rabbit run off the Donore Road. There the semi-naked and decomposing remains of Bettina Poeschel were found. Gardaí had gone off the beaten track to search this particular area and her body was very well concealed. The remains of the 28-year old could easily have remained hidden for ever. "There was a real determination to find her. Her body was deep in the undergrowth in dense bushes. We soon found out she had been raped and most likely strangled. He had made an effort to conceal her body. Forensics later found her clothes fibres in the bushes. She had been dragged 30 metres," says Finnegan. "He had also returned later that day and poured disinfectant over her to try and get rid of his DNA."

A post-mortem soon confirmed that she had died a violent death and a murder investigation was launched. Her family were informed of the tragic news, but they had already begun to reconcile in their minds that Bettina was gone. Because her body had been exposed to the elements for over three weeks, her family could not be asked to identify her remains. Instead, her glasses, mobile phone and bag were all returned to the family. They would have to wait two and a half years before Michael Murphy would stand trial for her murder.

Bettina had walked about four miles into her journey when she was attacked and murdered. Detectives began to compile a list of people whom she could have encountered along the way. "It was a difficult scenario because she had covered so much ground on foot. We immediately began a voluntary DNA programme and interviews. We were inundated with requests from men to give samples. We decided to begin with the people who were working on the roadway, which was under major construction for the new motorway," says Finnegan. "We estimated that we would need samples from between 12,000 and 13,000 men altogether. We were at the very beginning of the process when Michael Murphy volunteered. He was the 75th person to provide a DNA sample, a hair from his head."

The retired chief superintendent was present the day Murphy presented himself and volunteered to give a DNA sample. "It was about 5.30 pm. He was cool as a breeze. I believe he was quite satisfied he had destroyed all of his DNA on her body with the disinfectant. He also probably thought that her body was so decomposed that there couldn't possibly be any DNA still left. His sample was labelled and sent to the forensics lab. Within a couple of hours, we got a phone call saying he was a positive match."

Even before he gave a DNA sample, gardaí had their suspicions about the 40-year old. They knew about his criminal past. His propensity for violence towards women was of particular interest. They had spoken to his co-workers, who had told them that he had left work that morning saying he had to visit the doctor, and left several more times over the course of the day. They all said he acted out of sorts that day. Detectives had also found out from another colleague that Murphy had taken disinfectant from the construction site, on the pretext of needing it to clean out some kennels for his dogs. Even before semen found on the young woman's body was deemed to match Murphy's DNA profile, gardaí were building up considerable circumstantial evidence against him. Forensic tests also revealed that Jeyes Fluid, a type of disinfectant, was found on Bettina's black underwear. But his plan didn't work. Because he raped Bettina, he hadn't calculated the possibility that his DNA could therefore be kept intact internally.

At 8.10 am on 27 October 2001, gardaí arrested Michael Murphy at the home he shared with his partner Samantha Johnson and their three children. He was arrested on suspicion of withholding information. His partner was also arrested for withholding information but was later released without charge. She provided Murphy with an alibi for the day of the murder, telling gardaí that during his absences from work that day he had come home. "Initially, he made no admissions of significance and was still acting as cool as a breeze. He had himself convinced he would beat it. He genuinely did not think the DNA evidence was enough to convict him," says Finnegan. But by 7 pm that evening, he was formally charged with the murder of Bettina Poeschel after making some admissions. It had been a long day of questioning for Michael Murphy. Initially, when he was shown a photo of the German tourist, he claimed never to have seen her before. But in the course of the afternoon, Samantha Johnson, who was released from custody, was given a couple of minutes to speak to her boyfriend. The couple's following conversation was recorded:

Samantha: "Did you do it?"
Murphy: "What do you think?"
Samantha: "Tell me, did you do it?"
Murphy: "I'm sorry, Samantha."
Samantha: "Did you do it, Michael? Tell me the truth."
Murphy: "Don't raise your voice."

Murphy then asked for her to leave and she was taken out of the interview room by gardaí. This brief conversation with his partner seemed to be a turning point for the 40-year old.

Sensing he was on the verge of making a full admission of guilt, Detective Paul Gilton continued questioning him. It was the first time Murphy had shown any emotion since his arrest several hours earlier. He was visibly shaken. "I noted at the time that he was visibly shaking. He was trembling," the detective later told his murder trial. He then put his head in his hands and began sobbing. "I felt that he was going to admit to me what he had done to Bettina Poeschel and so I pressed on and asked him what happened," the detective added.

Detective Gilton: "Michael, will you tell us the full truth about what happened?"
Murphy: "I'm sorry."
Gilton: "Tell us what happened."
Murphy: "Just tell that girl's parents I'm sorry for taking her life and what I did to her. I'm so, so sorry."
Gilton: "How did you kill her, Michael?"
Murphy: "I don't want to say anything else about it. I'm just so sorry about it."

Through his sobbing, Murphy then asked to be returned to his cell. Gardaí were extremely pleased by what they saw as Murphy's admission of guilt for the murder of Bettina Poeschel. But the interviewing officers had failed to tape this interview with Murphy, an issue that would later be raised in court and for which gardaí would eventually be reprimanded.

Michael Murphy was refused bail after he was charged with the German's murder. On 12 January 2004, two years and three months after he committed his crime, the then 42-year old stood trial for her murder at the Dublin Central Criminal Court after pleading not guilty.

Cornelia and her parents Jürgen and Hermine returned to Ireland to attend the court case. "It was very difficult for us emotionally after nearly two and a half years to listen to what happened to her, to have the past so intensely pulled apart again," says Cornelia. "I have no feelings towards Michael Murphy. Not even hatred. That would only show that I have acknowledged him. He is not worth that."

Hearing in detail about the condition of Bettina's body was probably the most harrowing evidence the Poeschel family had to endure during the trial. "I came upon the body of a dead woman. She was lying face down and was naked from the waist down apart from black panties that were around the knees," Detective Inspector Brendan McArdle told the jury. "The upper body was covered in a blue jacket and initially her head was not visible as it was separated from the trunk of her body." The body had been hard to find, he added, and an attempt had been made to conceal it using thick ground vegetation. Dr Harpel Singh Glyral was called to the scene after gardaí made their discovery. "I found her lying on her abdomen face down. Her soles, calf muscles and palms were in an advanced state of decomposition," he said. "I lifted her head which was very, very stiff—her body was in a state of rigor mortis. Her head was detached from the neck and faced down. Her spinal cord was also detached. That's how I saw the body."

Detectives were surprised but not shocked that Murphy had pleaded not guilty. It was the view of gardaí that the DNA evidence as well as his own admissions in custody were overwhelming. Two weeks after he had been charged with murder, he made a second startling admission to Inspector Gerry O'Brien. O'Brien was supervising the prisoner while he ate his lunch at Drogheda garda station on 2 November 2001, when Murphy suddenly piped up: "Look, I went back to the body two or three days later. I took the red shoes and trousers and hid them in the skip at the graveyard in Donore. Have you found them?"

The inspector immediately dispatched Garda Thomas Flynn to go to the graveyard at Donore to see if there was a skip where Murphy had indicated. Garda Flynn found a skip at the Catholic church in Donore. Inside it was a pair of ladies' black trousers with German writing on them, black socks and red leather shoes. All these items belonged to Bettina.

Michael Murphy had enlisted the services of one of the country's top defence barristers, Patrick MacEntee. Again, gardaí did not record these comments made by the prisoner as he wasn't being officially interviewed when he made these remarks. But the facts spoke loudly to the jury. Michael Murphy's off-the-cuff comments led gardaí to recover the dead woman's clothing. Detectives knew nothing about a skip in the graveyard at Donore until Murphy told them about it.

Inspector O'Brien said that the prisoner's comments were spontaneous and he wrote them down in his notebook. "I merely recorded his unsolicited comments that he said to me. I merely recorded in writing the comments as he made them. At no time did I question him," he added. The inspector had given Murphy a cigarette and made a phone call to his solicitor on his behalf. He denied trying to ingratiate himself with the killer in a bid to get him to confess to returning to the dead body and removing and hiding her clothes. When the phone call was over, Murphy asked the inspector: "Why are you so kind to me after all I have done? I'm sorry for everything. How is that girl's family?"

There was more damning evidence to come. The head of the DNA unit at Garda Headquarters, Dr Maureen Smyth, told the court that the DNA profile from cells found on the body of the German tourist matched Michael Murphy's. "The DNA profile of the higher vaginal swabs showed the presence of profiles of more than one person. The major profile matched that of Michael Murphy," Dr Smyth told the court. The minor DNA profile was in fact Bettina's own DNA. The forensic scientist estimated there was a "less than one in a thousand million" chance that someone else could share the same DNA profile as Murphy.

One by one, the labourer's co-workers gave evidence against him. Pat McCahey, who worked with Murphy on the day Bettina disappeared, said he kept disappearing over the course of the day. His explanation was that he had to go see a man about a pump. "He could be away 20 minutes, half an hour or longer. He was away four or five times," he added. "There was a particular time we were talking about dogs. Michael Murphy said to me he'd have to take some disinfectant, that that was going to be good stuff for cleaning out the kennels. He wanted it for the dogs. It was a container of some liquid that was a cleaning fluid in the toilets." Despite the fact that her body was not found for 22 days, forensic tests on Bettina's black underwear revealed a "strong support that the smell was Jeyes Fluid", a type of disinfectant, according to forensic expert Mr John McCullough.

Murphy's three Latvian co-workers also spoke about how they barely saw him on the day the German tourist was murdered. He didn't take his 10 o'clock break with them as usual and later disappeared on the pretence of going to the doctor. They all gave similar evidence that they didn't think he was working on the site for most of that day. "I don't think so because we went out smoking and his car wasn't there," Audrey Krastinsh told the murder trial through an interpreter. Possibly in an attempt to make his story more believable, Murphy visited his GP the day after he murdered Bettina Poeschel and complained of a pain in his back.

It soon became clear that Murphy was having personal problems around the time he murdered Bettina. The week before he carried out his crime, he visited his father Larry and asked could he move back to the family home. "He just said to me that he was living with his girlfriend and anything he does doesn't seem to satisfy her," Larry Murphy said. "He told me that he hurt his back with the job and he was going to see the doctor. I think he said he hurt it when he came out from the toilet. I knew he was working on the road. He said he'd go to the doctor and that's the last I heard of it."

Bettina's final movements were also pieced together by the last people who saw her alive. Mary McCabe, who was in the Donore area that morning, saw Bettina walking along the road near the quarry at Donore. "She was on her own," she said. "She was wearing a mac jacket. She had a shoulder bag and glasses. I was thinking she didn't have an umbrella with her and it was raining and I was thinking, she'll get wet." Moments later, local businessman Kenneth Martin also saw the young German walking along the Donore Road. It was 11.35 am. She was never seen alive again. Three days after Bettina arrived in Ireland, she sent her sister a text message. "She said she was on the beach and that everything was okay," Cornelia Poeschel told the murder trial. "She said she was having a good time."

Her family were not surprised the 28-year old visited Newgrange on the last day of her holiday. She had read all about the ancient passage tomb and felt compelled to see it for herself. "I would see her as a girl who would like to meet a boyfriend as a companion but finds it hard as she expects so much," Jorgen Poeschel said after he had arrived in Dublin shortly after his daughter's disappearance but before her body was found. "In this I mean she is so intelligent and into things like literature, art and history and she finds it difficult to meet somebody with the same interests."

On the evening of 25 September, student Siobhán Byrne was sitting on a wall near Mullachrone Quarry with two friends when she noticed a black Honda Civic pull up outside a laneway, about 400 metres from where the body of Bettina Poeschel was eventually found. "A lorry drove by and its lights shone on this figure, which we presumed was a man from his build," she recalled. "We saw a man going up into the laneway. He was running up it. Then we heard this car drive off in the Donore direction. We never saw it again." Gardaí suspect that it was Michael Murphy whom the young woman had seen on one of his many visits to the spot where he murdered Bettina to ensure she was concealed.

The murder trial lasted four weeks. When the time came for

prosecution counsel Denis Vaughan Buckley and defence counsel Patrick MacEntee to address the jury, tensions and emotions were running high. In his closing submission, Vaughan Buckley put it to the jury that Michael Murphy made two admissions of guilt to the crime while in garda custody. "I would submit there's more than ample evidence . . . that you can safely come to the conclusion that the accused murdered Bettina Poeschel," he concluded.

MacEntee told the jury that they would have to decide what reliance they could put on Michael Murphy's admissions to gardaí on the day of his arrest. "What is he sorry about? Some sort of inappropriate move? Does it prove that he killed her? You're expected to construe 'I'm sorry' as guilt." That his client's semen was found on Bettina Poeschel's body didn't prove murder, he continued. "It proves perhaps that Michael Murphy had sexual intercourse with Fraulein Poeschel . . . does it prove that he killed her? Michael Murphy could get a very shoddy and very unjust trial. I think you'll find most of the evidence in this case is fantasy, isn't safe and based on a variety of fallacies."

But the jury disagreed. The seven men and five women returned a unanimous guilty verdict after deliberating for almost six hours. The recidivist killer sat emotionless in court and continued slowly chewing gum as the verdict was read out. Gone was the emotion he'd shown in garda custody when he confessed to the crime. He was handed down a mandatory life sentence by Mr Justice Aindrias O'Caoimh. Justice O'Caoimh told the family that he hoped the unanimous verdict would bring some sense of closure to a very difficult chapter in their lives.

Speaking outside the Four Courts afterwards, Jorgen Poeschel expressed relief at the verdict. "It made a closure of a bad chapter for my family," he said. "I want to thank the gardaí for their investigations and support. I want also to thank the local community in Donore and Drogheda for their assistance and for the sympathy they have shown us during all this time."

Inspector Gerry O'Brien also spoke about his satisfaction at the outcome of the trial: "It was a terrible tragedy that a young girl like Bettina Poeschel came to this country to see the historic site of Newgrange and this happened—it was an opportunistic crime. This man killed in the past."

The attack was one of the worst crimes against a defenceless woman gardaí had ever seen. More were to come. The rape and murder of Swiss teenager Manuela Riedo in Galway in 2007 has striking similarities to Bettina's case. Like Murphy, Riedo's killer Gerald Barry had struck before, having raped a French woman six weeks before he killed the Swiss teen.

Aside from his breaking down in custody on the evening of his arrest, Murphy has never shown remorse for his actions. That he had killed before angered and frightened the local community and Irish society in general. The following year, Murphy's appeal against his conviction was rejected. While Justice Nicholas Kearns dismissed the appeal, he also warned gardaí that all interviews with suspects should be recorded in future. Interviewing detectives failed to record Murphy when he broke down sobbing on the day of his arrest, made admissions and expressed regret for what he had done. With his last legal avenue exhausted, Murphy again showed no emotion as he was taken away from the Court of Criminal Appeal to serve the remainder of his life sentence. He is detained in Dublin's Arbour Hill Prison, which houses the country's most dangerous and notorious rapists and offers specialist treatment programmes for sex offenders.

The average time spent behind bars for lifers is 17 years. But for a small cohort of Irish prisoners, including Michael Murphy, life literally can mean life. Murderers and sex offenders whose crimes are so heinous that they spark public outcry and a media frenzy have major difficulties when trying to get parole, and Murphy is among that elite group. Unlike many other jurisdictions, the decision to release life sentence prisoners lies with the minister for justice of the day. To allow Murphy out of prison would be an unpopular political decision. His release would run the risk that he might repeat-offend, but the State will be forced to make this decision in the coming years. "Even aside from the sexual attacks on women, he's a man prone to extreme violence against anyone," says retired chief superintendent Finnegan. "I wouldn't want to see him back on the streets of Drogheda. He would create a lot of fear."

The Poeschel family have visited Ireland many times since Bettina's death. In 2002 a memorial to the young German woman was erected on the quiet country road where her body was found. Her father spoke of their pain in an open letter to the people of Co. Meath in 2001, and asked for their assistance in honouring his daughter's memory. He wrote: "I hope that we can erect a dignified memorial near the place she has been found, hopefully based on the ideas of young local artists. We want them to show how fate can meet anybody anywhere, for instance on a sunny afternoon on a frequented road amongst hospitable Irish people."

A stone monument was erected in May 2002 and a local priest held a service at the spot. For the Poeschel family, Ireland will always be associated with Bettina. "Every time I hear something in the news about Ireland, it leaves a tasteless aftertaste. But we received a lot of support from people in Ireland. Also, my parents are still in touch with people who helped with the memorial," adds Cornelia. Life goes on for the family but can never be the same. "We are all more closely connected in my family now. I am more precious to my parents and they are more precious to me. It has become easier from year to year. The wound has healed but the scar remains. That scar will be there for my whole life."

08 | ZHAO LIU TAO

The 16-year-old boy picked up an iron bar and stuck the Chinese man once over the head. The force of the blow was enough to knock him over, causing him to hit his head hard off the ground. He never got back up. Realising he had done serious damage, Darren Derwin and his friends ran from the scene of the attack at Beaumont Grove, Whitehall, on Dublin's northside. It wouldn't be long before gardaí caught up with them. It would take even less time still for the death of 30-year-old student Zhao Liu Tao to be condemned as a racially motivated killing. Despite a strong belief from within the Chinese and Irish community that the young man was killed by an Irish teenager almost half his age because of the colour of his skin, senior gardaí that led the investigation are adamant that this is not the case. Gardaí believe the real motive was not racism, but thuggery.

On 21 January 2002, Zhao Liu Tao went to a party hosted by some Chinese friends at an apartment in Grace Park Court on Beaumont Road in Whitehall. The English language student lived in nearby Summerhill and was well known and liked in Dublin among the Chinese community. He had been living in Ireland just nine months when he lost his life. At around 10 pm he left the party with two friends to walk to the nearby off-licence to buy some more alcohol to bring back to the party. On the way back, the men encountered two Irish teenagers, aged 15 and 16 years old. The teenagers were out looking for trouble. It started, as these things always do, with insults being traded on both sides. "It began with a bit of slagging. The two Irish guys started it. But we have no doubt that whoever they came across that night would have been verbally attacked. These guys were looking for trouble, looking for a fight and the first people they came into contact with were the Chinese men," according to a senior garda involved in the investigation. "It really was a case of the wrong place at the wrong time for Zhao Liu Tao. We are satisfied it was not a racially motivated attack, despite what has been said since. They didn't start a fight with them because they were Chinese; they started the row because they were actively looking for an altercation with anyone. They started a row with the first people they saw."

As the abuse intensified, the Irish youths threw a glass bottle at the Chinese men, who then chased them down the hill to the junction of Beaumont Road and Beaumont Grove. One of the teenagers then got out his mobile phone and called some friends who were drinking in a field near by. Within a couple of minutes, four of the teenagers' male friends ranging in age from 14 to 18 had arrived, in addition to a group of teenage girls. But the two Chinese students weren't without support either. Some of their friends came out of the party to look for them and heard the commotion outside. Suddenly there was a large number of people standing outside on the street, which inflamed the already volatile situation. "There was some squaring up and then more bottles were thrown by the teenagers as well as some punches on both sides. The teenagers had been drinking in a nearby field in Beaumont. It would all have happened very quickly," adds the garda.

Zhao stood 6 ft in height and was an expert in the martial art of kung fu. It is possible that Darren Derwin singled him out for attack because of his stature. The row between the two groups was not serious until the teenager picked up a 4 ft iron bar from roadworks near by and struck Zhao once over the head, hard enough to knock him to the ground. It was not a premeditated attack. The 16-year old acted on the spur of the moment when he picked up the iron bar, which was supporting a new footpath under construction, and chose to use it as a weapon.

As Zao fell heavily to the ground hitting his head, the group of teenagers fled the scene. Gardaí and emergency services were called by Zhao's friends and Garda Scott Tormey and Melissa O'Sullivan from Santry station arrived at the scene within minutes. Zhao Liu Tao was alive but unconscious. He would lose his battle for life three days later in the intensive care unit of Beaumont Hospital, just a couple of hundred yards from where he was attacked. His friends told gardaí what had happened and that the group had run away only minutes earlier. It was quickly decided between the two officers that Garda O'Sullivan would stay with the severely injured man while Garda Tormey would go in search of the youths, whose appearance the Chinese witnesses to the attack described. This decision later proved to be crucial.

Within ten minutes, Garda Tormey had apprehended two of the teenagers at Lorcan Avenue, Santry, about a mile from the scene of the incident. "He did well to find them," adds the senior garda involved in the case. "Finding them so quickly was instrumental in solving the case."

Darren Derwin was not one of the two youths apprehended in the immediate aftermath of the attack on Zhao Liu Tao. The arrested pair were taken to Whitehall garda station and during their 12 hours in custody told officers the names of their friends who were with them when the attack took place. Two days later, and one day before Zhao Liu Tao would lose his battle for life, Darren Derwin went voluntarily to Coolock station to make a statement about his role in the assault. His parents accompanied him and were deeply shocked that their young son, who had no previous convictions, could be capable of such aggression. Derwin told the officers: "I swung the pole at the Chinese fella but let it go. I saw the fella falling. I don't know where I hit him but it was close to the head. Then I ran away."

Within days of the assault, gardaí had interviewed the entire group who had been involved in the confrontation with the Chinese nationals, including the teenage girls who had witnessed it but had not taken part. All were forthcoming and generally co-operative. Detectives established that six male Irish teenagers were involved in the row. Two were aged 18, two were 16, one was 15 and the last was just 14 years old. Many came to the garda station with their parents and were genuinely shocked that they were involved in an incident where someone was killed. None of them was a serious criminal; they were just teenagers who got caught up in a row that took an unpredictable turn. The detectives questioning them did not have to deal with stonewalling and a refusal to answer any questions, a tactic commonly employed by those more accustomed to being in garda custody. Crucially, the main instigator of the violence confessed and some of the other teenagers admitted to varying degrees playing a part in the violence, from throwing punches to glass bottles. In this respect, it was a relatively straightforward case for gardaí as they had confessions within days as well as plenty of witnesses to the crime. Catching two of the teenagers within an hour of the attack was vital.

But while detectives worked overtime to track down all the teenagers who had been involved in the fight on the cold January night, controversy began to rumble over the motive for the killing, which deepened further after Zhao lost his fight for life. His killing sparked a major debate in Ireland over the issue of racial violence and his death was described by every newspaper as the country's first racially motivated killing, despite garda assurances to the contrary. The assertion that it was a racist killing ensured it got blanket media coverage and the broadsheet press were especially interested in the story. *The Irish Times* in particular wrote widely on the killing and its implications on society. "Some people in the Chinese community believed it was racially motivated and once that word got out there it was hard to change people's minds. But it's plain and simple to us, this was not the case," according to the garda. Senior detectives investigating the killing formed this opinion early on after interviewing all the witnesses and the teenagers involved. Shortly after Zhao Liu Tao's death, they met with the Chinese Ambassador to Ireland, her excellency Zhang Xiaokang, to assure her of this. "She did have some concerns that it was racially motivated because of what was being written in the papers and because of what some Chinese leaders in Ireland were saying," adds the garda. "But we were able to give her an assurance that this wasn't the case and she accepted it."

But some minds could not be changed. Dr Katherine Chan Mullen, director of the Chinese Information Centre, remains convinced the killing was racially motivated. "It was because of his death that I founded the Chinese Information Centre. I realised that Chinese people need somewhere to get information and to talk about problems they might be having in Ireland," she says. "I know all about the case. He had left the party to go to the off-licence and these boys just starting teasing him. He was very tall—6 ft—and was a black belt in kung fu. It was such a tragedy that he was killed. It really shocked the Chinese community here as well as the Irish community. His parents could not travel over, they were so distressed. Instead his brother and his cousin came."

Zhao Liu Yang made the arduous trip to Dublin from Shenyang city in the Lisaoning province of north-east China in the days after his killing to identify his older brother's body. His cousin Sang Ze Hui accompanied him to provide moral support. The State paid all their costs during their visit including their hotel, transportation and an interpreter. While he was here, Zhao Liu Yang attended the first hearing of an inquest into his brother's death and spoke afterwards of the deep sense of shock and loss the family were experiencing. Zhao Liu Tao worked as a property manager in China before coming to Ireland in March 2001 and was due to return home to China within six months. Such was their grief, his father Zhao Hing Li and mother Zhao Lyu Zhi had been unable to make the journey. "After hearing the news my parents have gone into hospital with shock. It has been very upsetting," said 26-year-old Zhao Liu Yang, speaking through an interpreter after an inquest into his brother's death was opened at Dublin City Coroner's Court. Zhao Liu Yang described his older brother and only sibling as an honest, hard-working young man, who had been enjoying studying in Ireland but was equally looking forward to going back home. "He was due to come home

around July/August of this year," he added. The family were told
the tragic news through the Chinese Embassy in Ireland.

How gardaí investigate a violent death differs hugely from how
the Chinese police would conduct their own enquiries, not to
mention the differences between how the two judicial systems
operate: in China, capital punishment is administered for a wide
variety of crimes and is almost always the sentence handed down
for those convicted of murder and manslaughter. Dealing with a
violent death is difficult enough for bereaved families, but trying
to cope with this in another country is all the more challenging.
After attending the opening and adjournment of his brother's
inquest, Zhao Liu Yang said at the inquest that he was satisfied
with the garda investigation. But he remarked on the many
differences between Chinese and Irish law. "I still have a few
questions," he said. He queried why more information was not
given about the attack on his brother. The coroner, Dr Brian
Farrell, explained to him that they could not give further details
until the garda's criminal investigation was completed and that
this could take some time. The inquest heard that Zhao Liu Tao
died from blunt force trauma to the head. Detective Inspector
John Dennedy from Santry station, now a detective superintendent at Ballymun, sought an adjournment of proceedings as
charges were being considered and a file was being prepared for
the Director of Public Prosecutions (DPP). The coroner agreed to
adjourn the inquest.

Before he left to return home after his week in Dublin, Zhao
Lin Yang was given a full briefing by detectives about the
circumstances that led up to his brother's killing. He also met the
neurosurgeon at Beaumont Hospital who treated Zhao Liu Tao,
and answered his questions about how his brother died.
Attending the inquest and identifying his brother's remains were
practical, necessary matters that had to be dealt with, but Zhao
Liu Yang and Sang Ze Hui also got some time to reflect on what
their loved one's death meant to the people of Ireland during
their few days in Dublin. An emotional service was held at the
spot where Zhao was attacked at Beaumont Grove, beside a small
park. Still in a state of shock, Zhao's younger brother and cousin

were comforted by over 100 supporters, many of them Chinese, during the ceremony. Bouquets of flowers were gently laid at the spot where the student had lain unconscious on the bleak concrete. In keeping with Chinese tradition, four cigarettes were lit and laid at the small shrine in front of a group of trees in the Beaumont cul-de-sac. The smoke will lead Zhao's ghost "to another, better place", explained a friend. A moment's silence was also respected during the non-denominational ceremony. It was here that his brother, a martial arts coach, got the opportunity to speak freely and openly about his loss. "We thought Ireland was a peaceful, friendly country so we are very shocked that this could happen," he said through a translator. His cousin Sang Ze Hui added: "It is so sudden, so sad. We did not really believe it. We could not, until we saw his body." Dr Chan Mullen remembers it as a poignant, touching and fitting occasion. "We wanted to have a plaque put up at the spot where he fell, but we couldn't get permission. It was a lovely service. I remember during the ceremony there was a bird in the tree for the entire time. I felt strongly that that was a sign that he was watching over us," says Dr Chan Mullen. "The bird flew away as soon as the ceremony ended." The 30-year old's remains were cremated in a non-denominational ceremony at Glasnevin and his brother and cousin then brought his ashes home. "In China, if the parents or the grandparents don't see the dead body of a loved one, the body is not flown home. It is seen as bad luck," she explains. "Everyone who knew Zhao Liu Tao spoke very highly of him. He was a strong and lovely person. His parents had placed a lot of hope in their eldest son, he had done so well for himself in his short life."

In the days after Zhao Lui Tao died, many other Chinese nationals living in Ireland began to speak out about instances of racism they had experienced as the media continued to be preoccupied with the story of the killing. At the time, there were 50,000 Chinese people living in southern Ireland and 20,000 of those were students. Many Chinese students spoke to the press anonymously and expressed a deep sense of growing fear within the community that Zhao's killing might spark further violence. "I really could not understand why such an innocent student was attacked. Such things have happened several times," one man who asked not to be named told *The Irish Times*. "Some young Irish have attacked Chinese with knives, iron bars, glasses and beer bottles, and I don't know why." Some of the 30-year old's friends that witnessed the row also spoke out about how they were racially taunted by the Irish youths that night. "They were saying very bad things," said his friend Nan, who was with him that fateful night and lived in the apartment where the party was being held. "There were two of them first," added Nan, "but then others arrived. They all seemed very young teenagers. One of them saw that my friend had a bottle of beer, and punched him in the face. My friend was very angry."

Nan's housemates, Xupeng and Qian, also came from Shenyang, the same province as Zhao. The three housemates had been studying English here for two years, more than a year longer than Zhao, who had only been a student at the Dublin International Language Institute for nine months. The Chinese community here have always stuck together, like most nationalities do abroad, and the students get to know each other easily. Nan, Xupeng and Qian had known Tao since he arrived. "It can be lonely here," explained Xupeng. "We have no parents or no families. So we get together and have parties. We have a few drinks and act the fool." Zhao liked the parties. He was a quiet and diligent young man, but he also liked to enjoy himself. Nan and his housemates lived for a while in Summerhill, in Dublin's city centre. But they made the decision to move after stones were thrown at their windows and doors by Irish kids. But up until their friend's death, they found Beaumont Grove a far quieter and less rough area.

Since China joined the World Trade Organisation in 2001, there has been a strengthened determination among people in the country to learn to speak English more fluently. As many students whose families could afford it began to send their children abroad, Ireland immediately became a popular destination. But with any major influx of new communities comes problems because of cultural clashes and the difficulties visitors have adapting to their new environment. The Chinese in Ireland have a track record of being eager to study and work, sometimes up to 80 hours a week. But Zhao's death forced the problems that Chinese people were experiencing in Ireland to the surface. Issues such as loneliness and isolation, often sensed acutely by teenagers studying abroad, began to be discussed in the wider society.

Zhao's death sparked a predicament in this country that needed to be addressed, regardless of whether Zhao Liu Tao's killing was race related or not. The tragic circumstances of how the student lost his life became a story of major national importance in the weeks following his death, and everyone had a view on the matter—from politicians to business leaders to groups opposing and supporting multiculturalism. Residents against Racism, a voluntary group of people working to curb racism in Ireland, placed the blame for the student's death firmly at the door of the government which, they said, hadn't done enough to promote anti-racism in this country. They also denounced the work of the Immigration Control Platform, which a few months previously had leafleted areas around north Dublin with pamphlets warning of the "invasion and colonisation of Ireland". In response, the group said it did not wish to comment on Zhao's death as an individual case, but added that the only way to end racial hostility was to ensure that all migrants from outside the European economic area were in the State strictly at "our invitation". But most people were keen to condemn the killing and were genuinely shocked and horrified by what appeared to be the country's first race-related fatality.

The level of outrage was such that five days after the incident, a demonstration was organised to protest against what had happened. Organised by Globalise Resistance, a couple of hundred people participated in the march on Dublin's O'Connell Street. Passers-by signed a book of condolence and a petition calling on the government to tackle racism. The protestors carried placards reading, 'Stop racist murders', and 'Chinese and Irish unite'. People had been galvanised. Even the Chinese Embassy in Ireland weighed in on the debate—before being fully briefed by gardaí—telling the press: "We are very shocked at the death of a Chinese student in what was apparently a racial attack." A grim proclamation was issued from the ICTU general secretary David Beggs: "Anyone who engages in racist behaviour cannot wash their hands of the death of this young Chinese man." The momentum seemed unstoppable. Victim Support widened the debate, saying it believed there were many racially motivated attacks which went unreported and the group announced plans to recruit volunteers from ethnic minority communities to deliver a support service for victims of racist crime. The Labour Party's then justice spokesman, Brendan Howlin, expressed his concern that the hostility "being directed towards refugees and asylum seekers is creating a climate of intolerance against non-nationals generally, which can soon escalate into physical attacks". Amnesty International stated that it was vital that racist attacks were taken seriously and such crimes should have an appropriate sentence.

Voices are often loudest in the immediate aftermath of an incident that rocks the public consciousness. But slowly these voices died down and the general public became preoccupied with other matters. On 6 March 2003—14 months after the attack—Darren Derwin and three others appeared at the Dublin Circuit Criminal Court to face charges relating to the incident that led to the death of Zhao Liu Tao. Derwin, of Ferrycarrig Road in Coolock, who was by then 17, pleaded guilty to manslaughter. Daniel Jones (19) from Gardiner Place in Dublin, along with two accomplices aged 15 and 17, pleaded guilty to violent disorder by using or threatening to use unlawful violence during the incident. Jones, who was 18 when he took part in the assault, was the only one who could legally be named in the media at that stage, as he was the only adult who participated in the attack. Marie Torrens, defending Darren Derwin, said her client was doing his Leaving Cert and requested he not be sentenced until some date after 12 June. Anthony Sammon, representing the 15-year old, said his client would turn 16 in April. He was anxious that the teenager not be sentenced before his birthday because of "a certain regime" in St Patrick's Institution for young offenders, letting those present draw their own conclusion about what was being insinuated. Judge Desmond

Hogan said he had to deal with each accused on the same date and adjourned the sentencing of all four until 24 June. He said he would put no other cases in for that day because the hearing would take some time and he wanted to give it his full attention. A fifth youth, aged16, had his case adjourned for arraignment until 19 March after his counsel, Mr Erwan Mill Arden, said he was not ready to enter a plea on the matter. The charges against this teenager were later withdrawn.

Daniel Jones was remanded in custody until his sentence date as he was serving a sentence on a different matter. The other youths were remanded on continuing bail. On 24 June, the four young men again appeared before Judge Desmond Hogan. Details of other serious charges against Daniel Jones emerged at this court sitting, which clearly showed the young man had a propensity for violence. He pleaded guilty to a number of charges of assault causing harm on a couple in their 50s in separate incidents on 11 July and 22 August 2001. These arose out of false allegations by Jones's girlfriend that she had been sexually assaulted by a man. Garda Cathy McNamara said Jones had savagely beaten a middle-aged man in his flat in Dublin in July 2001 because he wrongly believed this man had molested his girlfriend. He forced his way into the flat wearing a balaclava and attacked the man in his bed, she added. The following month he returned to the flat with an accomplice and burst his way past the man's wife and up to the room again. His accomplice detained the man's wife downstairs and she could hear Jones perpetrating acts of violence on her husband, said Garda McNamara. The woman managed to break free and as she ran up the stairs she met Jones coming down. He pushed her back and she fell down a number of steps and into a sofa. His accomplice picked up a chair and Jones shouted, "Kill the bitch." He then proceeded to hit her about five times before they left. She ran upstairs and found her husband lying in bed covered in blood, added the garda. Jones arrived back at the flat he shared with his girlfriend and said he had killed the man. His girlfriend then admitted that the allegations were false. Counsel Paul Coffey, for Jones, said his client came from a tragic background and most of his 22 previous convictions were for road traffic matters.

Judge Desmond Hogan said there were a number of reports on each of the four accused that he wished to read, as well as victim impact reports, and he would need time to consider those. He again adjourned sentencing of the convicted four until 30 July and ordered probation reports in each case. Det. Sgt Tom McCarrick told the court that Zhao Liu Tao died as a result of a head injury sustained from a single blow and then falling over and hitting the back of his head on the ground. He also told the judge that it was his view that the Chinese man's killing was not a racially motivated attack. On 30 July, having considered the various reports on each of the convicted young men, as well as the impact the 30-year old's death had on his family, the judge sentenced the four men. Darren Derwin was given a four year sentence for manslaughter, with two years suspended, while the three others received two year sentences for violent disorder, the entirety of which was suspended. The judge suspended the last two years of Derwin's sentence because of his "very young age and the fact that he has no previous convictions". Darren Derwin was the only one to spend time in jail for the killing of Zhao Liu Tao. The young men's sentences were handed down 18 months after the Chinese student lost his life.

There was no major outcry at the sentences decided by the courts and the media coverage was miniscule when compared with the extensive reporting at the time of the killing. But the office of the DPP did feel it was unduly lenient. The following year, the Court of Criminal Appeal rejected an application by the DPP to increase the sentences of Darren Derwin and Daniel Jones.

Dr Katherine Chan Mullen says the Chinese community were extremely disappointed by the sentencing. "We thought the prison sentences decided by the courts were very unfair," she says. "It was far too lenient."

Darren Derwin's actions did not provide the short, sharp shock to keep him on the straight and narrow after his release from prison. In 2007, he appeared in a UK court charged with another violent assault. In a strange, twisted kind of irony, he claimed racist abuse caused him to lash out in violence. In January 2007,

21-year-old Derwin was on a night out in Richmond, North
Yorkshire, with his 18-year-old brother Gary when they say they
were subjected to anti-Irish abuse. Derwin stabbed a young
Englishman named Dean Carter in the head with a broken bottle
in the altercation that followed. Teesside Crown Court in England
heard how Derwin screamed at Carter: "I am going to kill you.
You don't think I will do it, do you?"

When he was arrested, Derwin said he had been playing
snooker with his brother in the Fleece pub when a British army
soldier told him that he hated the Irish, so they left. Outside a
group approached him and one said "that's him", and they were
set upon, he claimed. Derwin pleaded guilty to wounding with
intent to cause grievous bodily harm (GBH) and he was given an
"indefinite prison sentence" for public protection by Judge Peter
Armstrong. The judge ruled that he must serve two years before
he could apply for parole.

After the intense media scrutiny following Zhao Liu Tao's death
died down, the detectives who led the investigation were invited
to dinner at the Chinese Embassy by ambassador Zhang
Xiaokang. While the ambassador initially believed it was a race-
related killing, she had by then accepted that the police
investigation had found no substance to support this assertion.
But if journalism is the first rough draft of history, then the 30-
year old's death will be remembered as Ireland's first racist
killing. "Sometimes, people's minds cannot be changed. But the
important people like his family know now that this was not the
case," adds the garda. "But really this was just a senseless killing.
If he had been struck twice with that iron bar there is no doubt a
murder charge would have been sought. But that's not what
happened. It started off as one of those rows between two groups
of people that should have ended with everyone walking away
after a bit of a scuffle. But sometimes these things take a nasty
turn."

Zhao's father visited Ireland in the months following his son's
death. He met with detectives involved in the investigation as well
as representatives from the Chinese community and friends of
his son's. While the family's grief can never be minimised, Dr

Chan Mullen agrees that some positive developments emerged from the tragedy of his death. "It did bring the community together. It did make us start talking and looking at problems with racism as well as problems Chinese people have adapting to life in Ireland," she says. "Because of Zhao Liu Tao, some positive things have happened and his family can be proud of what his memory represents."

09 | VAIDAS FRANCKEVICIUS AND VITALIJUS JASINSKAS

An alcohol-fuelled, savage attack ended the lives of the two Lithuanian men. Killed by a fellow countryman, the exact circumstances that led to their deaths has never been fully explained. The men's wives and children will never know what happened to their loved ones in the last few hours of their lives. All that is clear is that their last moments alive were filled with pain and suffering.

A man out walking his dog on a bright summer's morning found the bodies. He was taking a stroll along Mound Road in Warrenpoint, Co. Down, when out of the corner of his eye he spotted a semi-naked body in deep undergrowth. Upon closer inspection, the man saw two pairs of legs. Just one face was visible, which was disfigured as it had been so badly beaten. It just so happened that a police car was driving by and the passer-by immediately flagged it down and told the officers about his grim discovery. It was just before midday on Wednesday 15 May 2002. The bodies of the two Lithuanians had been dumped there in the early hours of Monday morning two days previously.

The dead bodies had been concealed in the undergrowth beside Warrenpoint golf course on the shores of Carlingford Lough. Within minutes, several police cars were at the scene and the area was sealed off. But because of the threat of dissident republicans and loyalists at that time, detectives could not immediately forensically examine the scene. It was protocol for the army bomb disposal team to examine the area first in case there were any concealed bombs and ensure the dead bodies weren't booby-trapped. After several hours, the army deemed the bodies and the area safe for examination.

The two dead men had suffered horrific injuries. Both of them had their throats slit and one of them had several teeth knocked out. Both bodies had been badly battered and their faces were barely recognisable. The cause of death would later be determined as blunt force trauma to the head and penetrating wounds to the neck. Both men also had defensive wounds on their hands. Their bodies were only partially clothed and their genitalia were exposed. Because of this, there were initial enquiries to determine if there was a sexual motive for their murder. This was later ruled out. There was no identification on either body and no one fitting their descriptions had been reported missing. Police were at a loss. There was also very little blood at the scene, suggesting to police that the men had been murdered elsewhere and their bodies were then dumped.

Within hours the Police Service of Northern Ireland (PSNI) got their first break in the case. In the early hours of Monday 13 May, two 13-year-old boys were on their way home. They lived in a residential care home in Newry and had snuck out without permission. As they walked along Sandy Street, about seven miles from where the dead bodies were found, they saw a man sitting in a car. They approached the window and asked the man sitting in the driver's seat for a cigarette. As they spoke to him, the two boys noticed the body of a partially clothed man lying in the back seat with blood dripping from his hand. Stunned, the two teenagers stopped talking to the man and walked quickly away from the car. But about halfway down the road, they couldn't resist turning around to take another look. They saw the same man who had been sitting in the driver's seat putting a body in the boot of the car with the help of another man. The car was parked outside 15 Sandy Street.

The two boys were so disturbed by what they had seen that they woke up the staff at their care home when they got back to tell them about it. Police were called, but a patrol of Sandy Street did not find anything unusual at the address. The car the boys claimed to have seen was gone. But two days later, the significance of this reported sighting became apparent to police and led them to visit 15 Sandy Street again. At the house they found two Lithuanian men and a local woman. Marks that appeared to be blood were visible on the walls. The two Lithuanians were taken to Ardmore police station for further questioning. Soon afterwards they were arrested at the station. The local woman, who didn't live at the house, also agreed to give a statement to police. It was soon established that the two Lithuanians in custody were friends of the dead men found at Warrenpoint golf course. Police also learned that two other Lithuanian men, housemates of the two men in custody, went missing shortly after the double killing.

The dead men were identified as Vaidas Franckevicius (27) and Vitalijus Jasinskas (30). Before their deaths, they were living at a caravan site at 21 Ryan Road, Mayobridge, with two other Lithuanian men. The two men who disappeared after their killings were Julius Aguonis (18) and Vitalius Sedovas (21). They lived at the house in Sandy Street with the two Lithuanian men who were arrested. Altogether, there were eight Lithuanians in the group and all were working as mushroom pickers for Mourne Compost. Four lived at the house in Sandy Street while the other four lived at a caravan site. The eight men all knew each other well from working together on a daily basis and they were friends. But tensions between some of the younger and older men had begun to develop. Police immediately went to the caravan site. They found the temporary home of the two dead men and the other caravan which was inhabited by their two Lithuanian friends. Despite their disfigurement, due to the horrific nature of their injuries, the Lithuanian men living at the caravan site were none the less able to identify their remains.

Soon, police had pieced together the final movements of Franckevicius and Jasinskas as well as what had caused Aguonis and Sedovas to flee the country. Sunday 12 May was a sunny day and the eight Lithuanian men decided to have a barbecue at the caravan site. The men all began drinking quite early that day and there were several trips between the caravan site and the house at 15 Sandy Street to collect more alcohol. Over the course of the afternoon, tension began to build between the two dead men and 18-year-old Julius Aguonis. Police have never been able to ascertain what the exact cause of the row was, but there was considerable ill-will between them that had been building for weeks. On the day of the barbecue, Aguonis said something offensive to his two older countrymen whom he would later admit to killing. At 10 pm the two men who would soon lose their lives gave Julius Aguonis and Vitalius Sedovas a lift home. Tilmantis Tamasauskas, who also lived at the caravan site at Mayobridge, went with them. Despite his young age, Aguonis already had a serious problem with alcohol and was extremely drunk that night. When the five men arrived at the house, they all went inside and there was a fight between Julius Aguonis and the two men he would later admit to killing. They gave the teenager a severe beating, while Tilmantis Tamasauskas held Sedovas back from defending his young friend. After the men left, the 18-year old was angry with Sedovas for not trying hard enough to help him while he was assaulted. They were supposed to be best friends. Aguonis was still very drunk and he accused his friend of being weak and unmanly for not sticking up for him.

That should have been the end of the matter. However, Vaidas Franckevicius and Vitalijus Jasinskas went back to their caravan site and had a few more drinks. The two men then decided to return in their car to the house at Sandy Street to confront Julius Aguonis once again. What exactly happened in the second confrontation that led to the death of both men is unclear as Julius Aguonis and Vitalius Sedovas steadfastly refused to tell police how events unfolded. But at the house police found plenty of evidence to link Julius Aguonis to the crime. Despite attempts to clean up the scene of the murder, Aguonis's bloody palm print was discovered at the house. The blood of the two dead men was also found in the kitchen, hallway, second floor back bedroom

and all over the walls. Some attempt had been made to hide the
crime. The walls had been washed but not particularly well. A
mop and a bucket containing traces of the victims' blood was
found at the scene. A golf club shaft with blood on it was also
found at the house. It was clear to police they had found the scene
of the double homicide.

Aguonis and Sedovas's housemates told police that both men
had left the house the morning after the barbecue, saying they
were going to southern Ireland. Police soon obtained CCTV
footage that showed the two men boarding a bus from Newry bus
station going to Belfast. The two men then caught the Larne to
Stranaer ferry and another bus before they arrived at London's
Victoria station. They had abandoned Vitalijus Jasinskas's Mazda
car in Newry some eight miles from where the bodies were
dumped.

In London, they were met by a blonde-haired woman, Julius
Aguonis's girlfriend Sylvija Muraliele. Again, they were captured
on CCTV and the 18-year old's hood was pulled up to try and
conceal his badly beaten face. Sylvija had previously lived with
Aguonis in Newry before moving to London. Soon after they fled,
they became wanted men in Ireland in connection with the
killings of Vaidas Franckevicius and Vitalijus Jasinskas. News of
the killings had spread to London and had appeared in
Lithuanian newspapers in the UK as well as Lithuania. Sylvija had
become close to another Lithuanian man in London. She was
involved in a brief relationship with this man and he became
aware that Julius Aguonis and Vitalius Sedovas had left the North
and were staying with her. He had heard that these two men were
in some kind of trouble. Police had put out an alert for the two
Lithuanians and were seeking to speak to them in connection
with the deaths of their fellow countrymen. This Lithuanian man
still had feelings for Sylvija and was wiring her money. He didn't
think she should be associating with Julius Aguonis. So he
decided to write anonymously to the immigration service in
London saying he had information about his two countrymen
who were wanted in connection with the deaths in Northern
Ireland. After his letter to the immigration authorities in London,

police in the North easily tracked Sylvija's ex-boyfriend and paid him a visit. He provided them with the address to which he had been wiring money to Sylvija. She had moved from London to Lancashire with Aguonis. The PSNI, assisted by English police, put this house under surveillance before raiding it on 3 September 2002 and arrested the young couple. Both were eventually taken to Banbridge police station. Sylvija was questioned in connection with assisting an offender and Julius Aguonis was within days transferred back to Northern Ireland where he was ultimately to face charges. He had spent almost three months on the run in London before police caught up with him.

Sylvija proved very helpful to the police investigation, something that would later be used against her. She told them she had got a phone call from Julius Aguonis the night of the double killing. He told her he was in trouble and was coming over because he needed her help. "We have got a problem, we need to come to England urgently," he told his girlfriend. She also spoke to Vitalius Sedovas. "This is no joke," he told her. "Can you find a place for us?" She agreed to help them. She was in love with Julius Aguonis. A few weeks after they arrived, she found the two men arguing in the kitchen of a house the three of them were renting in London. The pair were reading a Lithuanian newspaper. They wouldn't show it to her when she asked what they were rowing about. But she was not to be deterred and went out and bought it herself. In it, she learned about the circumstances of the brutal double killing in Newry and her boyfriend and Vitalius Sedovas's suspected involvement. Later, she asked her boyfriend about it. He admitted that there was some truth to the story. He told her they had both been involved in the deaths of the two men. He said it was self-defence and Sedovas had come to his rescue. Over the next few months Sylvija continued to ask her boyfriend questions about what happened. Bit by bit, he gradually told her some details about what had happened. He explained how he had been attacked earlier that night by the two men who would later lose their lives and that another one of his housemates had held back Sedovas while the pair beat him savagely. He was left bleeding and injured by the men, who then left. But a little while later, they returned and there was another fight. He and Sedovas were only defending themselves, he told Sylvija.

Police had Aguonis in custody and were obviously anxious to find Vitalius Sedovas. Sylvija was able to provide them with an address of a Russian shop in London where she knew he visited. The Baltika was located at Hugh Street, Walthamstow, London. Undercover PSNI officers assisted by UK police put the street under surveillance. Sylvija's tip led police straight to Vitalius Sedovas. He was arrested four weeks after Julius Aguonis was picked up as he was observed going into an internet café on High Street opposite the Baltika store. He had spent almost four months on the run from police and was transferred back to Northern Ireland to face charges relating to the double killing.

Sylvija was living illegally in the UK and was deported back to Lithuania after she assisted police. It was decided she would not face charges for assisting the two men in evading police; instead she would be a key police witness. The four other Lithuanian men living in Newry, who were friends of the two dead men and the men suspected of involvement in their killing, were also deported. All were illegally living and working in Northern Ireland as mushroom pickers. The four men gave statements to police about the night of the barbecue and the tension and violence between Julius Aguonis and the two dead men, before they were sent home.

In custody in the North, Julius Aguonis provided police with an explanation of what he claimed happened on the night his two countrymen were killed. He told them he had quite a lot to drink at the barbecue, as had everyone else. Along with his friend Vitalius Sedovas, he got a lift home from the two men who would later end up dead in the most brutal of circumstances. He said he went straight up to bed when they got home, but moments later the two men burst into his room and gave him a savage beating while Tilmantis Tamasauskas, who lived at the caravan site, held his friend Sedovas back. He had been rowing earlier in the night with the two men, he told police. He could not say what they had been fighting about exactly because he was so drunk, but detectives had already established that tensions had been simmering among the group of Lithuanians for several weeks. When the men finished beating him they left, he said, and he was angry that his friend had not helped him. But later the two men returned again. He said he opened the front door to them, and they immediately pushed him over and he knocked his head on the stairs. He was in an alcoholic stupor as they beat him and he could not fight back, he told police. Then he saw Vitalius Sedovas come down the stairs swinging a golf club, knocking both of the men over and beating them with it, he claimed. When they appeared to be unconscious, Julius Aguonis said he helped his friend move the two men's bodies to Jasinskas's Mazda 626 that was parked outside. He said that was the end of his involvement. He went back inside and cleaned up some of the blood before going to bed. A few hours later he said he was awoken by Vitalius Sedovas who told him, "We'll have no more problems with them." The two men then decided to leave Newry, packed their belongings and left. He denied any knowledge about a knife in the attack and said he did not see a blade of any description over the course of the night. Both dead men had their throats slit and Vitalijus Jasinskas also had several stab wounds to his abdomen.

Police had a number of problems with the teenager's version of events. First, he claimed his two countrymen were attacked at the foot of the stairs, but most of their blood was found in the porch. Julius Aguonis's blood was also found in the front seat of the car, but he claimed he only helped remove the bodies and nothing else. It was the opinion of police that one man alone would not be strong enough to kill both men and then dispose of the two bodies. It was a two-man job.

Vitalius Sedovas gave police an entirely different version of events. He claimed to know absolutely nothing about how his two friends had died. He said that after the barbecue he went to bed and was asleep when they were killed. He said he was wearing headphones in bed and taking painkillers for a toothache and heard absolutely nothing. When he got up the next morning, he said he didn't notice any blood anywhere and decided to leave Newry for London when his friend Aguonis suggested it because, as he put it, he was "bored in Newry". He totally denied any involvement in the double killing. Unfortunately for police, the two 13-year-old boys who had seen a body in the back seat of the car early that Monday morning could not identify Aguonis or Sedovas in an arranged police line-up.

Police felt there was enough evidence to charge both suspects in connection with the killings. By attempting to blame each other, both men had made admissions to police. Julius Aguonis clearly had motive and opportunity. Vitalius Sedovas certainly had opportunity and he was bigger and stronger than his 18-year-old friend. Both men were charged with two counts of murder at Newry and Mourne Magistrates' Courts within 24 hours of separately being returned to Northern Ireland. Both denied the charges. They were refused bail and 15 months later both appeared at Newry Crown Court to stand trial on two counts of murder. But just before the trial got under way, Aguonis and Sedovas had a sudden change of heart and changed their pleas. When the charge of murdering both men was put to Julius Aguonis, he replied: "Not guilty to murder but guilty to manslaughter by reason of provocation." His co-accused Sedovas told the judge: "Not guilty to murder but guilty of assisting an offender."

Justice Reg Weir was told that both men were now admitting some role in the deaths. But the circumstances of these killings still remained unclear. Having earlier blamed his friend Vitalius Sedovas for attacking the two men with a golf club, Aguonis now admitted that it was he who hit them with the golf club. He said he was acting in self-defence because the two older men had earlier given him a savage beating. His girlfriend Sylvija told police her boyfriend was severely beaten around the face when he showed up in London the next day. cctv showed he had his hood up to try and conceal his injuries and he asked his girlfriend to buy him sunglasses. "He admits he used the golf club," his lawyer Jim Gallagher told the court. "He says he didn't use a knife at any time. He does admit he used the golf club. Indeed, he believes that one if not the two deceased were alive at the time they left the house where he was staying." He also claimed his friend Vitalius Sedovas took the two men from the house and it was Sedovas alone who then dumped them at Warrenpoint golf course before the pair later decided to flee to London. Confusingly, he was simultaneously admitting to killing them while saying they were possibly still alive when Sedovas took them from the house. "He was 18 years old at the time, significantly younger than the deceased and, of course, the obvious thing is that the two of them were confronting him. So he was 18 years old, he had been confronted by two older, able and fit men. He was still, at the time the incident occurred, very drunk," his lawyer added. Aguonis sobered up soon after he arrived in London, and the depravity of his actions soon began to sink in, his lawyer told the court. "When he became sufficiently sober early the next day, he realised not only the enormity of what had occurred but the enormity of what he had done. To him it was effectively a nightmare scenario. Again this is reflected in the pre-sentence report. He feels great remorse, feels great sadness for the position of the deceased families." His lawyer said his client's grief was compounded by the fact that the two men he admitted to killing were his fellow countrymen and they came from impoverished backgrounds, as did he. "That is accentuated on account of the fact that the deceased are his fellow countrymen," his lawyer Jim Gallagher continued. "And he therefore, by reason of his own background and knowing their background and their families' background, can understand the implication of what has occurred."

Five months before the two men appeared in court charged with double murder, the PSNI's Detective Chief Inspector Derek Williamson travelled to Lithuania to meet the widows of Vaidas Franckevicius and Vitalijus Jasinskas. Police wanted to take statements from them about the impact the loss of their husbands had on their families' lives. It was September 2003 and 16 months had passed since the two men had lost their lives. As a result, both families had been left virtually destitute. The men were friends long before they decided to go to Northern Ireland together in search of work and both lived in Lithuania's Kuanas city. Like many Eastern Europeans, they had heard about the opportunity to earn good money in Ireland and left together on 18 March 2002 in Vitalijus Jasinskas's Mazda. They planned to

work hard in Ireland for as long as it took to save enough money
to return home and substantially improve their families' financial
circumstances. But two months after they left their homes, both
men were dead. Rita Jasinskas told police that she was earning
just £100 a month and had two children to support. Vitalijus
Jasinskas's daughter was 8 years old when her father was killed.
He also had an 18-year-old stepson Arunas Matiejunas, whom he
raised as his own child. "Vitalijus was the family's sole
breadwinner. Our family's financial situation was difficult, and
therefore Vitalijus wanted to earn more to support the children,"
she told detectives. "About a week before the killings, Vitalijus
rang me and complained that he was in poor health. He was short
of breath because he had an allergy and his work was with peat,
which activated his allergy."

Her husband had sent home £80 on one occasion and told her
that he had saved another £1,300. He told her he was planning to
return to Lithuania within a week or so with the money to visit
his family. She spoke to him about twice a week by phone. Rita
noticed that in the last week of his life, her husband seemed
unhappy. Up until this, he had been reasonably content living in
Ireland, working as a mushroom picker and saving money.
Maybe he was beginning to miss his loved ones back home more
acutely. Or perhaps he was simply beginning to tire of working
on the mushroom farm, which was tedious and physically
demanding. It is also conceivable that Jasinskas was troubled by
the bad feeling that was developing between him and some of his
countrymen in Ireland. "During the whole of that last week
Vitalijus was in a disturbed state. I noticed this while talking to
him on the phone. Up to then he was more communicative. He
used to tell me where he had been, whom he had visited and how
he was getting on. When he rang on Saturday, he only reacted to
what I was saying. He appeared to be both angry and frightened
and I could feel stress and uneasiness in his voice. I asked him
what had happened, but he explained that he was tired and
feeling unwell, but other than that everything was fine," she told
police. The next morning, he texted her to say he was having a
barbecue with his friends. It would be the last time she would

ever hear from her husband. "Vitalijus's murder is for me very difficult to bear, as I loved him very much and he also loved me. He was very fond of the children and took particular care of them. He was the sole breadwinner of the family. Our financial circumstances after Vitalijus's death are very difficult because, although I work full-time, my wages are low," she explained. "The total monthly income the family receives is less than £100. I spend half of this sum on [rent] for the flat. I would like Vitalijus's body to be cremated, because this would be cheaper than transporting his remains to Lithuania."

The death of Vilma Franckevicius's husband left her in equally unfortunate circumstances. The couple had a young son who she is now left to raise alone. She had spoken to her husband hours before he died and, like Rita, she noticed her husband was also acting strangely. "He rang me on the last day, Sunday 12 May. He rang me twice on that day. He rang me the second time during the night, about one o'clock in the morning. What particularly stuck in my memory were his words, 'You were and will continue to be the very best of wives, remember that.' He also said he had the very best of sons. I told him that we had not yet finished bringing up our son," she told police. "What he said made me feel very uneasy, particularly his use of the word 'remember.'"

In the week after her husband was killed, Vilma and other members of his family tried to phone him, but the line was disconnected. Then she read about the death of two Lithuanians in Northern Ireland in a newspaper. One of the descriptions of the men's appearance immediately reminded her of her husband. Concerned, she rang Rita Jasinskas. "We then saw a picture of the Mazda car on the internet and realised Vitalijus and Vaidas were the murder victims. Vaidas was the breadwinner in our family. I did not work before the event as I was bringing up our little boy. Our family therefore suffered a great loss both spiritually and financially," she told detectives. "Our financial circumstances are particularly stretched as I suffer from diseases of the joints, which makes it hard for me to work. I therefore cannot imagine how it will be possible to manage later on when my son will be going to school. My parents and parents-in-law help me out, but their financial circumstances are also difficult." Vilma Franckevicius also requested that her husband's body be cremated in Northern Ireland, as she could not afford to pay for his body to be transported home for burial.

But it wasn't just the lives of the Jasinskas and Franckevicius families that were irrevocably damaged by the killings. Sylvija Muraliele had assisted police with their enquiries; she had told them everything she knew about her boyfriend and Vitalius Sedovas's involvement in the homicides. Had the two men not changed their pleas, she would have been a key witness for the prosecution. She was deported back to Lithuania shortly after the PSNI tracked down the two suspects. But back home, the young woman's involvement in the aftermath of the double killing continued to haunt her. Despite the fact that her former boyfriend and his friend were in prison awaiting trial in the North, certain people seemed determined to remind her of her involvement in what had happened. In September 2003, she too gave a statement to Detective Chief Inspector Derek Williamson about how her life had been since her deportation back to Lithuania 12 months earlier. "On my return, I began to be threatened because I gave evidence to police. I was threatened by phone," she said. The intimidation the mother-of-one suffered took place before the two men changed their pleas in court and admitted some role in the double homicide. And they were not empty threats. "One phone call was particularly serious. He said that they knew the nursery school my son was attending and, if I did not want to lose members of my family, I should give evidence that was favourable . . . I understood this as a threat to kill me, my son or another member of my family. My son is 4 years old."

The 23-year-old woman was understandably terrified. Then things got even worse. "One incident took place at about 4 pm on 19 December 2002. I had fetched my son from nursery school and we only just managed to escape two men who had jumped out of a car that I did not recognise that was parked in the street. We managed to escape to my flat by running through narrow alleyways between some houses," she told police. "Apart from that, the door to the flat was frequently kicked during the night and I was even afraid to leave the flat. I used to look out the spyhole in the door to make sure that there was nobody on the stairway. I did not report these incidents to the Lithuanian police because I do not think that they are in a position to render me effective assistance."

Sylvija was still in touch with her imprisoned ex-boyfriend Julius Aguonis through letters and by telephone. While he was awaiting trial, she was living in a state of fear. "I received quite a few letters from Julius Aguonis. When I spoke to Julius on the phone, he emphasised to me that I should think about the contents of my letters bearing in mind that his letters were read by the prison authorities," she told police. "At present I am working in Lithuania and can make ends meet, with assistance from my family. However, in terms of how I feel, I am in a very bad state because of the constant threats. The people threatening me think I betrayed them . . . I am afraid that my situation could worsen. I am afraid for my own and my family's safety." When Aguonis and Sedovas changed their pleas at the last minute in court, this put an end to the threats made against Sylvija. She was finally allowed to try and rebuild her life.

At Newry Crown Court, Justice Reg Weir was told about the circumstances of Julius Aguonis's childhood. "His early childhood hadn't been a very happy one. It appears that his father was prone to very heavy drinking and domestic violence and that eventually led to the separation of the defendant's parents. It seems clear also that during his teenage years he started to drink excessively, got into bad company and that led him into conflict with the law," his lawyer Jim Gallagher told the court. Aguonis had convictions for theft in Lithuania when he was 14 and 16, as well as further brushes with the law for criminal damage and disorderly behaviour. Justice Weir listened at length to everything Julius Aguonis's lawyer had to say about his client, from the beating he had suffered at the hands of the two men to his regret over the killings. He then spoke his mind on the matter. "He made a dishonest case to police, sought to blame Mr Sedovas for what he now accepts were his own actions and generally obstructed the investigation." The judge was also unhappy that there were issues around the circumstances of the double homicide that remained a mystery. Aguonis completely denied stabbing the two men during the assault that led to their deaths. "If there are, as there were, incisions and stab marks on the bodies of the deceased, then by implication your client is suggesting that they were put there by Mr Sedovas," the judge added.

Vitalius Sedovas, who initially told police he knew nothing of the killings and was asleep the entire time, now admitted he had initially lied. He said he saw the two men injured and moaning at the bottom of the stairs at the house in Sandy Street, but denied being involved in attacking them. "His sole culpability is that after they were killed by his co-accused, Mr Agounis, he recommended that Agounis clean up the blood and assisted him by leaving Northern Ireland in his company and going to England," his lawyer Arthur Harvey told Newry Crown Court. Unlike his friend, Vitalius Sedovas was not a drunk, he added. "Mr Sedovas rarely, if ever, drank although the work that he had left his family and home to come to was anything but fulfilling for an otherwise intelligent young man . . . He was not part of any dispute, controversy or argument between Mr Aguonis and the deceased," the lawyer continued.

Sedovas, like all the other Lithuanians involved in the tragedy that unfolded, also came from an impoverished background. "Perhaps one of the difficulties that exists in the background to this case is the huge cultural gap that exists between citizens of a country such as Lithuania and here. There is not only a cultural gap," his lawyer Arthur Harvey pointed out. "One can see the tragic statements that have been made by the wives of the deceased which perhaps give some indication as to why people would leave a country such as Lithuania to come to Northern Ireland where mushroom picking on a farm in south Armagh provides a far more adequate and fulfilling economic life than that available to them within their own country."

Unlike Aguonis, Sedovas had no criminal record. "He also comes from an entirely respectable family. He has three brothers and one sister. They have been brought up by their mother basically on their own since he was 10 years of age. They are professional and business people within their own community and he left that community with the intention of obtaining a better life for himself," his lawyer said. "Regrettably, perhaps this case does give some insight into the desperately sad and isolated life of persons who are illegal immigrants in whatever community. But it simply means that they are dislocated from the mainstream of the community. When these events happened, the defendant [Vitalius Sedovas], because of those difficulties in language, in culture, in status, chose to leave and therefore assist Aguonis in evading immediate capture."

His lawyer also appealed to the judge that his now 22-year-old client's mental health had suffered during the 17 months he had already spent on remand in prison. "It has had consequences in terms of his own mental health as a result of this and he has found it very difficult to settle within that environment," his lawyer continued. "I would simply ask that perhaps he can be shown a degree of mercy and lenience that perhaps wasn't shown to his victims."

Justice Reg Weir had some questions and observations of his own to make. Sedovas initially claimed he knew nothing whatsoever of the death of his two fellow countrymen before drastically changing his story. "Mr Sedovas says that when he came downstairs having been roused from his sleep he saw two people lying at the bottom of the stairs, and he is adamant that at this point both bodies had movement and there were sounds of moaning. Is that the case?" the judge asked. His lawyer confirmed that this was what Vitalius Sedovas had told him. "Your client's response to that was to go back to bed. Is that right?" the judge asked. Again, his lawyer confirmed that this was what he had been told, adding that Sedovas said he had an argument with Aguonis before going back to his bedroom. "He admits he gave no consideration to calling the police or ambulance service," the judge noted. "Can your client throw any light on the stab and cutting marks that were found on the bodies?" Absolutely not, his lawyer Arthur Harvey replied. Sedovas also denied driving off in the car to dump the two bodies, despite Julius Aguonis's claim to the contrary, and the statements by the two 13-year olds who saw two men placing the bodies in the boot of the car. It also remained unclear if the Lithuanians were dead or alive when they were taken from the house. Justice Reg Weir expressed his deep unhappiness that the court had not been told the full circumstances that led to the double killing. Both men denied stabbing their fellow countrymen and dumping their bodies. "One way or the other, Mr Harvey," said the judge, "we are not getting the full picture of what happened here, are we?"

The Crown Court prosecution accepted the pleas of the two men. This meant that no trial was necessary or witnesses needed to give evidence. But the judge wanted to know if the prosecution had a view on who inflicted the stab wounds both men sustained. "The position of the prosecution has to be that the evidence is insufficient for us to be able to specify the exact circumstances in which those wounds came into being," prosecution counsel Gordon Kerr QC told the judge. Justice Weir also asked if police knew who moved the bodies from the house and dumped them near Warrenpoint golf club. Both men were claiming the other was responsible for transporting the bodies. "There were inconsistencies. Based on that evidence, we believe the two persons were involved at least in the removal of the bodies from the house to the car. We are not in a position to say who was involved in the driving of the car to Mound Road, but we are in a position to say, my Lord, that there was no forensic link between Mr Sedovas and the vehicle or anything in the vehicle. There was, however, blood from Mr Aguonis inside the vehicle on what appears to have been a weapon, that is, part of a golf club," Kerr told the court. "The difficulty that we had is quite clear, my Lord. There is clear forensic evidence to show the involvement of Mr Aguonis in various respects in this offence. There is no such evidence that relates to Mr Sedovas."

Justice Reg Weir considered all the evidence before returning to the courtroom to pass sentence. He was clearly unhappy that the circumstances of the double homicide remained unclear. Justice Weir said that by assisting Aguonis to cover up the killings, Sedovas deliberately obstructed the course of justice and tried to prevent police from catching the person responsible for the double killing. "The problem with both of your accounts is that neither explains how the deceased came to be found lying together in woodland near the road in a rural location some miles distant from the house in Sandy Street where their injuries were sustained. Nor do they explain how the deceased received their slash and stab wounds. There are also many unanswered questions about Sandy Street itself," the judge continued. "I regret to have to say that, having carefully considered the matter, I have concluded that neither of you has, even now, been prepared to give a complete account of your involvement in and knowledge of these ghastly events. Had you chosen to do so, the families of the two men, for whom through your counsel you have professed sympathy, might have gained some small consolation from hearing a full explanation of how their relatives came to meet their deaths and what happened to their bodies thereafter."

Justice Weir then sentenced Julius Aguonis to eight years' imprisonment for the double killing. He jailed Vitalius Sedovas for three years for assisting his friend in the aftermath of his horrific crime. Both men have since been released from prison and deported back to Lithuania. Unsurprisingly, their friendship did not survive their incarceration. While Julius Aguonis eventually took responsibility, many question marks remain about how a teenager of his stature, not to mention his drunkenness and the fact that he had received a severe beating earlier, would have been able to kill two men much bigger and older than himself.

Toxicology reports found that both Vaidas Franckevicius and Vitalijus Jasinskas also had a high level of alcohol in their system at the time of death. And Julius Aguonis admitted to being extremely drunk when he carried out the assault that killed the two men. While a firm motive for the double homicide has never been firmly established, there is no doubt alcohol played a major role in the tragic events that unfolded in Sandy Street in Newry that fateful night in May 2002.

Over the past decade, north and south of the border there have been dozens of instances where Eastern European men have stabbed each other to death in drunken rows. Often these men (and it is usually men) are friends and show deep remorse for their actions afterwards. Feelings of isolation and a lack of integration into Irish society, mixed with copious amounts of alcohol, have been a major influence in many of these fatal stabbings. The double killing of Vaidas Franckevicius and Vitalijus Jasinskas by 18-year-old Julius Aguonis was more gruesome and violent than many similar killings of Eastern Europeans in Ireland. But all loss of life through violence results in grief and damaged lives, sometimes beyond repair, of loved ones left behind. Justice Reg Weir probably encapsulated the essence of this particular tragedy that befell the group of Lithuanian mushrooms pickers best: "It is a cruel irony that two men who felt driven to leave their homes to come to this country so as to try and provide a better life for their family should have here met such violent deaths at the hand of their own fellow countryman who had himself come here for the same purpose."

10 | QUI HONG XIANG

Armed with knives and machetes, the Chinese gang members assembled for battle on Dublin's O'Connell Street. It was a warm July night in 2002. Witnesses to the street fight watched in disbelief as up to 40 Chinese men brandishing weapons started to brawl in the street. When the dust finally settled minutes later, one man was left murdered and another was minus his scalp.

The street battle was waged over an unpaid brothel bill. Twenty-six-year-old Zhang Da Wei had visited a brothel in south Dublin with a friend a few weeks earlier. After both men had availed of the sexual services offered by the Chinese women working there, they left without paying. It appeared to be both a brave and stupid move. Zhang knew the brothel was run by a Chinese triad gang from the Fujian province. Triad gangs are branches of larger Chinese criminal organisations based all over Asia and in countries with significant Chinese populations.

But Zhang Da Wei didn't care if he offended the triad criminals; he was aligned with other Chinese gang members from north China. He knew men that would be prepared to fight with him should the need arise. Zhang Da Wei was also involved in criminality himself and had previously targeted his fellow countrymen for protection money in Dublin. Some of his associates were also involved in prostituting Chinese women and had a long-running dispute with the triad gang from the Fujian province over control of the Asian brothel market in Dublin. Detectives have not ruled out the possibility that Zhang Da Wei's refusal to pay at the brothel was designed to antagonise the gang and initiate a vicious battle.

Twenty-two-year-old Qui Hong Xiang was a good friend of Zhang Da Wei. He had arrived in Ireland less than a year previously on a student visa. He had been living at Mulberry Park in Castleknock with a host family before he moved into the city centre. He wanted to be closer to the Chinese community and his friend Wei in particular, whom he met shortly after he arrived in Ireland. Detectives say the 22-year old was associated with criminal elements in the Chinese underworld in Dublin and seemed particularly in awe of the older and wiser Wei, who took him under his wing. It was for this reason he agreed to take part in the organised gang fight, ultimately leading to his murder.

The Chinese triad gang that ran the brothel were enraged by Wei's attempt to undermine them by refusing to pay. The group of criminals ran several brothels in the capital and were relatively well organised. Some of them had links to the infamous 'Snakeheads' Chinese triad gang, who also hail from the Fujian region. Snakehead gang members are predominantly involved in human trafficking into Western Europe, North America and Australasia. The gang is renowned for its brutality.

The Chinese triad gang hired an associate, Chen Long, to go and speak to Zhang Da Wei and his friend and recover the money owed. The debt collector located Wei's friend, who had visited the brothel, and demanded the cash. But he refused and a row broke out between the two men. Afterwards, Wei was contacted and told about the developments. Angry that his friend had been attacked, he vowed to never pay the debt. It was decided by both sides that the only way to resolve the dispute was a gang fight, which is how it would be handled if they were living in China.

It was arranged to take place the next night at the top end of O'Connell Street. Both groups of men came into the city centre that night and spent the evening drinking at the Parnell Mooney pub on Parnell Street. They needed Dutch courage for the violent clash they knew lay ahead of them. A Chinese cultural evening was being held at the pub. The gang members socialised within their factions, while tensions between them simmered all night. At 1.30 am they quietly left the pub and walked to the corner of O'Connell Street and Cathal Brugha Street.

Many elements of the arranged confrontation were not well organised. They chose to stage their gang fight on O'Connell Street, one of the city's busiest areas that is well covered by CCTV and is close to Store Street garda station. Many of the Chinese men involved were known to gardaí and the vast majority were young men—older Chinese criminals were not inclined to get involved in a gang fight with weapons. The brawl was an opportunity for up-and-coming Chinese gang members to flex their muscles, advance their reputations and gain respect in the Chinese underworld among their elders. On one side were the triad members from the southern Fujian province who ran the brothel. On the other were Zhang Da Wei and his criminal associates who were from various regions around northern China, including the Hebei province, Qui Hong Xiang's original home place. Historically, politically and culturally, there remains some division between north and south China. Within its criminal underworld, this divide is far starker and there is considerable mistrust between northern and southern Chinese gangs. Fierce rivalry between these gangs also exists abroad as they vie for control of the Asian brothel market.

For about a minute, the two groups stood at opposite sides of the street and talked amongst themselves. Zhang Da Wei and his friends stood beside the Charles Stewart Parnell monument at the north end of O'Connell Street. Qui Hong Xiang was among the group. He stood close to Zhang Da Wei and, as one of the youngest present, he was probably feeling apprehensive. Little did he know he would be pronounced dead within an hour. Debt collector Chen Long and his associates stood outside the Eircom building at the corner of Cathal Brugha Street and O'Connell Street. The men on both sides appeared calm. There was nothing in their demeanour to suggest a gang fight was about to break out.

Taxi driver Anthony Shields watched from his car as the groups of Chinese men began to assemble. He didn't pay much attention until he saw weapons being produced and the vicious fight got under way. Gardaí at Store Street were monitoring O'Connell Street by CCTV that night as the row broke out, as is normal practice. Detective Garda John O'Donovan noticed that a large group of Chinese men had suddenly congregated on the street. Then officers noticed that one of the Chinese men appeared to be holding a knife behind his back. This man was later identified as Zhang Da Wei, whose refusal to pay at the brothel had sparked the row. As patrol cars were promptly radioed and told to make their way to the scene, gardaí watched as Zhang Da Wei walked to the traffic island in the middle of O'Connell Street and stood facing a large group of his fellow nationals. He then brandished his knife in full view and many of his rivals then produced their blades and machetes in response. Within seconds, the gang fight broke out. Because gardaí had watched the row unfold, they were at the scene within two minutes. Had it been any longer, Qui Hong Xiang most likely would not have been the only man to lose his life. But even within that short space of time, two others sustained serious injuries. Qui Hong Xiang's last moments were captured during the street fight. The video footage shows a man armed with a knife approaching the student, but the pair then became partially obscured by a phone box. At this point gardaí believe the 22-year old was stabbed fatally in the chest. After he was stabbed, the student stumbled away in the direction of Parnell Square. But he didn't make it very far. He collapsed outside the Rotunda Hospital in the consultants' car park.

In the heat of the battle, 23-year-old Yang Wang was accidentally knifed in the neck by one of his own gang. He was fighting on behalf of the triad gang from the Fujian province. The young man was himself wielding a knife when he was stabbed. One of his gang screamed, "Wrong person, wrong person", after his associate stabbed his friend in the neck. Zhang Da Wei also suffered horrific injuries. Part of his scalp was cut off by an unidentified rival during the fight. It was later found on the street by gardaí and was successfully reattached at the Mater Hospital. Debt collector Chen Long was also clearly visible in the CCTV footage. He too was brandishing a knife and at one point fought with Zhang Da Wei.

The arrival of garda squad cars scattered the two gangs. Some of them dumped their weapons along the way while others bundled them into a Mercedes parked near by belonging to one of the triad gang members from the Fujian region. Detectives later recovered nine types of knives, several machetes and meat cleavers, as well as a Walter PPK pistol.

A chaotic aftermath followed the gang fight. Zhang Da Wei was lying in a pool of blood in the middle of O'Connell Street, with part of his scalp lying beside him on the road. He was screaming in pain. Yang Wang lay near by, bleeding profusely from his neck and gardaí tried to stem the blood loss before the ambulances arrived. Garda Anthony Brady, who was attending to Zhang Da Wei, was then told there was another injured man at the Rotunda Hospital. A man walking past had found the 22-year old lying outside the hospital and muttering to himself in Chinese. Patrick Flannery had stopped to help him and appealed to other Chinese people who had been socialising at the Parnell Mooney pub to help him and speak to the man. But they refused, saying they didn't want to get involved and rushed quickly along. As Zhang Da Wei was at this stage receiving medical attention, Garda Brady ran up to the Rotunda Hospital. He found 22-year-old Xiang lying on the ground with a superficial knife injury to his forehead as well as a deep chest injury. An ambulance was called and he was rushed to the Mater Hospital. But the wound had pierced his heart and he was pronounced dead on arrival.

Yang Wang and Zhang Da Wei were also rushed to the Mater Hospital. Both had suffered serious injuries, Yang Wang's neck wound particularly so. The reattachment of Zhang Da Wei's scalp was a complicated operation but was deemed a success. Zhang Da Wei was arrested after he was released from the hospital, as was Yang Wang after he recovered from extensive surgery for the stab wounds he suffered from a member of his own gang. He later thanked gardaí, who he said were responsible for saving his life. Medics told detectives if he hadn't received such prompt medical attention as he lay injured on O'Connell Street, he would certainly have died. Debt collector Chen Long, who had been living in Dublin for four years and managed an internet café on Parnell Street, was not injured in the fight and fled the scene when gardaí arrived. The father-of-two was arrested on Parnell Square four days later. The three men all admitted violent disorder and producing knives during the street battle when questioned by detectives. They didn't have much choice; they were clearly identifiable in the CCTV footage. But they refused to identify any of their fellow gang members in the footage. Chen Long and Yang Wang would later be jailed for four years. Zhang Da Wei, who learned about the death of his closest friend Qui Hong Xiang while in garda custody, was later handed down a five year prison sentence.

Seasoned murder detectives based at Store Street were astounded by what had occurred on one of the capital's busiest streets. They were used to investigating serious gangland criminality in nearby Sheriff Street and its surrounding areas, but they had never witnessed a group of 40 men, all armed with blades, prepared to fight each other to the death. Significant resources were deployed to solve the murder. A team of detectives from Store Street worked with officers from the National Bureau of Criminal Investigation (NBCI) and the Garda National Immigration Bureau (GNIB). Over 200 statements were taken, including those from many members of the Chinese community who had been socialising with gang members in the Parnell Mooney pub earlier that night. Soon detectives pieced together that the row stemmed from Zhang Da Wei's refusal to pay up at the brothel. Many Chinese people not involved with either gang were wary of passing on too much information to gardaí, fearful of repercussions from triad gang members. But after extensive interviewing, gardaí were able to build up a picture of how the disagreement between the two groups culminated in the fatal stabbing of the 22-year-old student. "There was an indication suggesting that there was a dispute between two rival groups over a sort of territory type of thing towards females who were under their control," Detective Inspector Nicholas McGrath told an inquest into Xiang's death in 2005 at Dublin City Coroner's Court. Some of the Chinese nationals captured on CCTV were known to gardaí, he told coroner Dr Brian Farrell. The inquest was held after the three Chinese men were convicted for their roles in the mêlée. Footage of the brawl was shown at the inquest. The jury were forewarned that they may find the images disturbing. Some chose to look away.

Detective Garda Martina Shields pointed out to the jury in the CCTV footage the Chinese man whom gardaí suspected of fatally stabbing the 22-year-old student. But because Xiang and his killer were partially obscured behind a telephone box when he received his fatal stab wound to the chest, the evidence wasn't definitive. The footage showed a man wearing a black jacket and T-shirt with a light coloured design fighting with the 22-year old. The pair then momentarily disappeared from view behind the phone box before Xiang reappeared and stumbled away, having been stabbed. Despite analysing the footage frame by frame, it would have been impossible for gardaí to prove in a court of law that their main suspect was responsible for the fatal strike as it was obscured. Detectives did identify who they believe was responsible for the student's death. But after consultation with the DPP, he directed that no one be charged with the student's killing. The jury at the inquest returned a verdict of unlawful killing by a person unidentified. None of the other Chinese men witnessed the fatal stabbing; all were preoccupied fighting. The only person who could have identified the killer was now dead.

Ten months after the gang fight, Zhang Da Wei and his two rivals were jailed for their role in the street brawl. All admitted producing a knife. Zhang Da Wei, who was living on North King Street in Dublin city, had obtained a student visa to come to Ireland. He had already got himself into serious trouble with the law despite only being in Ireland a year. Two nights before his friend was stabbed to death on O'Connell Street, Wei held a group of his fellow nationals at gunpoint and robbed them. He was found guilty of falsely imprisoning and robbing the group of

Chinese people after he broke into their flat in Clarinda Park, Dún Laoghaire, on 8 July 2002.

He appeared to be the leader of the four-man Chinese gang who raided the apartment in Dún Laoghaire. He carried an imitation 8 mm pistol and demanded bank cards, PIN numbers, mobile phones and other property. The four Chinese men and one woman were terrified by the gang and handed over what was demanded during their hour-long ordeal. The gang threatened the victims not to report the crime, but they ignored their warning and went to gardaí. The 26-year old denied the charges, and also denied robbing property and cash worth €405 from one of the men. But he was found guilty by a jury at the Circuit Criminal Court in March 2003. He had been in custody for the O'Connell Street gang fight since July 2002. Two months later while he was awaiting sentencing for the false imprisonment and robbery of Chinese nationals, he appeared at the Dublin Circuit Criminal Court in front of the same judge, Yvonne Murphy, and pleaded guilty to violent disorder for his role in the O'Connell Street brawl. She jailed him for five years for the gang fight. He was then also jailed for four years for the false imprisonment and robbery in Dún Laoghaire, both sentences to run concurrently.

Debt collector Chen Long (23), of Dublin's Sherrard Street, and Yang Wang (23), of no fixed abode, were both jailed for four years in relation to the fatal knife fight at the same court hearing. At the sentencing hearing, Chen Long's barrister Erwin Mill Arden said his client regretted the death of his fellow national and wished to apologise to the Irish people and the Chinese community for his actions. All three men have since been released from prison.

The killing of Qui Hong Xiang was proof that bubbling below the surface of Dublin's Chinese community lay the palpable threat of gang warfare. The authorities were already aware of several cases of extortion and kidnapping by Chinese gang members demanding protection money from their own countrymen. Other gang related killings of Chinese nationals had already taken place in Ireland, but the brawl on O'Connell Street showed gardaí that there were many young criminals who were willing to lay down their lives for their cause. Qui Hong Xiang was not involved in criminality to the same extent as his friend Zhang Da Wei, but he lost his life out of loyalty to his gang.

The threat posed by Chinese triad gangs in Ireland exists largely within its own community and rarely impacts the rest of Irish society. Like most foreign gangs, they operate independently of Irish criminals and are predominantly concerned with controlling criminality within their own communities. Chinese triads are involved in the trafficking of women into Ireland for prostitution purposes—they've cornered a sizeable proportion of brothel-running in Dublin. A significant number of Chinese restaurants and takeaways also pay protection money to Chinese criminals, such is their concern about reprisals from the gangs if they refuse. But the anticipated criminal impact Chinese triad gangs were expected to make on the Irish crime scene at the turn of the century has never materialised.

Qui Hong Xiang was a young Chinese man who came to Ireland to learn English. He got involved in low level criminality as his friendship developed with Zhang Da Wei. Like many other young foreign students far from home, he felt isolated. He was happy to be accepted by criminal elements within the Chinese underworld in Dublin. Yet he was very much on the outskirts of organised crime. But by trying to fit in with his countrymen, he paid the ultimate price.

11 | NATASHA GRAY

S everal undercover armed detectives quietly entered the courtroom unbeknown to the jury and media. Such precautionary security is usually only required for criminals at gangland murder trials and terrorists at the Special Criminal Court. But these were highly unusual circumstances. Nigerian man Goodwill Udechuckwu, on trial for the murder of his wife Natasha Gray, had shown such contempt for the state prosecutor that it was feared he was planning to attack her. Pauline Walley was the Director of Public Prosecutions (DPP) senior counsel appointed to prosecute Goodwill. The Nigerian man's agitation was rooted in the fact that a woman had the power to lead a trial that would put him behind bars. Armed gardaí and investigating detectives braced themselves when the foreman of the jury announced they had found the Nigerian guilty of bludgeoning his wife to death with a lump hammer in 2003, before leaving her body upside down in the cot of their five-month-old baby. Goodwill's reaction shocked everyone. Instead of lashing out in violence, he stood up and made an extraordinary speech protesting his innocence and claiming he did not get a fair trial because of the colour of his skin.

It was an unexpected end to one of the most bizarre trials ever held at the Dublin Central Criminal Court. When not eyeballing Pauline Walley and muttering inaudible but seemingly sinister things under his breath, the Nigerian attempted to hex gardaí. During his 17 day trial in 2006, he took turns staring intently at the senior detectives who charged him with his wife's murder. Once he held their attention, he pretended to summon evil spirits from his own body through a sequence of elaborate hand movements and gestures. He then threw these evil spirits in the direction of the detectives to curse them, all the while smiling broadly. Detectives say his behaviour was somewhat comical. But at the same time they were also conscious that this man was a dangerous sociopath with no respect for women whatsoever. In his mind, women were far inferior to men and his criminal past suggested he felt entitled to inflict violence upon them at will.

Goodwill soon displayed the aggression detectives felt he was harbouring during the trial. Within 24 hours of being convicted of his wife's murder, he found himself at the centre of a violent altercation in Dublin's Mountjoy Prison. He was stabbed above his right eye, back and stomach by a mob of inmates after he deliberately antagonised them. Moments before he was attacked, he stood in the centre of the D1 landing and announced at the top of his voice: "I am king." He began to remove his T-shirt to display his physique and sense of superiority when a prisoner standing behind him pulled his T-shirt back down, rendering him temporarily immobile. A group of up to ten inmates then swarmed around him stabbing and beating him repeatedly in a planned attack. When the mob parted, the Nigerian was left staggering along the landing, clutching his bleeding stomach. He was taken to the Mater Hospital and although he suffered serious injuries, he made a full recovery. His was one of the most savage beatings in Ireland's toughest prison and there are several reasons he was targeted. The inmates would not allow a Nigerian to appoint himself the "king" of Mountjoy and wanted to put him in his place after his attempt to assert his authority. Many knew he had murdered his wife in savage circumstances, and killing a woman is seen by some prisoners as a cowardly crime deserving of a beating. Goodwill had spent 11 months in Cloverhill Prison between 2002 and 2003 in relation to another crime and earned the reputation of being a violent man with a bad attitude. He spent another 11 months in custody awaiting trial for murder and had made enemies of some very dangerous criminals.

Goodwill Udechuckwu arrived in Ireland in 2001 seeking asylum. At that time all asylum applicants' fingerprints were not cross-referenced with international crime agencies to determine if they were being sought for a crime in any other jurisdiction. Goodwill was wanted elsewhere. Police in Austria, where he had previously lived, having originally sought asylum there, had issued an international arrest warrant for a serious assault the authorities say he inflicted on his common-law African wife. He bit off part of her nose in a savage attack. The registration process for asylum seekers has now changed—fingerprints are now cross-referenced to determine if any outstanding international arrest warrants exist. This anomaly in the system allowed the Nigerian to enter Ireland. Within two years he would meet, marry and have a child with Jamaican woman Natasha Gray. He would then brutally murder her in 2003 and go on the run before finally being apprehended in London two and a half years later.

Natasha Grey moved to Ireland from Jamaica in 1998 with her sister Nicola. She came to Ireland to build a new life and she was happy to work hard to achieve it. At the time of her death, she was a trainee nurse working full-time at various hospitals, as well as raising her two sons, Jayden (five months) and Jordon (3½). She had her first son with Guy Mboze, who also lives in Ireland, but their relationship ended in 2001. At just 5' 2" tall, she was a slight woman. In comparison, she was dwarfed by Goodwill's 6' 3" and 18 stone frame. The pair met soon after Goodwill arrived in Ireland in 2001 and started a relationship. On 20 January 2002, when Natasha was one month pregnant with his child, the couple wed in a small ceremony in Dublin. Her sister and friends were surprised by their nuptials. Goodwill had not made a good impression—her family and friends found him an unsettling man with a violent streak and never understood what Natasha saw in him.

Within three months of their marriage, Goodwill had a serious

run-in with the law. On 16 April 2002 the Nigerian visited
Rathfarnham health centre to enquire about rent allowance.
When he didn't like the information he was given, the Nigerian's
temper got the better of him. He began to threaten staff and they
phoned gardaí. A violent struggle ensued when the officers from
Rathfarnham tried to remove him from the premises and
Goodwill bit a garda sergeant on the hand, cutting deep enough
into his flesh that the garda required hospital treatment. He was
immediately arrested, charged with assaulting the garda and
taken to Cloverhill Prison, where he was held on remand. It
wasn't the best start to married life for Natasha and her 29-year-
old husband. They began fighting during his incarceration. He
demanded that, as his wife, she should visit him every day. She
wasn't willing or able to fulfil this demand. Eleven months later
in February 2003, Goodwill was handed down a six month
suspended sentence at the Dublin Circuit Criminal Court for his
assault on the garda and walked free from court because of the
time he had already served. Within a week he would murder his
wife in a premeditated attack.

After he was released from prison, Goodwill returned to the
apartment where his wife lived with her sister Nicola, her
husband Ian Curtis and their friend from Jamaica Sharon Facey.
Sharon and Nicola each had a child, while Natasha had two, and
these four children also lived with them. Nobody wanted
Goodwill there, particularly his wife. The entire house was on
tenterhooks as the Nigerian was an imposing presence and his
behaviour started to frighten his wife. Their marriage, which had
barely had a chance to begin, was destined to fail in the most
horrific of circumstances.

When Goodwill buzzed the door of the apartment on Royal
Canal View, Phibsboro, on the day he got out of prison, 12
February, Sharon Facey threw him down the keys. She then went
to tell Natasha that her husband had arrived. Natasha was in bed
after working the night shift and her reaction to the news was to
pull the covers over her head and say, "Jesus Christ, or something
like that," Sharon Facey would later tell Goodwill's murder trial.

The following morning, Goodwill was still at the flat and he was shouting at his wife, frightening her. "She wanted him out of the flat because she was not expecting him to come back," added Sharon. Because of her husband's presence, Natasha did not return from work on Friday until Sunday morning, but did phone her sister to tell her she was safe and to arrange care for her children. Natasha also confided to her friend that she wanted her husband to leave their apartment because he had become abusive towards her. However, he refused to go. While she was away, Sharon saw Goodwill go through his wife's belongings where he found an itemised phone bill. He became upset and said his wife had phoned her ex-boyfriend Guy Mboze, the father of her first child, 85 times. Sharon said she watched as he then spent hours on a computer at the apartment trying to access his wife's emails by trying different passwords. Goodwill then began to badmouth his wife to her friend, saying she had given him AIDS. Sharon disagreed with him. They had been pregnant at the same time, gone to hospital appointments together and read each other's medical notes. "He always say 'your friend is a whore, she sleeps with men, she's dirty', and stuff like that, always swear words against Natasha . . . She slept with one eye open in fear," she said. The state pathologist Dr Marie Cassidy was able to confirm that Natasha did not have HIV.

Goodwill's relationship with his wife's sister Nicola Curtis also became increasingly volatile in the days before he murdered his wife. They had many rows and he even threatened to murder her and drink her blood during one heated argument. "He's a liar, a thief and a serial killer . . . One day he say he going to kill me and drink the blood. He told me from his mouth he drank blood in Nigeria. That's why I said he's a serial killer," she told the court. "She always planned to run away but she never wanted to leave her children."

When Natasha returned to her apartment after spending the weekend with a friend to get away from Goodwill, she asked her husband to leave once more. She told him their relationship was over. Again he refused. But he knew their marriage was damaged beyond repair. So in a perverse attempt to gain control and power in the relationship, Goodwill Udechuckwu reverted to what he knew best—violence. The day before he killed his wife, he visited a hardware store on North Frederick Street with murder on his mind.

Peter Foran, who worked at Central Key & Hardware, recalled assisting a black man with broken English who enquired about buying a hammer on 17 February. He showed this man a number of claw hammers, which Goodwill complained were quite expensive. He asked if there was anything cheaper and was shown a Chinese claw hammer which was lighter. But Goodwill said he needed something heavier and was then shown a lump hammer for €5. He weighed it in his hand before saying: "ok." He then picked out a small hatchet priced €5.50 and was sold both items for the discounted price of €10. CCTV footage captured him entering the hardware store. His brother-in-law Ian Curtis identified Goodwill Udechukwu as the person in the video footage. The hatchet was found hidden in a suitcase in a wardrobe at the flat with the price sticker still on it, enabling gardaí to track its purchase.

While Goodwill was shopping for murder weapons, his wife was making plans of her own.

On the morning of her killing, a distraught Natasha Gray telephoned a solicitor's office looking for an immediate appointment. Mary O'Reilly, of FH O'Reilly solicitors on the North Circular Road, agreed to see Natasha after speaking to her at 10.30 that morning. "She was distressed. That's why I did see her. I wouldn't normally see someone without an appointment," she told Goodwill's murder trial. During their consultation she advised Natasha to get a protection order or a barring order if possible. She sent out letters that day to Goodwill and a barrister who deals with family law. She wrote to the barrister because she felt the matter was urgent and she thought an application could be made to the Circuit Court to protect Natasha from her husband. Later that day, Mary O'Reilly heard that a young woman had been killed. Immediately she thought of Natasha. She was so concerned that she got her secretary to ring the mobile number Natasha had left, but it went straight to voicemail.

Since Goodwill has continuously denied killing his wife, it is unknown what exactly happened between the couple that led him to hit her repeatedly on the head with the lump hammer. But detectives believe that Natasha told Goodwill she had visited a solicitor that day and was in the process of obtaining a barring order. Gardaí later found a solicitor's letter at the house addressed to Goodwill and which referred to "our client Natasha Gray". It read: "Because of your behaviour, our client can no longer expect to live with you." It also asked him to vacate the premises and advised him that his wife was seeking to take legal action.

Sharon Facey was downstairs in the flat when Natasha got into her final confrontation with her husband in the bedroom. Pathology evidence later found that he hit her eight times with the lump hammer on her head. The force of the blows knocked her backwards into their infant's cot. The patterns of the blood spatter in the room suggest she had been struck repeatedly after she was driven into the child's cot. Sharon had gone to answer a knock at their front door while Goodwill murdered his wife. By the time she returned after speaking for a minute at the door, her friend was dead. She was in the kitchen when Goodwill suddenly appeared. "I recall he was breathing a bit fast," she told the court. He told her he was leaving, that Natasha had ordered him to leave. She noticed that he had changed his shirt, was carrying a black bag over his shoulder and seemed extremely agitated.

Goodwill left the flat immediately and made his way towards Cathedral Street in the city centre, gardaí believe. He was last seen on Talbot Street, which runs parallel to Store Street where the bus terminal Busaras is based. Detectives believe he boarded a bus to Belfast and from there fled to the UK by ferry. But before he disappeared he made some phone calls to try and cover his tracks. He telephoned his wife's flat and spoke to Sharon Facey. She had not yet discovered her friend's dead body upstairs. During this call he repeated to Sharon that his wife had given him AIDS and that she was "dirty" and "a whore". He also asked to speak to his wife, but Sharon did not call her. Goodwill also phoned his brother-in-law Ian Curtis. He told him he had moved out because Natasha had asked him to leave. It was to be the last time anyone would see or hear from the 29-year-old Nigerian for two and a half years.

A few hours passed before Sharon Facey found her friend's body that afternoon. She had been minding her sons Jayden and Jordan. Natasha's elder sister Nicola was also in the flat. When it was time for Jayden's nap, Sharon went into Natasha's bedroom to put him down. She did not notice Natasha's dead body immediately. It only became clear to her as she went to lay the baby down. Natasha had fallen backwards into the infant's cot because of the force of the blows from her husband. Her frame was so small that she fit into it and was partially covered by a blanket. The lump hammer lay beside her on the ground. Sharon let out a piercing scream, waking Natasha's sister who was asleep in the next room, having been working earlier. In the horror and panic that unfolded, the women made a 999 call to gardaí and the murder scene was soon sealed off.

In Natasha's bedroom, detectives found the lump hammer and a blood-stained white shirt, which Sharon Facey told them Goodwill had been wearing earlier that day. After interviewing Sharon Facey and Natasha's sister Nicola Curtis, they immediately put out an alert to find Goodwill Udechuckwu. But he had already left Dublin and was on a bus to Belfast. He had dumped his phone shortly before he got on the bus. It is most likely that from the North he caught a ferry to the UK, possibly using a false identity, which he had done in the past.

Fitzgibbon Street Detective Inspector Christy Mangan (now detective superintendent with the Cold Case unit) led the murder investigation. He was assisted by officers from Mountjoy garda station. Detective Garda Adrian Murray, Detective Garda Kenneth Keelan, Detective Garda Dave O'Brien and Detective Sergeant Walter O'Sullivan (now a detective superintendent at Blanchardstown) were all involved in the murder probe.

Gardaí issued an appeal to the general public, and specifically members of the Nigerian community, for information about the whereabouts of Goodwill. But he was gone. Detectives soon learned that the 29-year old had few friends in Ireland and was considered a loner by Natasha's friends and family.

Detectives began to build a case of circumstantial evidence against the Nigerian man. They extensively interviewed Sharon Facey, Natasha's sister Nicola and her husband Ian Curtis, as well as everyone else who came into contact with Natasha and her husband in the last week of her life. They soon learned of the problems in Natasha's marriage and her fears that her husband would harm her. As Goodwill was the last person to see Natasha alive, and had left behind the murder weapon before disappearing, the evidence against him was mounting. The solicitor's letter addressed to Goodwill initiating a barring order against him was also found at the apartment. Detectives also learned that the 29-year old was wanted in Austria for the assault on his common-law wife before he came to Ireland. The bloodstained shirt and lump hammer were sent for forensic analysis and gardaí issued an international warrant for the arrest of Goodwill Udechuckwu.

Given his criminal past, detectives suspected that the Nigerian wouldn't be able to stay under the radar for long. True to form, Goodwill was arrested in London in August 2005 for shoplifting. Two and a half years had passed since he murdered his wife. Initially, the Nigerian told Bow Street Magistrates' Court that he would not agree to Ireland's extradition request in relation to his wife's murder. But after a break in proceedings he returned to the court and gave his consent. The judge asked him if he understood what he was agreeing to and he replied that he did. "Yes, because I have got a son in Ireland which I have missed so much," he said. Dressed in a dark suit and white checked shirt, he added: "I haven't got any other matter in Ireland. I have got my son in Ireland."

On 19 August 2005, the 31-year old appeared at Dublin District Court and was charged with his wife's murder. Eleven months later in July 2006, Goodwill stood trial for the murder of Natasha Gray.

The court proceedings got off to a curious start, setting a precedent for the remainder of the trial due to the behaviour of the defendant. In the middle of the first day, Justice Kevin O'Higgins asked the jury if anybody had tried to contact them or interfere with them in any way in connection with the case. It had been reported to the judge that Goodwill kept winking at one of the female jurors. No one had any idea why he would do this. It was possibly a bizarre attempt at flirting to try and ensure this juror would find him not guilty.

Justice O'Higgins asked whether anyone had winked at one of the female jurors. Following a brief discussion, the jury foreman replied: "No member of the jury has had any contact in any way with anyone."

On three occasions during the 17 day trial, Goodwill broke down in tears and the jury had to momentarily leave while he was given the opportunity to compose himself. He chose to give evidence during his trial and managed to shock and scare some of the jury as a result. Detectives believe that his unpredictable behaviour in the witness stand may have done him more harm than good.

Giving evidence, he said he came back from England because he wanted justice for his wife and child and was shocked when he was told he was wanted for her murder. "I was gobsmacked. I said that can't be." At first, he thought they were joking and just wanted to deport him. He said he agreed to his extradition because he was innocent and he hoped to help the State with its investigation. He then broke down, saying: "Because I am black, because I have no father, because I have nobody I came back to bring justice for my wife and my children." His crying turned into sobbing and the jury were asked to leave the court for a short time. After he composed himself and proceedings had reconvened, he insisted that he loved his wife very much and the couple enjoyed a good relationship. He insisted he had not killed his wife. "Absolutely not. I have no reason whatsoever to do such a thing. We were very happy together. She mean a lot to me. Why would I do that?" he asked. He claimed that gardaí wanted to convict him "at all cost" and that the people who committed the murder had managed to deceive everyone. He also said that gardaí force-fed him on the plane back from London to Dublin to be charged with his wife's murder. Asked about the CCTV footage from the hardware store—in which his brother-in-law identified him—he denied it was him. "No I can see that person is wearing something like a sports shirt," he said. In the first of many attempts to blame others for his wife's murder, Goodwill said he dressed as a professional and that the person in the CCTV footage was wearing the type of clothing that Guy Mboze—his wife's former partner—often wore. As the trial proceeded, Goodwill would try to implicate his wife's sister, her friend Sharon Facey and even gardaí in the killing of Natasha.

But the father of his wife's first child seemed to particularly preoccupy the Nigerian's mind. On the witness stand he took off his shirt and vest to show the jury a scar he claimed had been left as a result of Guy Mboze attacking him with a bottle. But his demeanour as he stripped from the waist up shocked the jury. He finished his bizarre testimony by claiming the media coverage of the case had been controlled by "the truth police". A senior detective present in court for the entire trial believes his antics and claims in the witness box put the jury on edge, and the way he removed his shirt was aggressive and menacing, scaring some jurors.

Goodwill again became overcome with emotion during the testimony of a forensic scientist. Unusually, a small proportion of people leave behind very little DNA. Goodwill is one of those. Scientists do not know why this is, but it is a fact that one person can deposit a full DNA profile after brief contact with an object, while others can leave virtually no forensic profile with the same level of contact.

Dr Dorothy Ramsbottom gave evidence that Goodwill's DNA was not found on the bloodstained shirt found in Natasha's bedroom. She got a partial DNA profile from the Nigerian by developing it from a cup he was believed to have drunk from. As the scientist spoke, the Nigerian began to cry loudly: "I said it to Irish police, I didn't do this. I said it many times." Again the jury had to briefly leave the courtroom while the Nigerian was comforted by his barrister Pieter Le Vert. Natasha's blood was found spattered on the white shirt, which Sharon Facey said she had seen Goodwill wearing earlier that day. On the day of the murder, Natasha's sister saw Goodwill behind the door in her sister's bedroom. She said his shirt was wrapped up in his hand. "He had no top on. He looked at me and I looked at him and he closed the door," she added. She was very tired at the time, did not think anything of it and went back to sleep. The only DNA, other than Natasha Gray's, found on the shirt was on the left sleeve and belonged to another male. Another partial profile was also found on the back of the shirt, but it could not be determined if this was from the same person. Natasha's former partner Guy Mboze, her nephew Steaveroy Steer and her brother-in-law Ian Curtis gave DNA samples and were ruled out as being the source of DNA on the shirt. The only forensics present on the lump hammer was a partial fingerprint. Again, this did not match Goodwill's partial DNA profile.

Despite the lack of forensic evidence, the jury ultimately accepted that Goodwill murdered his wife because of the testimony of her friends and family as well as the CCTV evidence of the Nigerian buying the murder weapon. He was also the last person to see his wife alive. While forensic evidence has become increasingly important in solving crime, detectives say proving means, motive and opportunity remain pivotal in modern policing. Goodwill told his legal team an elaborate story that Sharon Facey had started a relationship with Natasha's former partner Guy Mboze and they had plotted the young Jamaican's murder. He also claimed to have had sex with Sharon Facey himself. Natasha's flatmate spent four long days in the witness box being questioned and cross-examined. She emphatically denied having an affair with Goodwill. "Am I that desperate?" she exclaimed in court. "I'd rather go to a dog or to Moore Street and prostitute myself. That's what I'd rather do."

Shortly before he murdered his wife, Goodwill suggested to Sharon that she put his name on the birth certificate of her child so they could both get residency to remain in Ireland. She did not go through with this plan. But she did toy with the idea and told Holles Street Hospital and a social welfare officer that Goodwill was the father. She admitted in court that this was untrue. "That was a big fat lie I told the social welfare office."

Goodwill also tried to convince the jury that he was not living at the apartment at the time of his wife's death; that she had already kicked him out. But Sharon Facey was proving herself to be a formidable witness. "That's a lie. He stays there," she said with conviction. Natasha Gray's nephew Steaveroy Steer was also staying at the flat at the time of the murder. He too saw Goodwill at the apartment on the morning his aunt was killed, despite his insistence that he had already been thrown out.

Goodwill also told his lawyers that Guy Mboze had arrived at the apartment a couple of days before the murder and pushed a newspaper aggressively into Natasha Gray's face. "That is a definite lie. Nothing like that happened. That's a made up story, an absolute lie," Sharon Facey told the court. She rejected Goodwill's allegation that she was involved in her friend's death. "Your client murdered Natasha," she told senior counsel Blaise O'Carroll with authority. "He's making up lies to get out of it but God in heaven see what he does." She also denied she had been in a relationship with Guy Mboze, saying his claims were ridiculous. "Why would I have to take Natasha's two men?" she asked. "That's a stupid, silly question."

Guy Mboze also took the witness stand and denied that he had any part in the murder of the mother of his child. He also rebutted several other outlandish accusations Goodwill Udechuckwu made against him. His son Jordon was 3½ at the time of his former partner's murder. He admitted being involved in family law proceedings with Natasha over access and maintenance and that she had taken a barring order out against him. In the week before she was killed, he had twice called to the house to collect his son. It was Guy that Sharon answered the door to when he dropped his son back, while Goodwill was murdering his wife upstairs. He denied that he went upstairs to the apartment that day. "I formally put it to you that you and Sharon Facey were involved in the demise of Natasha Gray," Blaise O'Carroll said to him. "I'm not involved," he replied.

He also denied that some of his companions were involved in the murder and that the reason for Natasha's death was because he would not allow his son to leave the country with Goodwill. Shaking his head in disbelief, Guy Mboze told the court quietly that there was a court order preventing his son from leaving the country with anyone. He was also forced to deny that he was in a relationship with Sharon Facey.

Investigating detectives found Goodwill's attempts to blame anyone he could for his wife's murder to be the actions of a desperate, unscrupulous man. His attempts to implicate others in his crime were ultimately utterly rejected by the jury.

On 20 July 2006, after deliberating for just over an hour, Udechuckwu was found guilty of his wife's murder. Armed gardaí and senior detectives braced themselves for a violent reaction from the 32-year old, which never came. Instead, the judge and jury listened to Nicola Curtis give a tearful account of the impact her sister's death had on her entire family. Shortly before her death, Natasha had returned to Jamaica to visit her father, who was ill. "When my family told him, the only thing he could say was 'Natasha, Natasha' and he never spoke again and then he died. When I went home I had to bury them both together."

She had just one question for her sister's murderer, which she did not expect him to answer. "I want to ask Mr Udechukwu in my heart, but I don't think he will answer it. I just want to ask him, did she cry? Did she call for her child? What did she say when he hit her? But I know I won't get that answer."

Nicola Curtis thanked the jury for its verdict and said it had been a very difficult time for her and her family. Her sister was killed when her two sons were just five months and 3½ years old, and since then she was raising these two children with her husband, along with her own baby. She was also working and studying. "It hasn't been easy for us. I know I can't bring her back." Outside the court Natasha's elderly mother, who had flown over from Jamaica for the verdict, got down on her knees and proclaimed, "Thank you, Jesus."

Nicola Curtis was right about one thing. Her brother-in-law would give her no answers about her sister's last words. His immediate reaction to the guilty verdict was one of stunned silence. But he soon found his voice and made an extraordinary speech after the judge ruled that he be jailed for life. "All I have to say to everyone in this court is I didn't kill my wife. This is total injustice. I am from Africa. Everybody in this court is from Ireland," he shouted. "Everybody know Goodwill did not commit this crime. If justice is being done, I am not supposed to be pronounced guilty. I did not kill my wife. God knows it. The person who give me life will find justice from the air, the sea and from Irish motorway. My justice will surely come."

But despite his protestations of innocence, there was to be no redemption for Goodwill. Within 24 hours of being convicted of his wife's murder, he would be stabbed in Mountjoy prison after antagonising his fellow prisoners. And the following year, his appeal against his murder conviction was rejected.

In his customary fashion, he sobbed in court and shouted his innocence after his appeal was turned down in May 2007. Five prison officers surrounded Goodwill as his bid for freedom was rejected by the Court of Criminal Appeal.

As his legal team tried to argue that he was racially discriminated against by the jury, he burst into tears and pleaded his innocence to the court, saying: "Please let me go. I didn't kill my wife. I am telling the truth." Justice Hugh Geoghegan was forced to call a halt to the appeal when he continued to sob loudly and protest his innocence. Chained to a prison officer, he began to raise his arms erratically in the air and shouted that he was serving time for a murder he didn't commit. "I wasn't there at all," he shouted in the courtroom when only the media remained. He then pointed at the ceiling and shouted: "Papa, Papa, I love you." Flanked by guards, the prisoner was warned to behave himself and to stop hurting a staff member's hand. After the appeal resumed, the three-judge court took just 15 minutes to throw out the case. The court rejected the argument that a white judge and jury hampered a fair trial. His legal team also complained about the refusal to admit evidence in his trial of a videotape of Goodwill and Natasha's wedding day. "It is claimed that he was denied the opportunity to show that he and his wife were happy on their wedding day," Justice Geoghegan said. "But the learned trial judge was quite correct in ruling out the evidence, which is neither here nor there and it proves nothing. The court is quite satisfied that in general it was a very fair trial conducted meticulously by one of the most experienced judges and finds no fault in it."

Goodwill was still protesting as he was led back to prison, all his legal avenues exhausted. He will never walk the streets a free man in Ireland again. Upon his eventual release from prison here, he will immediately be extradited to Austria to answer charges of seriously assaulting his former partner while living there.

Natasha continues to raise her sister's two sons in Ireland with her husband Ian Curtis. "Her family were all really lovely people, gentle and kind hearted," adds the senior garda who investigated the murder. "Natasha was a lovely young woman by all accounts. She was very hard-working. It's just so unfortunate that she ever came into contact with Goodwill Udechuckwu. He is a cancerous human being."

12 | LINDA WANG

He stood over her dying body and asked if she had any final words. "All of the time she said, 'I'm sorry mum and dad,'" These—if the man who killed her can be believed—were the dying words of Xiang Yi Wang, who was also known as Linda. "She told me I was the only person she loved. I said I loved her and 'I go with you,'" 25-year-old Hua Yu Feng told detectives, with tears streaming down his face. He admitted to stabbing the young woman several times in the upper body with a carving knife and said he then tried to end his own life: "I found an empty can of beer to try and cut my wrist. I did not find the artery."

It was the early hours of 4 July 2003. Hua Yu Feng left the woman he claimed to love with fatal injuries in the small wooded area in Bray, Co. Wicklow, close to where she lived. The pair had gone to the secluded area to talk. Perhaps realising the enormity of what he had done, the young man fled to Belfast later that evening, and tried again to end his own life six days later. He was admitted to hospital after slitting his wrists in a Belfast hostel. His cousin journeyed to Belfast to visit him in intensive care and then brought him back down to Dublin voluntarily where the dental student was arrested over Linda's death. Two years later in July

2005, the Chinese student was sentenced to ten years for the manslaughter of Linda Wang. He was charged with her murder but a jury found him not guilty of this crime.

Seven years have now passed since Xue Xia Qin and De Jiu Wang lost their only child. They have since been blessed with the birth of twin boys. But time has not healed their pain. Their bitterness remains as tangible as their daughter's death. "I remembered the date we got the news of her death; we were having a family gathering. We were looking at the photos of Linda who participated as a volunteer in the Special Olympics 2003. Linda's mum got the call from the Irish Embassy in China. She fell into a coma with the photos scattered everywhere and my mind went blank for the day," says her father De Jiu Wang, speaking from their home in Fuxing city, China. "I could not forgive the killer. He not only took away the life of our daughter, he also took away our happiness. If there is reincarnation, he will still be my most hated enemy and I will curse him for ever. This ache in our heart will not fade away with time and will not lessen at any time."

Twenty-one-year-old Linda had been living in Ireland for two years when she was killed. She knew Hua Yu Feng from their hometown in Fuxing city. The day she arrived in Ireland, he met her at the airport. He had completed a diploma in dentistry in China and intended continuing his dentistry studies. Linda wanted to perfect her English, so her parents agreed to send their only child to Ireland. It wasn't long before the young student had found a home away from home when she moved in with a Chinese family in Bray. Summy Wong met Linda, a talented musician, when she began giving her son piano lessons at their home in the Valley, Woodbrook Glen, in Bray. She soon became close to the entire family. Summy invited her to move in when her flatmates moved out of the house they was sharing and she began to look for somewhere else to live. It was an invitation Linda readily accepted. "She called me her sister and soon it was like I had another daughter. It felt like I was her mother in Ireland," she recalls. "She called me her godmother. We became very close but she never really talked about any boyfriend. I wish she had talked to me. Maybe I could have helped. Maybe it never would have happened." On the night Linda was stabbed to death, Summy Wong got an email from Linda's father, De Jiu. "He said, 'since she has come to Ireland, she has been so happy. She is a gift from God.' But Linda never came home that night."

On the evening of 3 July 2003, a polite young man knocked on Summy Wong's front door. He asked whether Linda was home. It was the first time Summy had ever met 25-year-old Hua Yu Feng, who within hours would knife Linda Wang to death. Because she didn't know this young man, Summy asked who he was. "'A friend,' he replied. I told him I thought maybe she was out for dinner. He looked sad. I felt a bit sorry for him. The last thing he said was 'thank you' in Chinese. I thought he was a very polite boy. He had a very polite manner."

Summy closed her front door and didn't think any more about it. It was just after 7 pm on 3 July 2003. But instead of going home, Hua Yu Feng stayed lurking in the shadows of the Wong family home, leaving only to go home and retrieve a carving knife and some cans of beer. Feng's murder trial heard that he had been in a relationship with Linda for 18 months before he killed her. But the idea that her daughter had been dating the 25-year old has been dismissed out of hand by her father. "It was said in court that theirs was a lover's relationship. This was totally wrong as we understand it from Linda's letters home. Linda never loved him," he says. "Can you understand how a killer who waited outside for hours with a knife and stabbed our daughter eight times is considered as manslaughter? A disappointing Ireland. An unforgivable Ireland."

Linda had begun to date someone. His name was Seán Lynan, a garda. She had met him two weeks before her death when she volunteered at the Special Olympics. The garda told Feng's murder trial that he exchanged text messages with Linda and that she had told him how much she liked him. She never mentioned having ever been in a relationship with Feng, telling him she used to have a boyfriend in China, "but that was over".

On 3 June Linda was out on a date with the garda when Feng called to her home in Bray. Garda Lynan collected her from

Portobello College in his car that evening and they drove to Enniskerry where they took a walk. Later that night, the pair decided to go to a hotel and left at about 12.30 am. Garda Lynan then dropped Linda home at around 1 am. "For a long time, I blamed myself for her death. I encouraged her to volunteer in the Special Olympics. That's where she met the garda," says Summy. "She asked me, 'is it ok to have an Irish boyfriend?' I said of course it was." Linda never mentioned to Summy that she was dating Feng, despite his claim that they were in a relationship for 18 months. Summy has since met with Garda Lynan, who also feels a sense of guilt that he did not wait in his car for a few extra moments to make sure Linda got safely inside.

Summy, who had already gone into her bedroom, heard the porch door click open that night and assumed Linda then came into the house. But she hadn't. Feng, who was lurking in the garden, called her back. In his statement to the gardaí, Feng said he called Linda as she was going inside and she came back out to meet him. It appears that the 21-year old went willingly with him and the pair walked to a nearby public garden area, a place they sometimes went to talk. "We always go to the garden to talk," he told detectives. "Is it in the garden where you killed Linda?" Feng was asked. "Yes," he replied. He said they had been arguing for a few days because Linda had told him about another man. "She told me she was seeing somebody. She told me some love stories. That made me very, very crazy, very angry," he said. "I told her if you loved me you wouldn't tell me that secret about that person."

He tried to contact Linda earlier that day while he was at work to apologise for the quarrelling, but she was not there. He later learned she was out with somebody else. After failing to reach her all that day, he went home and got a carving knife from his kitchen. "What did you intend to do with the knife?" he was asked. "I don't know. I just got very, very drunk and wanted it with me," he said.

Asked if he intended to harm Linda, he said: "No, I never meant to do that." The Central Criminal Court heard he then left his house with the knife to go to Linda's house, but he did not recall how he was carrying the knife. "At that moment I got very, very drunk and I was mad. I just remember the stories she told me of that man," he said.

When he called out Linda's name as she was going into her house that night, she agreed to take a walk with him, he said. One of the first things she asked him was if he had seen a man hugging her on the road, he told gardaí. What the 25-year-old man was suggesting was that Linda was deliberately goading and provoking him when she knew he was in love with her.

"Did you kill Linda Wang?" Sgt Patrick Campbell asked him.

"Yes, I did. Last Thursday night I killed her by knife in the garden," Feng replied through an interpreter.

"Did you love Linda?" Sgt Campbell asked.

"Yes," he replied.

"What part of the body did you stab her?" came the next quick-fire question from Sgt Campbell.

"I don't know," he replied.

"How did you kill her?" Sgt Campbell asked.

"At the start I didn't use the knife. I just used my hands," he said.

"Where?" the sergeant asked.

"On her neck," Feng replied.

He said he did not know how many times he had stabbed Linda. He told detectives he tried to pick Linda up in his arms to get help. "But I thought she was very painful . . . At that moment I knew she would die."

Before he left, he said he asked Linda if she had any last words. "All of the time she said, 'I'm sorry, mum and dad.' She told me I was the only person she loved. I said I loved her and 'I go with you'," Feng said during his interview with detectives. Despite the fact that he had a knife, Feng told gardaí he had tried to slit his wrists with a beer can. "I found an empty can of beer to try and cut my wrist. I did not find the artery."

Feng made two attempts to phone the emergency services, but his calls were not understood. His distressed state, his imperfect English and his drunkenness were all factors in his 999 call not making sense to the person on the other end of the line. Soon after, he fled the scene. Linda's parents and Summy Wong have always found it difficult to believe what he claims were her last words—why would she tell a man who had just stabbed her that she loved him? To them, and many others, it sounded like delusional, self-indulgent rambling.

The next morning, a passer-by found Linda's body. She had seven "deep and penetrating" stab wounds to her upper body, six of which were inflicted from behind. The state pathologist Dr Marie Cassidy also found she had compressions to her neck, from Feng's attempt to strangle her, but these did not cause her death. Her death was due to "haemorrhaging, shock and breathing difficulties" from the stab wounds.

Feng went home after committing his crime and looked for a sharper implement to take his own life. The beer can he had tried to use hadn't done much damage. "I went to kill myself," he said. But again his attempts were unsuccessful. He fell asleep in his own bed and was woken up by one of his housemates at 7 am who asked why there was blood all over the kitchen and bathroom. That evening, he fled to Belfast. "I stayed there and I tried to finish my life," he said in his statement. "Why Belfast?" Sgt Campbell asked. "I just wanted to finish my life where nobody else knows me," he replied.

On 10 July, the manager of ARC youth hostel in Belfast, Paula Quigley, received a phone call to tell her that a suicide attempt had been made at the hostel. "There was a lot of blood on the floor and bed of his [Feng's] room, and he'd vomited on the centre of the floor," she said. He had more or less kept to himself since he had arrived at the hostel four days previously, she said. After the incident, they found knives, a bottle of wine and a half-eaten burger in his room. Liam Cutting, who was staying at the hostel on the night of 10 July, heard a loud noise and then saw the Chinese student lying on the floor. "At first I thought he was drunk," he told gardaí, until he noticed the blood on his wrists. When the ambulance arrived, Liam Cutting said Feng struggled with the ambulance crew when they tried to help him. "They had to put him in straps," the court heard. He was taken to the Royal Victoria Hospital in Belfast and treated by Dr Peter Watson. In his statement, Dr Watson described the accused as "very uncommunicative" when he was admitted to the ward. "All he said was that he came from China and wanted to go back to China." The doctor could not determine if he was suicidal or not, the jury heard. "We all formed the impression that he was frightened of something and anxious," Dr Watson said.

Feng's cousin travelled to Belfast and brought him voluntarily back to Dublin when he was discharged from hospital. Apparently defeated, he admitted his crime to gardaí when he was arrested on 13 July. Feng, who had been in Ireland since 2000, was enrolled at an English language school and was employed as a cleaner when he carried out his crime. He had planned to perfect his English before continuing his dentistry studies.

He pleaded guilty to Linda's manslaughter, but not guilty to her murder. This plea was not accepted by the DPP, and he stood trial for Linda's murder. But on 11 February 2005, after deliberating for two hours and eight minutes, the jury of seven men and five women returned a unanimous verdict of guilty of the manslaughter of Linda Wang due to provocation, but not guilty of her murder. The jury accepted that Linda had in some way provoked Feng, possibly by discussing her new boyfriend. On 1 July 2005, he was sentenced to ten years for his crime. Feng's sentence was backdated two years since he had been in custody since 14 July 2003.

When the verdict was delivered, Linda's mother Xue Xia Qin collapsed in tears, inconsolable. Addressing the court through an interpreter, her father spoke of the family's anger and disbelief at the jury's verdict. "We strongly felt very unfair and upset about the verdict brought by the jury. Our hundreds of Chinese friends and family felt very upset. All the Chinese students in Bray felt very upset," said De Jiu Wang. "On behalf of my daughter, I strongly protest the unfair verdict given by the jury." He also spoke of his shock at how little time the jury spent on the verdict. "The court has spent more than ten days hearing the evidence; gardaí spent over a year and a half investigating such a big case; and the jurors only spent two hours on their verdict," he added. "You didn't even have enough time to review the evidence." He told how in 2001 he and his wife, along with relatives and friends in China, decided to send their only child to Ireland. "You should know what a big decision this was for us. She was our only child, our hope and our future." He said they chose Ireland for two reasons. "Irish people are peaceful and full of kindness, and the social security system is good. Second, Ireland is a beautiful country."

He spoke with heartfelt passion and emotion about the impact his daughter's death had on the loved ones she left behind. "How could she have been killed in such a peaceful country?" he asked. "We sent our child alive to Ireland. She was full of energy and wishes for the future. And we got back only ashes." He recalled a dutiful daughter who had excelled in school and was loved by her teachers and classmates. He told the court of her talent as a musician, how she had begun playing piano at 4 and had qualified as a piano teacher. The killing of his daughter was "an unforgivable evil" and it had left his family in a painful abyss. "My wife wanted to die many times after hearing the news of her death." He also addressed his daughter's killer, saying: "The shameless coward has won. You can run away from punishment, but you won't run away from God. My daughter's eyes will look at you for ever."

Feng's trial heard that he had been in a relationship with Linda for 18 months, but they had been estranged since she began dating Garda Seán Lynan. This has never been accepted as truth by Linda's parents. She had also never mentioned to Summy Wong that she was romantically involved with the young Chinese dental student, yet she told her excitedly about her new relationship with the garda she had met at the Special Olympics. Neither had Linda mentioned to Garda Lynan anything about being previously involved in a relationship with Feng in Ireland.

Feng's defence counsel spoke of his client's regret for his actions. "For what it's worth, Mr Feng suffers from the deepest remorse and grief for what he has done," said his counsel Diarmaid McGuinness. "This was a crime of passion and it's very clear from the probation report that he should be given therapeutic treatment. It was a classic, if not tragic, crime of passion. That's not to excuse it or justify it."

When passing sentence, Justice Paul Butler said he could not but be deeply affected by the harrowing evidence of Linda Wang's father. But on a matter of principle, he added that he had to treat the sentencing the same "as if Linda were an orphan . . . Linda was an entirely innocent person. She was female and defenceless against the attack." There were also mitigating factors in the case, he added. Feng had no previous convictions and was otherwise considered to be of good character. The judge also took into consideration the fact that the student voluntarily turned himself in and fully co-operated throughout the investigation and trial. Justice Butler said he hoped the young man would receive proper therapy for his anger management. "The base of the problem of his anger is still there," he said. "The accused is a foreign national who is going to serve a term of prison in Ireland."

When Feng was sentenced, he had already spent two years in prison. He has been extremely isolated in prison. At the time of his sentencing, he had received just one visit, from an aunt who travelled specifically to see him. Feng's parents have refused to speak to him, but he is in contact with his uncle on the phone.

He has chosen to spend his time wisely while incarcerated. He completed his Junior Cert from behind bars, as well as studying social science through the Open University. He is due for release in January 2011, when he will be deported back to China. It is unlikely he will return to live in his hometown of Fuxing city as it is also Linda's hometown.

At their home, Linda's parents have surrounded themselves with memories of their first-born child. They feel they cannot ever find it within themselves to forgive Feng for taking her life so cruelly and suddenly. They have still been unable to tell Linda's grandmother about the fate that befell the young student in Ireland. "She was a most outstanding girl. Most of her childhood was extraordinary. Linda was the first grandchild of our family. She was spoiled but she was always well mannered," recalls her father De Jiu. "When she was young, Linda's mother was working as an accountant at a factory and did not have much time to raise Linda, so during a lot of her childhood she was cared for by her grandma. We are still afraid to tell her about Linda's misfortune. She loved Linda in a very special way."

Eighteen-year-old Inga-Maria Hauser was murdered in an unsolved
killing in Co. Antrim in 1988.

Swiss student Manuela Riedo was murdered by Galway man Gerald Barry in 2007.

Gerald Barry is serving a life sentence for the murder of Manuela Riedo. He was also handed down two more life sentences for orally and anally raping a French student just seven weeks before he killed Manuela. (*Irish Times*)

Polish mechanic Mariusz Szwajkos was murdered in a vicious screwdriver attack along with his fellow countryman Pawel Kalite by 17-year-old David Curran.

Charlotte and Linda Mulhall were christened the 'Scissor Sisters' by the media following their gruesome killing of Kenyan Farah Swaleh Noor in 2005. (*Courtpix*)

Farah Swaleh Noor was bludgeoned to death and cut into eight pieces by the Mulhall sisters before they dumped his headless torso in the Royal Canal.

Malawian Paiche Onyemaechi was decapitated and her body dumped in bags on the banks of a river in Kilkenny in 2004. (*The African Voice*)

Nigerian Chika Onyemaechi, the husband of Paiche, disappeared shortly after his wife's murder. Gardaí are anxious to speak to him about his wife's killing. (*Press Association Images*)

Rwandan Regina O'Connor was murdered by her son Moses in a frenzied stabbing in 2005.

Moses O'Connor was convicted of his mother Regina's murder and handed down a mandatory life sentence after pleading guilty. (*Courtpix*)

Chinese national Yu Jie was convicted of the double murder in 2001 of his two friends, Yue Feng and Liu Qing, following the longest jury trial in Irish legal history. (*Courtpix*)

Summy Wong has endured many sleepless nights wondering if she could have done something to save Linda's life that night. That she was stabbed to death just yards from her home has intensified her feelings of responsibility. "He has said things about what they said to each other that night. But who knows if he is telling the truth. Maybe she told him she didn't love him." Could she ever forgive him for taking Linda's life? "I think jealousy could have led him to have mental health problems. I think the man that killed Linda, he had no belief, he had nothing to turn to." But by taking Linda's life, Summy understands why Linda's parents feel they cannot forgive Hua Yu Feng. "He took away all their dreams, all their future."

When Linda's parents visited Ireland, a cherry tree was planted in her memory beside Summy's house and close to the laneway where she was killed, which Summy tends. It is also the place she goes to when she wants to feel close to the 21-year old. "This is always where I go to talk to Linda. I asked her to do something to help her parents. I always think that her parents being blessed with twins had something to do with Linda." Summy hopes the twin boys, born in 2007, have helped ease their pain. "I have seen pictures and they are identical to Linda. Since the twins have been born, it has been a new life for them."

Summy says that because of the one-child system in place in China, grandparents are deeply bereaved too by the loss of a grandchild. "It can be as if six people have lost a child. It is such a difficult thing for anyone. I know why it is so hard for Linda's parents to forgive," she says. Since her death, Summy has tried to use the experience to achieve something that will help the Chinese community. "I still do things for Linda. I set up the Irish Chinese Federation of Ireland. I feel that since she's passed away, she's given me a lot of support and strength. If I gave it up, I would feel like what happened to Linda could happen to someone else. Sometimes I don't feel like she's gone. I feel like she's still with me."

Summy now works with Chinese students, helping them come to grips with life so far from home. "A lot of them are very lonely here. I can't sleep properly since Linda passed away. I had to try and do something positive and not just keep crying all the time. Maybe she was so good, God wanted her back early. It's good you didn't know her because if you did, you would miss her. After it happened, every time my son sat down in front of the piano, he would cry. He doesn't play it any more. He can't because it reminds him too much of Linda."

The community in Bray was also deeply affected by the death of the young woman. Hundreds of local people joined her mourning parents to bid an emotional farewell to the Chinese student a week after her death. Local people also expressed their support by contributing over €10,000 to a fund created to assist her parents with the cost of travelling to Ireland to cremate their only daughter. The outpouring of support from the Irish and Chinese community here was not lost on her parents. Members of the Special Olympics committee organised the special memorial service as a mark of respect to Linda, who acted as an interpreter for the Chinese team based in the town for the tournament. Pat Vance, the chair of the town's Olympics committee, spoke fondly of the young woman. They worked closely together for the two months prior to the tournament and over the six days of competition; Linda had worked 12 hours a day without a word of complaint. "She was a beautiful young woman, very pretty and a talented musician. She was outgoing, yet quiet," said Vance, a Bray Fianna Fail councillor. During his daughter's memorial service, Linda's father expressed his thanks through a translator for all the support his family had received. The commemoration was held at the Valley in Bray, the secluded area where Linda's body was found, and a cherry tree was planted in her memory. Three days later, Linda's parents returned home carrying with them the ashes of their daughter, as well as a memorial book signed by hundreds of sympathisers. It would not be their only journey to Ireland. Two years later they would again travel to Ireland for Hua Yu Feng's murder trial.

Music was a huge part of Linda's life. She regularly played with Ceoltas Éireann in Bray, as well as at various other events. She also played at a reception hosted for the Chinese delegation of the Special Olympics. She had been scheduled to play the guzheng, a

Chinese plucked instrument named for its sound, at the National Museum, Collins Barracks, as part of their China week of culture. She had also agreed to present a musical evening for the Irish-Chinese Cultural Society three months after her killing. Summy offered to stand in and played the guzheng in her absence. The instrument has 21 strings and is played by plucking with special artificial fingernails.

Linda showed a talent and interest in music from an early age. "She loved music since she was very young. She was taught to play the keyboard at the age of 5 and the piano at 6. Later she learnt the Chinese flute and then the Chinese guzheng. Maybe it was because of her talent in music that she picked up things easily academically as well," says her father. Her parents were also protective of her, booking her taxis to get to her music lessons as she was growing up, rather than walking or travelling alone on public transport. "Later, Linda said she could get to her music lessons by bicycle so we bought her one. Now we keep it as our memory of her."

At senior high school, Linda excelled in her studies and her parents expected her to get a secretarial job. But Linda had other plans. "She did not disappoint anyone by achieving her best both musically and academically in those three years of senior high. Later, she was recruited as one of the 500 teachers to teach the guzheng. It was a very well paid job. But she refused the offer and decided she had a lot more she wanted to learn before she got qualified. She said she must travel to a foreign country to learn another language. This idea was the beginning of her fate."

Linda's parents did not like the thought of their only daughter leaving China at just 19 years of age. "Our family did not like this idea as she was so young and on her own. But Linda gave a very good reason to go. As her parents, we eventually gave her permission to go. We really regret that now."

While De Jiu says the support his family received from Linda's friends and the community in Ireland was unforgettable, he feels his family has been utterly let down by the judicial system. "After she was killed, we expected the Irish government would give a just trial. We always learned the western world has better justice and more democracy. But we were very disappointed with the final judgement as manslaughter and that he only got ten years in prison. Linda and Feng were never lovers. He is only an evil killer."

Her father cannot let go of his anger. Perhaps with time it will lessen. But eight years on from her death it is still as raw as the dark days that immediately followed her death. "I know my daughter is grateful to Summy for tending to the cherry tree we planted for her. Now, my girl is in heaven and we will never forget her. In our house I have assigned a special area for all her belongings and a 20 inch photo of her in the middle on a stand. We have placed all her beloved books and her clothes there. We have fresh cut flowers for her every day. She is still very much with us in our house. If there is justice, Linda will settle peacefully in heaven."

13 | PAICHE ONYEMAECHI

For three days, she was simply an unidentified female body, cruelly decapitated and discarded. Her decomposing remains were discovered in bin bags on the banks of a river in Kilkenny in 2004, shocking and scaring the community in equal measure. Only when Paiche Onyemaechi's identity was confirmed did one of Ireland's most gruesome and unsolved murders begin to unfold. In life, the 25-year old was renowned for her beauty. In death, her killers desecrated her image in a crude attempt to almost nullify her very existence. Her head has never been found. In her short but complicated life, the young Malawian woman meant many different things to the people she shared her life with. To her two young sons, she was a loving mother. To her father, the chief justice of Malawi, she was a wayward, strong-willed child. To TJ Carroll, then one of Ireland's wealthiest pimps, she was an extremely lucrative prostitute. And to her second husband Chika—who disappeared days after her headless body was discovered on the banks of a bridge in Kilkenny—she was the less than dutiful wife he desired. A couple of weeks after he disappeared, gardaí intercepted two packages addressed to the Nigerian-born Chika. One was sent from Belgium, the other from Austria, and neither had a return address. Both packages contained jars filled with liquid, twigs and earth. The parcels baffled gardaí. Following analysis, the substances in the jars were deemed to be natural soil-based matter and fluid. Senior detectives probing the unsolved murder believe the Malawian woman was murdered in a ritualistic killing and her head was offered up as a sacrifice.

On 10 July 2004 at 11 am, Chika walked into Waterford garda station and reported his young wife missing. The couple had moved from Dublin to Waterford in May 2001 after Paiche left her first husband, Malawian Abiodun Lambe, for Chika. He told gardaí that his wife had left their home in Herblain Park, Waterford city, two nights earlier to go to Limerick in search of work. He gave them a photograph of Paiche. Before she disappeared, Chika told gardaí that he had spent the day with his wife and their two young sons Anthony and Andrew, who were 3 years and 18 months old at the time of their mother's murder. That evening, after the family ate dinner together, he "made love" to his wife who later received a phone call at 9 pm, he told gardaí. At 9.30 pm she left the house abruptly to go to Limerick and he hadn't seen her since. Two days later, Chika met Detective Garda Gerry Howe by appointment at the station to give a more detailed statement about his wife's disappearance. However, this time he gave a slightly different version of events. He told the detective that his wife left the family home on 7 July, not 8 July as he had previously told them. He also said his wife left their home by taxi at 8.30 pm, an hour earlier than the time he had told gardaí two days earlier. Detectives have extensively checked with taxis and hackneys servicing the area and none has a record of a booking to the Onyemaechi family home at 27 St Herblain Park.

Chika also told Detective Howe that his wife worked as a prostitute and that she would often go away for a week at a time to "meet men" for "lots of loving". He then informed the detective that a few nights before she disappeared, his wife was arrested for drink driving in Waterford and was in the company of another Nigerian man he did not know. But this was not entirely correct. Gardaí have since established that on 6 July, Paiche and her husband had an argument. He decided to go down to Galway to cool off and visit his close friend, 26-year-old Chijioke Ezekwem. Paiche told friends that she had thrown her husband out and later went out for a few drinks with a Nigerian man, who gardaí are now satisfied was a platonic friend. They went to a couple of pubs in Waterford town, including Fletcher's and Muldoon's. The 25-year old was a sociable woman who had many friends. At 1.55 am on 7 July, Paiche and her friend got into his car outside Muldoon's and he attempted to drive. But the Nigerian was stopped by gardaí and breathalysed. On failing the intoxication test, he was arrested and taken to the station. Paiche, as a passenger, was not arrested. After her friend was released from custody, the pair went back to Paiche's house, where the Nigerian man stayed the night in a separate bedroom. By this stage, Chika had returned from Galway and the next morning he gave the Nigerian man a lift home. Detectives have since interviewed this man closely and are satisfied he was a friend of both Paiche and her husband. Chika also told Detective Howe that his wife drank, smoked and regularly went out socialising. Once, he said, she was dropped home by a man driving a black BMW. Detectives later established that this car belonged to wealthy pimp TJ Carroll, for whom Paiche was working. At the time of her murder, he was one of the most well-established pimps in Ireland. His fortunes have since waned. In February 2010, 48-year-old Carroll, originally from Bagenalstown, Co. Carlow, was jailed for running a multimillion euro prostitution ring. Over 70 women across Ireland were working in Carroll's brothels, which he ran from a quiet Welsh village. He was jailed for seven years at Cardiff Crown Court after pleading guilty to organising prostitution and money laundering. Detectives did probe extensively whether Carroll was involved in the young mother's murder, but have now fully ruled him out as a suspect. What use would one of his most profitable prostitutes be to him if she was dead? Paiche was one of the few girls he considered important enough to personally give a lift home to.

In his second meeting with gardaí, everything Chika told the detective was again taken down in a statement and his young wife officially became a missing person. At that stage, there was no reason whatsoever to believe she was dead. According to her

husband, she often left her family for a week at a time to work as
a prostitute, so this seemed like the most likely explanation for
her absence. No one except the person or persons who chopped
off her head and dumped her body on the banks of a canal 20
kilometres away could have guessed that she had met her end in
the most merciless of circumstances.

The last known sighting of Paiche was in Tramore, Co.
Waterford, on 8 July, three days before her husband reported her
missing. She travelled with Chika and their two young sons to the
town for a swim. The row the couple had two days earlier seemed
to have been put behind them. At 5 pm, as they drove home, a
woman garda stopped their car at Pickardstown. Paiche was
driving. The car's road tax had expired and the garda asked the
driver to ensure this was rectified as soon as possible. The garda
took note of Paiche's name and her husband gave his name as
Pater Jack, not Chika Onyemaechi. It is common among the
African community to use more than one name in official
documentation. Paiche herself used several different identities.

Thirteen days after Chika reported his wife missing, her
dismembered body was discovered in bin bags on the banks of
Brenar Bridge in Co. Kilkenny. Two elderly women contacted
gardaí when they noticed a foul smell coming from the canal and
local gardaí were stunned when they uncovered the decapitated
body of a black woman in the bin bags. She was fully clothed and
there were no other injuries on her body. From the positioning of
her body, she was most likely thrown from the bridge. On the
other side of the canal bank, Paiche's vanity case containing some
of her jewellery was discovered. Detectives believe her killer may
have discarded it to give the impression that the 25-year old had
been murdered in a botched robbery. Gardaí do not believe theft
was the motive for the murder.

Her body was identified through fingerprints and it then
emerged that Paiche had several identities. According to the
fingerprints, the remains belonged to Regina Vasslatos from
Mozambique. When she arrived in Ireland as an asylum seeker in
1999 with her first husband, this was the false name she gave to
the authorities. She also regularly used the names Gina and

Cassandra—many locals in Waterford knew her as Gina. It is common for Africans and Chinese people in particular to adapt English names. Paiche's mother's maiden name was Willis and after her murder, gardaí found a forged French identity card at her home that stated her name was Gina Willis. Her various identities complicated an already puzzling murder.

She was born Paiche Unyolo in Malawi on 14 April 1979. One of five children, her father Leonard Unyolo was the chief justice of Malawi at the time of her murder. She met her first husband Abidun Lambe when she was just 16 years old and her father was strongly opposed to the relationship. Despite this, Paiche and Abidun married two years later in 1997 in a traditional ceremony attended by her mother, brother and sister, but Paiche's father refused to attend. He felt his daughter was too young to marry and her husband was from a lower social class. Her father was happy when his daughter said she wanted to leave Malawi and continue her studies in the UK. She left Malawi with her husband in 1998, but stayed in the UK only briefly before coming over to Dublin. On 15 December 1999, the couple arrived in Dublin and sought asylum saying they faced persecution in their homeland. She told the authorities her name was Regina Vasslatos from Mozambique. The couple were housed at asylum accommodation at Beechwood Avenue hostel in Rathdrum, Co. Wicklow. They later moved into a flat on Rathdrum's Main Street. But cracks were already beginning to show in their marriage. On 3 March 2000, she went to gardaí after her husband assaulted her. He was arrested and charged with the crime and, on 9 June 2000, his case was heard at Rathdrum court. At this stage, the couple had resolved their differences, were back together and Paiche indicated she wanted to withdraw the charges. What had happened was still taken seriously by the court and Judge Donnchadh Ó Buachalla told Abidun that he could not impose his will on his wife whenever he wanted to.

Garda Seamus O'Neill told the court that Abidun had locked his wife into their flat after he had assaulted her. He said that Paiche had blood on her temple and nose. Solicitor Mary Miley said that the couple had resolved their differences and were back together again. She said that Abidun had been under a lot of stress in adjusting to their situation here and the couple now planned to move to Dublin together. After finding the facts proven in the case, Judge Ó Buachalla struck out the charge against Abidun Lambe after hearing that a conviction could have an important impact on his asylum application, which had yet to be decided.

Back together, the couple duly moved to Dublin and into Chester House on the North Circular Road, which was used for housing asylum seekers at that time. It was here that Paiche met Chika Onyemaechi and she struck up a friendship with the Nigerian that would eventually lead to an affair. In October 2000, Paiche and her husband moved out of the hostel accommodation to a flat on the Old Bawn Road in Tallaght and later moved again to a flat on Chesterfield Avenue in Ranelagh. At that stage, Paiche and Chika had begun an affair. On 23 March 2001, Abidun spotted his wife on Parnell Street with the Nigerian. He confronted them and a fight broke out between the two men. Paiche took her lover's side in the dispute and struck her husband several times in the row. After this incident, the marriage effectively ended. She moved out of the flat they shared and moved in with Chika. After a few months, the couple decided they wanted to move out of Dublin and chose Waterford as a place to begin their new life. One of the main reasons for the move was because Paiche was pregnant. In May 2001, the couple moved into 53 John's Street, Waterford. Anthony Leonard Onyemaechi was born in August 2001. His middle name is the same as his grandfather's, suggesting that although Paiche and her father had a troubled relationship, she still felt an attachment to him. In November 2001, the couple were married at the registry office in Waterford. Strangely, although Paiche had married Abidun in Malawi, the paperwork had not been filed correctly, so technically she was still a single woman. While there is no doubt that the ceremony with her first husband took place, it was not recognised officially in her home country.

The couple moved three times around Waterford city in the next three years. They lived in Johnstown, then Prospect Mews before finally settling at 27 St Herblain Park on 9 August 2003. It was to be the last place Paiche would call home. By then the young parents had welcomed another son into their family. Andrew Kuzoni was born on 12 April 2003. When the couple first moved to Waterford, they were both asylum seekers but were granted full refugee status following the birth of their sons. It didn't take Chika long to secure employment in Waterford. At the time of his wife's death, he was holding down two jobs. He was working in an Italian-run takeaway as well as the Tower Hotel in Waterford city. In both places of employment, his employers and co-workers knew him as Patrick Jack. Chika was reasonably well liked by Irish people, but many Africans living in Waterford expressed reservations about him. But everyone loved Paiche. She was well known around the town and always had a smile and a kind word for everyone. She became involved in prostitution soon after she arrived in Waterford, and gardaí believe her husband encouraged her into this murky world. She had a few regular clients in Waterford whose homes she visited for sex. One of these men was an Italian who worked with her husband at the takeaway. He later told gardaí that he handed over €120 each week to Chika to have sex with Paiche on a regular basis.

In the beginning Paiche only worked in Waterford, but her eyes were opened when she met a middle-eastern woman, who also worked as a prostitute. They became fast friends and she told Paiche that she was beautiful enough to be earning thousands as a prostitute, rather than earning a few hundred each week with clients in Waterford. This woman introduced Paiche to her pimp TJ Carroll and one of his associates, who happily took her on. Soon the two women were travelling around the country together to work in various brothels run by TJ Carroll in Galway, Limerick, Carlow and Kilkenny. She also worked in lap dancing clubs and massage parlours. Chika initially encouraged his wife, as she was now earning considerably more money, much of which was handed over to him. She enjoyed the independence of being away from her husband, who could be quite controlling, but she soon tired of the unglamorous life of a prostitute. Her two young sons were well looked after during her absences, but

Paiche's friends later told gardaí she sometimes talked about returning with her sons to Malawi. "She talked about returning home. She'd been on the game for about three years. She was sick of it," according to a garda source involved in the investigation, who spoke on condition of anonymity as the murder investigation is ongoing. "She was an absolutely stunning woman. She could have been a model. We looked at various different motives for her murder and the investigation has been extensive. After carrying out considerable research, we believe she was killed in a ritual killing and her head was offered up as a sacrifice as it was believed it would bring riches. These kinds of sacrifices take place mainly in Africa among some of the tribes. We believe that more than one person was involved in the murder."

At the post-mortem, there were no other injuries on Paiche's body and it could not be determined by state pathologist Marie Cassidy if the mother-of-two had been strangled before she was beheaded. She was wearing a pink top and jeans and had not been sexually assaulted. Her husband Chika was then contacted to identify the body. "He barely looked at her but did identify her as his wife," adds the garda. It was 23 July 2004. The next day, Chika boarded a bus bound for Dublin, effectively abandoning his two young sons. He has not been seen since. On board the same bus was one of his employers from the Tower Hotel, who later told detectives that Chika did not speak to him and got off the bus at O'Connell Street. It is believed that a couple of days later, Chika visited a recruitment office in Phibsboro. There was later a false sighting of him in Belfast and detectives believe the Nigerian man is now living in the UK. Despite appeals, Chika has not come forward to assist gardaí. In the days after her body was discovered, gardaí released a statement: "We would be particularly interested in speaking to Paiche's husband Chika who may be able to assist us further with the investigation. We are concerned for Chika's welfare as he has not been seen since a number of days after his wife's body was discovered."

After the discovery of her headless body and Chika's disappearance, Anthony and Andrew were taken care of by friends of the couple. The Garda Technical Bureau carried out an extensive five-day forensic trawl of the family home. It was clear that the banks of the bridge in south Kilkenny where Paiche's remains were discovered was not the scene of her murder. But it was soon determined that neither did it occur in the family's rented house. No forensic evidence was found when technical experts removed flooring and carpets for fibre and other analysis. When the family home was later examined by gardaí, it was noted that it was remarkably clean. It is unlikely the young mother was killed at her home. As forensics are now so advanced, it would be practically impossible to behead someone, which would result in a major loss of blood, and not leave behind some forensic evidence.

Gardaí liaised with Interpol and soon contact was made with Paiche's family, who were informed of the tragic circumstances of the 25-year old's death. Paiche's father, Leonard Unyolo, flew to Ireland immediately and was joined by his daughter Lucy, son Leon and Paiche's sister-in-law Thoko.

The family decided not to fly their daughter's body home for burial, but to have the funeral in Waterford. Eight days after the headless body was discovered, Paiche's funeral was held. Around 150 mourners attended and Chika's absence was conspicuous. The mixed service of hymns and readings took place in St Patrick's United Presbyterian and Methodist church in the city. Her father led the mourners and the Malawian honorary consul, Fr Patrick O'Mahoney, also attended. Her two sons Anthony and Andrew were also at the service and being cared for by their relatives.

Rev. Dr John Parkin told the mourners that Chika's whereabouts were now unknown. He appealed for anyone with information to come forward to either himself or gardaí. At the same time, he urged members of the African community in Waterford not to engage in the spreading of rumours. "Leave the investigation to the police," he said, "who will leave no stone unturned. So far, they have conducted themselves with extreme sensitivity and I've every confidence that justice will be done."

At the start of the service, Rev. Parkin expressed his deepest sympathies to the family, describing as "evil" what had been done.

"Evil has been done and now many questions are remaining, including what is the meaning and purpose of what has happened," he told the congregation. The purpose of the ceremony, he continued, was to give dignity to one who was denied dignity in death. Paiche's brother Leon Unyolo also spoke fondly of his sister and how she would be remembered. She had touched the hearts of many, he said, through her compassion and kindness. A strong gathering from the community of Piltown, Co. Kilkenny, where her body was discovered, also attended the funeral service. Fr Paschal Moore, parish priest of Piltown, said: "When Paiche's body was discovered last Friday, not only were the two people who found her saddened and shocked, but the whole community was devastated." He assured her family that when they returned to Malawi, they should know that their daughter and sister would always be in Piltown's prayers. After the service, a cavalcade of black cars brought the family to St Otteran's Cemetery where the private burial took place.

A couple of days before the family returned to Malawi, bringing with them Anthony and Andrew to be raised far away from the country where their mother lost her life, Paiche's brother made an appeal to the Irish people. Speaking on behalf of his family, he asked anyone with information on his sister's disappearance and subsequent murder to come forward. Leon Unyolo said the family was deeply shocked at what had happened and praised gardaí for their thorough investigation. "We last spoke to Paiche in June and she was full of life and joyful," he said. "All of this is very upsetting for us and we are still struggling with it." During his visit, Chief Justice Unyolo also met with the then Justice Minister Michael McDowell to discuss his daughter's murder. The meeting was at the request of the chief justice, who was anxious to make sure there was a system in place to ensure the family were kept up to speed with the inquiry.

Detectives found Paiche's family to be respectable and dignified people, deeply shocked by the brutality of her murder. But when gardaí told them that she was involved in the sex industry, her family found this difficult to accept. They refused to believe it. Their decision to have her buried in Waterford rather than returned home is telling. "They were very polite, nice people. But they didn't want to know anything about her background in Ireland. When they were told she was involved in prostitution, they said this was not true and refused to accept it," continues the garda involved in the investigation. "They told us that she had been a troublesome child. They didn't want to bring her body back to Malawi but took her two sons home to be raised there. We haven't had much contact with them since, but we keep them up to date with any developments."

After Paiche's funeral, detectives continued with their extensive enquiries. Chika's disappearance aroused their suspicions and gardaí interviewed all the Nigerian man's friends and acquaintances that he came into contact with from the day he reported his wife missing to the day he himself disappeared. Just as he had given gardaí different versions of events, Chika had also given his friends and co-workers varying accounts about his wife's disappearance. A couple of days after he reported Paiche missing, he called to the home of two of his wife's friends, an African man and woman who weren't fond of Chika. Shortly before her death, Paiche had confided to these friends that she was tiring of life as a prostitute and was considering moving back to Malawi with her sons. They had never trusted her Nigerian husband, but allowed him into their home as he was worried about his wife, as were they. He explained that she had left in a taxi to go and earn some money and that he had reported her missing. While he was at their house, they telephoned Paiche's sister Lucy in Belgium. He told his sister-in-law that Paiche wore "dirty clothes, prostitutes' clothes . . . I pray that they will kill her and she will not return to me." After the telephone conversation ended, Chika told his wife's friends that he was happy to now be alone and living as a bachelor. He also asked them, "If you kill someone and put them in the river, will police detect it?"

The next day, 11 July, Chika bumped into the Nigerian man who had been out socialising with his wife a few days before she went missing. He told his countryman that his wife had gone to Limerick to work in lap-dancing clubs and massage parlours. "Limerick is a dangerous place. They could kill her," he said, before adding with disgust. "I didn't know my wife was an *Ashawo*." *Ashawo* is the Nigerian word for prostitute. The day after that, Chika called into his next door neighbour's house and borrowed some cleaning products to clean his home.

The day after, Chika met a Nigerian woman in Waterford whom he was attracted to. "My wife ran away from me. I'm a bachelor looking for a girlfriend," he told her. "My wife ran away back to Malawi to marry a rich man." The 31-year old seemed unable to keep his own counsel. He told a work colleague at the Italian takeaway that his sister had gone missing and had gone to Limerick. He told another colleague that it was his sister who was missing but that she had gone to Kilkenny with some friends. And to a third colleague, Chika said that he believed his wife's father was coming to take Paiche and their two sons back to Malawi.

Gardaí were amazed by the varying stories he told people about his wife before he disappeared. It seemed that he told everyone a different version of events. All of these people, most of them African, happily co-operated with gardaí after the Nigerian's disappearance. Gardaí were also able to determine whom Chika had been in contact with during the period when his wife went missing. It was of interest to gardaí that Chika was often in touch with his close friend, Nigerian Chijioke Ezekwem, who went by the name CJ and who then lived in Galway. The pair were from the same Igbo tribe in Nigeria and grew up together. "They were like blood brothers," explains the garda. "They were from the same tribe in Nigeria. When he had a fight with Paiche a few days before she went missing, it was Chijioke he went to see."

Detectives believe that CJ came back to Waterford with Chika after his friend visited him to discuss his marital problems. The two Nigerians arrived back in Waterford on 7 July, and Chika went home while CJ stayed somewhere locally in Waterford for a few days. Three days later, Chika reported his wife missing.

At the height of the garda investigation, 40 detectives were involved. Throughout their exhaustive enquiries all avenues and theories were explored. A couple of weeks after Chika's disappearance, gardaí intercepted two packages addressed to the

Nigerian. One was sent from Belgium, the other from Austria and neither had a return address. Both packages contained jars filled with liquid, twigs and earth. Following analysis, the substances in the packages were deemed to be natural soil-based matter and fluid. It initially baffled senior officers, but they have now formed their own views on what was the intended purpose of these substances.

Detectives believe that Paiche was not targeted by her pimp or by a violent client. Their belief is that she was killed in a ritualistic murder and those who beheaded her offered up her head as a sacrifice, believing it would bring them riches. Gardaí researched beheadings in Africa and found that similar decapitations still take place within tribes in various parts of the continent. It is also likely that more than one person was involved in her murder. "It wasn't a conclusion we came to lightly," says the garda. "It seems so far-fetched but we believe that she was murdered in a ritualistic killing."

Over two years after her dismembered body was discovered, gardaí charged CJ with withholding information in relation to Paiche's murder. On 8 September 2006, the 26-year old appeared at Letterkenny District Court charged with failing to disclose information which was believed to be of assistance in securing a prosecution in the case. Arrested the day before and brought to the Letterkenny station, he asked gardaí, "Why me?" when he was charged. The father-of-one was living in Donegal. He was granted bail. But he was later taken back into custody after his High Court action to prevent his deportation failed and gardaí felt he was a flight risk. In 2007, the charge of withholding information was withdrawn. Detectives did not have enough evidence against CJ to secure a conviction. The main basis on which he was charged was that CJ was found in possession of Chika's mobile phone sim card after he disappeared. CJ was not able to provide gardaí with any information about his friend's whereabouts. "We simply didn't have enough evidence against him," explains the garda. "All his avenues fighting his deportation had run out at the time when the charges were withdrawn. I expect he was deported not long afterwards."

It took detectives several months to track down the middle-eastern woman who had befriended Paiche. She was initially reluctant to talk to gardaí as she feared she could face prosecution for her involvement in prostitution. But detectives eventually earned her trust and she told them about how she had encouraged Paiche to get more deeply involved in the world of prostitution. She also said that Chika was pressuring his wife to get as much work as possible selling her body.

As far as gardaí have been able to determine through Interpol, Chika has not returned to Nigeria and they believe he is most likely living in the UK. Before coming to Ireland, he lived in France for a few years, and at one stage he worked as a professional footballer. It is unlikely he will return to Ireland as he is still sought here for questioning in relation to his wife's murder. But gardaí have no evidence against Chika. "He'll probably turn up in another country at some stage," adds the garda. "But we do not have enough evidence against him to charge him and then extradite him if he does. The only way this can progress is if he comes back to Ireland. We took hundreds of statements and not one person said a bad word about Paiche. That's very unusual. She was friendly, fun-loving and outgoing. It seemed that people couldn't not like her and her beauty was striking."

Anthony and Andrew are Irish citizens and will have the right to return to Ireland if they so wish when they are adults. While Andrew was just 18 months when his mother died and his father disappeared, he probably has little recollection of his early life in Ireland. But as Anthony was 3, he would have clearer memories of both his parents and his life in Waterford. As they grow up, both children will question their family in Malawi about how their mother lost her life. They will also wonder why their father then disappeared without trace.

In July 2009, to mark the fifth anniversary of the discovery of her body, gardaí in Clonmel reissued an appeal for Chika to come forward. The community of Piltown once again united in prayer to remember the young mother. When Paiche's dismembered body was discovered, it shocked the small community to its core. Rumour, speculation and fear abounded, particularly in the three days before she was identified. What horror visited their peaceful village in the dead of night to dump a mutilated body over the stone-built bridge across the River Pil? It frightened people. Locals were anxious that someone—or something even—was lurking among them and carrying out atrocities in the shadow of nightfall. At Sunday mass in Piltown the day before Paiche was identified, Father Paschal Moore tried to verbalise to his parishioners the sense of abhorrence the community was experiencing. "This is an outrage against God and the community, that a person would be dumped over a ditch like a dog. This was somebody's daughter, maybe a mother . . . Somebody somewhere is going to be traumatised." He told the community that they would adopt and accept this woman into their hearts and the community "as one of our own. She will be included every day in our community prayers. She is now one of ours."

14 | FARAH NOOR

Husna Said has one wish. To travel to Ireland and visit the three women serving prison sentences for killing her husband Kenyan Farah Swaleh Noor. She is not looking for an apology. But she wants answers from Charlotte, Linda and Kathleen Mulhall about why they committed and then covered up their brutal crime. She also wants the Mulhalls to come face-to-face with Farah's 19-year-old son Mohamed, who she says is the living image of his father. She feels the women responsible for ending her husband's life should be confronted with the devastation left in its wake.

The killing of Farah Swaleh Noor by Charlotte and Linda Mulhall is the most notorious murder of a foreigner on Irish soil. The 38-year-old Kenyan was stabbed and bludgeoned to death by the women in a drink and drug-fuelled haze. First, Charlotte cut his throat with a Stanley knife and then stabbed him a further 21 times while her elder sister hit him repeatedly with a hammer. The sisters then spent hours hacking him into eight pieces before they dumped his headless torso in the Royal Canal at Ballybough Bridge. His head and penis were detached from his body and have never been recovered. Charlotte and Linda Mulhall were christened the 'Scissor Sisters' by the media during their sensational trial in 2006. They have maintained that they attacked the Kenyan, who was in a relationship with their mother Kathleen, because he attempted to rape Linda. Details of their gruesome crime appalled the nation. Linda was convicted of the Kenyan's manslaughter and was sentenced to 15 years, while her younger sister Charlotte was convicted of his murder and handed down a mandatory life sentence. Their mother Kathleen fled to the UK to avoid being arrested by gardaí, but eventually returned and was jailed for five years in 2009 for helping to clean up the scene of her boyfriend's murder.

The grotesque killing and subsequent cover-up was one of almost unimaginable brutality. The 'Scissor Sisters' have been vilified in the media for their monstrous crime. But their own background is equally tragic. While senior detectives investigating the murder were all horrified by their actions, opinion amongst gardaí over their motive and the vulnerability of the women has been divided. Farah was murdered at the economic height of Celtic Tiger Ireland, something which had bypassed the Mulhalls entirely. The sisters existed within an underclass far removed, disconnected and untouched by the economic boom. Problems within their own family unit damaged their lives before they reached adulthood and were intensified by their drug abuse. In Linda's case, her subsequent relationships with men dismantled further her already vulnerable psyche. Her former partner is serving a lengthy jail sentence for inflicting sadistic cruelty upon three of her four children. Photographs of Linda and Charlotte, always wearing heavy make-up and stark black eye-liner during their trial, became iconic images that represented the dysfunctional underbelly of Irish society most people were unaware existed. The sisters both horrified and enthralled the general public in equal measure. While their crime was truly shocking, so too were the circumstances of their lives. Charlotte and her mother regularly worked as prostitutes on the streets of Dublin together, while Linda cut something of a helpless figure, abusing drugs not for enjoyment but to function each day.

The media have predominantly been obsessed with the

Mulhalls while their victim Farah Swaleh Noor has had far less attention. An examination of Noor's life is detailed in Mick McCaffrey's book *The Irish Scissor Sisters*. The Kenyan man was a violent, sexual predator. That a man like Noor was murdered shouldn't have been too shocking given his own crimes against women, but the circumstances of his killing ensured that it was. Yet his wife does not recognise the man who has been labelled a violent rapist as her husband. Speaking from her home in Mombasa, Kenya, in a rare interview five years on from her estranged husband's murder, she remembers an entirely different man. "When he first left, we were supposed to join him eventually. He said he would send for us but he never did," says Husna, who lives in severe financial hardship raising the couple's two remaining children. Their eldest, 17-year-old Somoe, died shortly after she heard her father had been murdered. The teenager had been suffering from health problems since childhood. Husna is now raising 19-year-old Mohamed and 16-year-old Zuleh alone.

Husna Said married Noor when she was 17 and the couple lived in Mombasa. Noor left the family in 1993 saying he was going to Europe to set up a base and would then fly his wife and children over. Husna was pregnant with their daughter Zuleh at the time. "He was a really caring father and husband. He never hurt me in any way. He loved his family. I don't know what happened to him in Ireland. He must have changed," she says. "Maybe it was because he didn't see his family. I have nightmares all the time about what happened to him. He stopped calling me after he went to Ireland. But he still called his mother. He told her Kathleen [Mulhall] didn't know about his wife and children in Kenya and that's why he stopped calling us. He still spoke to his children when he called and they were at her house. The last thing he ever told his son was, 'I will come and see you soon, my son.' A few months after that, we were told he was dead."

It seems the Kenyan never had any intention of including his wife and children in his new life. He lived in London until 30 December 1996 when he boarded a flight to Dublin and claimed asylum. His real name was Sheilila Said Salim. He told the

authorities upon his arrival in Dublin that his name was Farah
Swaleh Noor, that he was fleeing war-torn Somalia and wanted to
claim political asylum. He said his date of birth was 2 July 1967
and he carried no passport or other identification. He was
photographed and fingerprinted and his asylum application was
duly processed. After his death, gardaí discovered his true
identity, nationality and age—he was two years older than he
claimed to be.

He desperately wanted to get out of Kenya. He felt he had no
future there and had heard it was easy to get refugee status in
some European countries if you concocted a convincing story
about fleeing persecution. In his application form for refugee
status that he filled out in detail a few weeks after his arrival, he
claimed to be a Somalian from the Muslim Bajun tribe. He said
he had married a woman named Hajila in 1988, but she had been
murdered. He gave the correct names and dates of birth of his
three children, one of the few truths in his asylum application
form. He claimed to have fled his native Somalia for Kenya,
before leaving that country and journeying to Rome, before
taking another flight to Dublin. He wrote on the final section of
his asylum application form: "When I reach Mogadishu [in
Somalia] I went to my family house. The door was open, when go
inside nobody was in. The only thing I saw was the dead body of
my wife, she was having a bullet in her chest ... I don't know what
to do because the war destroy my house. I don't know where's my
family are they live or dead. No government to protect me ... So
I will be very happy if you allow me to stay in this country."

Husna learned later of her husband's lies on his asylum
application, as well as his relationship with Kathleen Mulhall and
other women. But at the time of his death, she still hoped he
would come home. "He told his mother he could not talk to me
because Kathleen did not know about his family. That did make
me jealous. I still loved him. I did not ask for a divorce even
though he was not in contact with me any more. I hoped he
would come home to his family soon," she says. "Life has been
very hard since he died five years ago. I work in a restaurant but
it is not enough money. He had been sending money to his

mother and she helped me. Now he is gone, his mother tries to help me when she can but it is very difficult."

Husna applied to the Criminal Injuries Compensation Board for monetary compensation in March 2007 following Farah's death. She detailed the expenses she has had to bear alone to raise her family since her husband's death. But as she does not live in Ireland, she is not entitled to any compensation. "It is not just about money but life has been very hard for us. My son has been very traumatised and troubled by what happened to his father. He is almost a man now himself. I want the Irish authorities to bring me to Ireland. They offered to bring me soon after they told me about his death, but I could not go because my daughter became suddenly very sick when she heard about her father and I had to stay in the hospital with her. Then she died. But I want to go now. I want to visit Kathleen and the others in prison. I want them to meet my husband's son. He looks exactly like his father."

She is not looking for an apology from the Mulhalls. "That would not take away our pain. But they should meet his family and explain. I was told by police what happened. But they should tell me. They should face me and my son."

In December 1998—two years after he arrived in Ireland—Farah's application for refugee status was rejected. He appealed this decision and this appeal was upheld. He was officially granted refugee status on 30 July 1999. During the two and a half years his application had been going through the system, Farah had been settling into Irish life. He liked Ireland, its people and its customs. But he had a problem with alcohol, and this worsened considerably in this country. When he was granted refugee status, he was entitled to claim social welfare benefits, which enabled his drinking to become progressively worse. As the Kenyan's alcoholism deepened, his phone calls to his mother lessened.

He became well known around the pubs in Dun Laoghaire and Dublin city centre. It was not unusual for him to drink three bottles of vodka in one day. He also used drugs including cannabis, cocaine and ecstasy. People who came into contact with him described a nice man when sober but completely changed when drunk. He was a serious alcoholic. Most people knew him as Farah, but he also socialised within the Somalian community, and they knew him by his real name, Sheilila Said Salim. His father, who died when Farah was a young man, was a Somalian and this was no doubt one of the reasons he pretended to be a native of the country. His Somalian friends in Ireland did not know he was a Kenyan using an assumed identity. While he made friends and acquaintances in the nine years he spent in Ireland before he was murdered, he also kept himself apart from people. He had quite a few nicknames including 'American' and 'Abawa'. He could regularly be found drinking in the Blessington Street area and was a huge soccer fan. He followed the Irish national team, as well as Manchester United, religiously. In fact, if he had not been wearing an Irish soccer jersey when he was murdered, it is likely he would never have been identified. A Somalian friend saw him on the day of his murder with the Mulhalls and later recognised the jersey when an appeal was issued to the African community in a bid to try and identify his corpse.

Long before Farah met Kathleen Mulhall, whom he systematically, physically and sexually assaulted, he had raped and attacked other women. He was only in the country eight months when he met a 16-year-old Chinese student in Dr Quirkies amusement arcade on O'Connell Street in the city centre. The teenager had mental health problems and the Kenyan preyed on her. She was playing pool when Farah walked up to her out of the blue and asked her to be his girlfriend. They had never met before and the teenager refused the 29-year old. But she did go back with him to his flat. He then forced her to have sex with him on the couch. It was to be their only sexual encounter, but the 16-year old fell pregnant by Farah. When she told him about their child, a son, he wasn't interested in being involved. She later told the Mulhalls murder trial in 2006 about her encounter with the Kenyan: "He tried to do something on me. He tried to do something, make sex to me." Asked if she had wanted that to happen, she said: "No, he forced me to do it."

The same month the mentally impaired Chinese teenager gave

birth to Farah's son, he met and fell in love with another 16-year old. It was April 1998 and the Kenyan met the third-year secondary school student out celebrating her birthday. Her identity was protected in court when she gave evidence about her relationship with Farah. The Kenyan told Sarah* he was 20 years old. Within three months, she was pregnant and she gave birth to their son in March 1999. In the beginning, their relationship blossomed. He stopped drinking to excess and was devoted to his son and girlfriend. He even moved into her family home in south Dublin and got on well with her family, particularly her father.

But when his son was three months old, Sarah and her family began to notice a change in Farah. He began drinking heavily again and would disappear for days on end. He also began to beat his girlfriend. But the teenager didn't want to give up on their relationship. The couple applied and were soon provided with a council house and moved out of her family home. Over the next three years they resided at three different county council houses in the same area as Sarah's family. The teenager hoped that if the couple had their own space, their relationship would improve. But living with Farah only became more dangerous. When he was sober, he was kind and loving, but he became a completely different person when intoxicated. The next three years of her young life were a living nightmare. She was forced to call gardaí on a number of occasions but never pressed charges. She received a particularly savage beating from him when she was 17 years old.

The couple were on a night out with some of Sarah's friends when Farah began to abuse one of her friends, calling her a lesbian and accusing her of trying to steal his girlfriend. That night, she did not go home with Farah, she was too afraid of his temper. When she returned the next day, he beat her until his own arms ached. This pattern continued for the rest of their relationship. When he was drunk, he was particularly violent. He was clever enough to beat her around the top of her head and drag her by her hair, so as not to leave visible marks. On a few

*name has been changed

occasions, she complained to gardaí at Tallaght garda station about his abuse, but never made a formal complaint. She was terrified of the Kenyan, but still too young to realise she had other options.

She also noticed that her boyfriend was self-destructive. He would often burn himself with cigarettes on his arms and chest if something was troubling him. He also had several scars on his wrists. He would slash himself every time someone from home passed away. Life with Farah continued to deteriorate. The beatings had progressed to violent rapes, which soon became a daily occurrence. On two occasions she did build up enough courage to leave him. But both times, he begged her to come back and she did. She desperately wanted him to become the partner and father she believed he was capable of. Sarah later told gardaí that he had an obsession with knives, had threatened to stab her, and carried at least one knife with him at all times. It wasn't just his girlfriend he was violent towards. He regularly got into fights over the smallest of disagreements. Farah was the only boyfriend Sarah had ever had; she didn't know what a normal relationship was. As well as raping her, he had begun taking photos of her tied up around different parts of the house as he forced her into degrading poses. All the while, their young son slept upstairs.

Finally, in 2001, Sarah got the reality shock she needed. A friend of hers, Jane,[†] moved in with the couple. The 25-year old only stayed for three weeks. She left because she was afraid the Kenyan was going to start beating her also. He became convinced she was trying to turn his girlfriend against him. But three weeks was long enough for her to witness Farah's violent and dangerous behaviour towards his girlfriend. As well as the constant physical and sexual violence, he also controlled his then 18-year-old girlfriend's every move. He had turned an outgoing young teenager into a damaged and timid young woman scared of her own shadow. Jane told her friend she needed to get herself and their 22-month-old son away from him.

†name has been changed

Eventually, Jane phoned Sarah's parents to tell them the extent of the abuse their daughter was suffering at the hands of the domineering Kenyan. Her father went immediately to the house and took his daughter and grandson away. Back in the safety of her family home, she finally saw that it was not safe for her or her son to ever live with Farah again. She got a barring order against him and slowly began to rebuild her life. She was awarded full custody of their son in April 2001.

He still had parental access to their son, but soon Sarah became concerned about marks on the young boy's body after he returned from visits with his father. He had burns on his skin, which his father couldn't explain. Sarah knew about Farah's history of self-harming. She was also worried about her son's behaviour after he returned from spending time with Farah. Immediately after returning from visits with his father he acted highly sexualised, despite the fact that he was only 3 years old. She worried that his father had been trying to teach him sexual behaviour. At first Farah would not accept that his relationship with Sarah was over. He stalked his ex-girlfriend and made threatening phone calls to her. Then Sarah began dating another man. Eventually Farah came to the realisation that she would never take him back. Then, in late 2001, he met Kathleen Mulhall. His interest in his son and ex-girlfriend soon began to wane. It was a lucky escape for Sarah and her son. And for Farah Swaleh Noor, it marked the beginning of the end of his life.

From the beginning the relationship between the Dublin mother-of-six and the Kenyan seemed an odd pairing. She was 11 years his senior and the Kenyan had previously shown an interest in women far younger than himself. Kathleen was married to John Mulhall and living in Clare Gardens in Tallaght when she met him. Before she met Farah, there were problems within the marriage, as well as in the family unit itself. She left her husband for the Kenyan, but instead of her moving out, her husband John left the house and some of the children left with him. Farah then moved into their home in Tallaght. In working-class Dublin, it was very unusual for a middle-aged woman to throw out her Irish husband and move in her young African lover. But theirs was a dysfunctional family.

Eventually, Kathleen and Farah decided they wanted a fresh start and decided to move to Cork. In September 2002, they left Dublin and John moved back into the family home. Before they left for Cork, Farah had already beaten Kathleen. But his violent and controlling tendencies intensified as they attempted to set up a new life together. In the three years before his death, he subjected Kathleen to continuous physical violence. He hospitalised her on more than one occasion. He cracked her ribs several times. He burnt her with cigarettes while she was sleeping. Eventually, Kathleen would beg her daughters to kill her boyfriend. But before she reached that point, she phoned Farah's ex-girlfriend Sarah in 2003 asking for advice on how to deal with him. She had found her number in Farah's phone and confided in her that he was beating her regularly. She was looking for answers about how to get him to stop. But Sarah only had one piece of advice. "She was looking for advice. I advised her to leave him. I said he would never change. She wanted to know if he had ever beaten or attacked me. I told her about the abuse," Sarah later told gardaí. "She knew I was in a new relationship but I told her to leave him. I remember telling her that he would never change and that something awful would happen if she didn't."

Her prediction was correct, but no one could have imagined just how awful the final outcome would be. After Farah's disappearance, but before the remains of his mutilated body were found, Kathleen was interviewed by detectives and shed some light on the cruelty and sadism that he was capable of. "I had two very different relationships with Farah. When he was sober he was a beautiful person, a beautiful man, but when he was using both drink and drugs he was like the devil. He attacked me nearly every day. He was totally crazy when he was drinking. He'd beat me with his hands, his fists or with a belt. He'd mostly use a belt. He'd say, 'I wouldn't beat you if I didn't love you.' I believed him. He told me on a number of occasions that if I told anyone about the attacks, he would kill me. I believed him when he said this."

While the detectives know that Kathleen initially lied to them about the circumstances of her boyfriend's disappearance and death, they have no reason to disbelieve her account of his abuse towards her. Acquaintances of the couple in Cork regularly saw Farah beating her in public and hospital records confirmed her injuries. The two mothers of his sons in Dublin also attested to his violent nature.

On 14 September 2004, after almost two years living in Cork, Farah and Kathleen decided to move back to Dublin. The fresh start they had dreamed of hadn't worked out. A month later, on 24 October, three garda on patrol witnessed Farah repeatedly hit an older woman on the Old Bawn Road in Tallaght. He was arrested on suspicion of assault and taken to Rathfarnham garda station. The woman he was beating was Kathleen and she refused to co-operate with gardaí and make a statement about her boyfriend's behaviour. He was released without charge. Six months later he was murdered. The brutality he inflicted at will on the women he encountered finally caught up with him.

On the day he was murdered, Farah was drinking in the city centre with Kathleen when her two daughters Linda and Charlotte joined them. It was 20 March 2005. All four were on the dole and couldn't afford the luxury of a pub. So they bought vodka and beer from an off-licence and were drinking it on the streets, wandering around the city centre. It wasn't a conventional way for a middle-aged woman to interact with her two grown-up daughters. But they were not a typical family. Charlotte worked occasionally as a prostitute, as did Kathleen, and the mother and daughter sometimes even worked the streets together as they enjoyed each other's company.

The four of them ended up drinking along the Liffey Boardwalk, a place habituated by drug-addicts, drug-dealers and alcoholics. Linda had brought ten ecstasy tablets with her and Charlotte happily took one with her older sister when she told her about the drugs. When their mother saw what they were up to, she also took one and they washed the pills down with vodka. They didn't give one to Farah. He was already very drunk. Linda had a strained relationship with her mother. She wasn't happy when she walked out on her father John after 29 years of marriage, effectively ripping the family apart. It bothered Charlotte less. She felt her 49-year-old mother should do whatever made her happy.

As the day turned into evening, it got cold and Kathleen and Farah began to row. As the four made their way back to the couple's flat in Ballybough, they screamed and roared at each other drunkenly, embarrassing Linda and Charlotte. On O'Connell Street earlier, Farah had bumped into his Somalian friend Mohamed Ali Abubakaar. Mohamed could tell immediately that Farah was very drunk and told him to take it easy. He knew he got aggressive with drink taken. He then watched his friend stumble on up the road with the three women. He was the last person to see him alive and later told gardaí that Farah was wearing the Ireland soccer jersey he was so fond of, and which led to his identification.

The group arrived at 17 Richmond Cottages in Ballybough and continued drinking. The three Mulhalls had taken two more ecstasy tablets each. Kathleen then crushed up the last tablet and put it into a can of beer that she gave to her boyfriend. She wanted him to be on the same buzz as the rest of them. He then went into the sitting room and began to harass Linda, while Kathleen and Charlotte remained in the kitchen.

He put his arm around Linda's shoulder and began to whisper in her ear, "We are two creatures of the night." She tried to push him away, but he wouldn't let her out of his tight grip. She shouted for her sister and mother who ran in and saw Farah with his arms locked around Linda's body and refusing to budge. She was scared and eventually stood up to try and get free from his grip. But the African refused to let go. At this stage Kathleen and Charlotte had both begun screaming at Farah. But he was in a different world and had begun chanting Linda's name as his grip tightened around her waist. She was crying and desperately trying to get free of his grip when her sister began to prise his hands away. Eventually he let go. Immediately, he lunged for Kathleen and made slitting motions with his hand, indicating he wanted to cut her throat. "Please kill him for me, just please kill him for me," Kathleen began to plead with her daughters as she struggled with the Kenyan. Charlotte ran to the kitchen and found a Stanley knife. She then walked up behind Farah, who still had her mother in his grip, grabbed him by his hair and slit his throat from behind. He staggered forward into the bedroom, falling and hitting his head hard. Charlotte followed him and continued to stab him 21 more times, puncturing all his major arteries. Her elder sister had joined her, armed with a hammer, and struck him ten times all over his body with the blunt object. It all happened in a matter of minutes.

Had the Mulhalls immediately telephoned gardaí and told them what had happened, Linda and Charlotte would most likely have escaped such lengthy jail terms. Some gardaí have questioned the veracity of the women's story about Farah's attempt to attack Linda. But as one senior detective involved in the case pointed out, if they were going to make up a story, then surely they would have concocted a better lie and said that Farah had actually succeeded in raping Linda?

Kathleen said it was Charlotte's idea to cut up the body, while her daughter insisted she did it with Linda's help on her mother's instruction. Regardless, the Kenyan ended up in eight pieces after being hacked apart, which included the removal of his head and penis. They then dumped his limbs and torso in the nearby Royal Canal before taking his head on the bus to Tallaght where it was hidden in a park, before being disposed of in another location by a guilt-wracked Linda.

It wasn't just the end of the Kenyan's life. The crime set in motion a chain of events that damaged beyond repair the already dysfunctional Mulhall family. The murder destroyed Kathleen's estranged husband John, who helped the women cover up their crime. He later committed suicide. Charlotte's life has also been effectively shattered by the brutality of her actions that night. A jury convicted her in October 2006 of the Kenyan's murder, while Linda was convicted of his manslaughter. The jury took the view that as Charlotte slit the Kenyan's throat, she intended to end his life. Charlotte gave birth to her first child, a son, five months before she was handed down a mandatory life sentence. He is now in care and will most likely be an adult by the time she is released. Linda's four children are also now in care and will be grown-ups by the time she completes her 15 year sentence. In May 2009, Kathleen Mulhall was jailed for five years for helping to clean up the scene of her boyfriend's murder to protect her two daughters. And in Mombasa in Kenya, the estranged wife of the Kenyan says she still weeps for the loss of her husband who walked out on his family. The brutality of his killing upsets her deeply and she worries for her two remaining children. "I want to meet the women in prison. I have got no justice," she says. "Is this too much to ask?"

15 | REGINA O'CONNOR

Moses O'Connor went into his mother's bedroom armed with a breadknife. As she lay in bed unable to defend herself, the 24-year old stabbed his Rwandan mother Regina O'Connor repeatedly in a frenzy of violence of which she always feared her son capable. She suffered fatal stab wounds to her back, neck and arm. He also fractured her larynx and broke ten of her ribs in the savage assault. Afterwards, Moses removed the bloody sheets from his mother's bed, washed them and hung them out on the washing line in the back garden of their upmarket home in Castlebyrne Park, Blackrock, south County Dublin. Instead of fleeing the scene, he stayed alone at the house for the next three days until gardaí arrested him after discovering his mother's dead body. Moses O'Connor's bizarre actions and delusional demeanour in the aftermath of his crime led senior gardaí to the conclusion that the young man was mentally deficient.

Regina O'Connor had made a last will and testament. It stated that Moses, her only child, would receive most of her money when he turned 25 under the strict condition that he was drug-free. Moses was just a few weeks shy of his 25th birthday when he killed his mother. He was still abusing drugs. Detectives found the will in Moses' bedroom after he was arrested on suspicion of her murder. As he never admitted to gardaí that he was responsible for her death, the exact circumstances that led to the fatal stabbing remain unknown. Only two people know what happened between them that spurred Moses to kill the woman who gave him life. One of them is dead and the other has never explained his aberrant crime. It appears that Moses killed Regina when he learned he was to receive nothing from his mother in her will, as he was still using drugs. But whether it was a premeditated or spur-of-the-moment attack will never be known.

It has never been definitively determined, but it is most likely that Moses O'Connor stabbed his mother to death on 23 November 2005. The next day, an ambulance arrived at the house to pick up Regina and take her to Tallaght Hospital for her dialysis treatment. Regina had serious kidney problems and was attending hospital three days a week for dialysis. Moses didn't answer the door when the ambulance crew arrived. Concerned, staff contacted nearby Blackrock garda station as they feared she could be inside the house possibly unable to answer the door due to her debilitating illness. Regina was a tiny woman—as was her son standing at just 5' 6"—and her illness had left her weak and fragile. Two gardaí arrived at the house and knocked on the front door. This time, Moses answered. They asked if his mother was at home and he told them she had gone to the countryside with a friend. Gardaí then asked Moses if they could look around the house and he let them in. But the officers found nothing out of the ordinary. They even looked into Regina's bedroom but did not notice her dead body. Her remains were concealed by bedclothes and the room was badly lit.

Satisfied, gardaí left the house. But the situation struck them as somewhat strange and the following day they again called to the house. This time one of the officers noticed that Moses was acting edgy. The day after that, gardaí got another call from the Tallaght Hospital ambulance crew. The medics were concerned because Regina had missed another appointment, which would have left her in a critical condition.

For the third time in three days, gardaí knocked at the front door. No one answered. Officers then spoke to one of the neighbours and when she knocked on the door, Moses allowed her into his home. A more thorough garda search of the house was carried out and detectives discovered Regina's dead body covered by bedclothes in her bedroom. It was clear she had suffered a violent death.

When gardaí made their grim discovery, Moses became extremely agitated. He repeated that he thought his mother was down the country with a friend and had no idea she was lying dead upstairs. Initially, gardaí interviewed him as a witness, but his behaviour was decidedly strange and one of the gardaí interviewing him noticed blood on his tracksuit bottoms. A few hours after his mother's body was found in the afternoon of 26 November, her son was arrested on suspicion of her murder. Gardaí had at this stage carried out a background check on the 24-year old and learned that his mother had a barring order out against her son since January of that year as he had threatened her. But despite this, she allowed her son back into her house when he was released from a prison term several months previously. The young man had accumulated 26 previous convictions in his short life, several of them for assault. Gardaí also established that Moses was the only person at the family home between 23 and 26 November.

In custody, Moses O'Connor's erratic behaviour alarmed gardaí. He was agitated, irrational and delusional. He continuously denied having killed his mother and blamed various other people for the murder, including gardaí. He ranted and raved in a nonsensical way making wild claims and accusations that disturbed senior gardaí to such a degree that they did not repeat in court what Moses said in custody. So bizarre was his demeanour that Moses was seen by a doctor, but the GP found that he was not suffering from ill-health. While in custody, he made certain admissions about being in the house around the time his mother was murdered and told them he had washed his mother's bed linen. His fingerprints had also been found in blood on the radiator in his mother's bedroom. Investigating officers were also perplexed as to why Moses had remained at the scene for three days with his mother's dead body instead of fleeing. Despite two previous visits from gardaí before they found his mother's body, Moses did not leave the house to escape detection. Detectives felt this was another indication that he was mentally unstable. Moses also knew that an ambulance called to collect his mother three times a week but, despite this, he stayed at the family home ignoring the knocks on the front door. It did not appear that these were the actions of a man trying to get away with murder. The knife believed to have killed Regina O'Connor was found by gardaí at the house, but as it had been wiped clean, it was never conclusively confirmed as the murder weapon.

As Moses O'Connor's 12 hour arrest period on suspicion of his mother's murder drew to a close, there was not enough evidence to charge him in relation to her killing at that point. Detectives were preparing a file for the Director of Public Prosecutions (DPP) seeking that he be charged with murder. But gardaí did not have to release Moses from custody after his arrest period came to an end, as other bench warrants were outstanding for his arrest.

Two days after he was arrested in connection with his mother's murder, Moses appeared in court charged with assaulting a garda and a security officer in Dun Laoghaire in 2003. He pleaded not guilty and was denied bail while he awaited trial. In October 2006, he was jailed for three years at Dublin Circuit Criminal Court for assaulting security guard Bobby Jenkins and Garda Kian Long on Dún Laoghaire's Marine Road. Despite his size, he injured both men as they tried to restrain him after he stole a mobile phone from an O2 phone store. On 25 May 2006—six months after he was arrested on suspicion of murder and while he remained in custody awaiting his assault trial—the DPP directed that Moses O'Connor be charged with his mother's murder.

He was taken to Dun Laoghaire courthouse and when the charge was put to him, he replied: "I'm not happy with that." He was granted free legal aid and assigned a solicitor. It would be another 18 months before the murder trial would get under way and gardaí began their preparations by learning as much as possible about both Regina and Moses O'Connor's background.

The outpouring of grief in Blackrock following the murder was testament to the popularity of Regina O'Connor. She is remembered as a beacon of selflessness who always had a smile and a kind word for anyone she met. She was well known in the community for her charity work, and her garden was the envy of keen gardeners in all of south Dublin. Before and after her murder, her friends wondered how such a kind-hearted and gentle woman raised a son who seemed the polar opposite.

Regina Nyibhabarugira was born in Rwanda and grew up on a large farm where she tended to her own patch of garden. Both of her parents were teachers. As a young woman, she moved to Kenya and at the age of 22, she gave birth to her only child, Moses. A few years later, she met Irishman Andrew 'Teddy' O'Connor in Kenya. Her future husband was a widower in his 70s travelling around the African country. The pair struck up a relationship and in 1986 Andrew, Regina and Moses moved to Ireland and settled at Castlebyrne Park in Blackrock, a property Andrew owned. Moses was 6 years old. When Regina first saw the neat, suburban lawn in their front garden, she remarked to her new husband, puzzled: "I can't eat it." Soon she had replaced the grass with rows of vegetables and flowers that became renowned in the area. "I thought I would be painting my nails and letting my hair down . . . Now I find that I just work in the garden like an African woman, and I appreciate it," she told a newspaper two years before her death.

For Regina, creating a beautiful garden was her way of staying connected to her homeland. In later years, when she became ill with kidney failure, she did not stop toiling in her garden. Instead, she worked even harder alongside a Chinese gardener she hired to help manage it. Every year she had a massive flower and vegetable exhibition and sale with all the proceeds going to the Irish Kidney Association. She was an active member and fundraiser for the association and the exhibition took several months of preparation. She was also a practising Catholic and friends and neighbours remember a woman who embodied a true Christian spirit in how she lived her life.

Despite living so far from home, Regina would travel to Rwanda frequently to visit her elderly father and extended family. On each of these visits, she would arrive laden down with clothes and other necessities for her villagers. "She used to go home to her village every year. But there is no dialysis in Rwanda, so she could only go home for four or five days," recalls Mark Murphy, chief executive of the Irish Kidney Association, who got to know Regina well in the last few years of her life. "Once, she got delayed and it was six and a half days before she came back and she had to go straight for dialysis. But it never stopped her going. She used to bring huge amounts of things back to her village for the people living there. Anything they needed, she'd bring it over to them from wheelbarrows to soccer balls and everything you can imagine in between. Aer Lingus were always very good to her. They used to ignore the baggage allowance. Her illness was failed kidneys."

In 1994, Andrew died. Moses was 14 years old and the death of his elderly stepfather hit him hard. When he was alive, Andrew had been a steadying influence in Moses' life. He had been the only father Moses had ever known. His parents tried to give Moses every opportunity in Ireland, but his life began to unravel in his early teens and he became friendly with people his parents didn't approve of. Moses had been sent to the prestigious Blackrock College but, unlike his mother, he never adjusted properly to life in Ireland and seemed unable to settle. Being a black child growing up in Dublin during the 1980s meant that Moses would have stood out, and in some ways he always felt an outsider. He was an African child trying to come to grips with life in an affluent south Dublin suburb. He showed considerable promise playing League of Ireland soccer, but as he began to abuse drugs in his early teens, he abandoned his talent. Moses was already going off the rails and displaying aggression before his stepfather died from natural causes, but things spiralled out of all control following his death. Regina found it hard to cope with her son. Although he left Africa when he was just 6 years old, he resented his mother for taking him away from his home to live in another country where he could not settle. At age 16, Regina was forced to put her son into foster care as their relationship had completely broken down. Moses felt that his mother was too strict and that he was now the man of the house. Regina told friends she was afraid of her son. He stayed with several foster families and as the teenager grew into a young adult, his problems intensified. His drug experimentation had progressed to heroin and he had had several spells in jail before he murdered his mother. Moses fought every system. Many of his 26 convictions were for assault as well as stealing cars and theft of goods from shops. Each time he went into prison, he came out worse, railing against a system he could not beat. Moses also managed to amass convictions from within prison, including attacks on prison officers. When he was sentenced to three years for his assault on a garda and security guard, Judge Michael White expressed his concern at the number of previous assault convictions he had accumulated.

When he was just 17 years old, he robbed a Spanish student of just £1 in Shankill, Co. Dublin, and was convicted the following year. On the same day in 1998, he robbed a black leather bag worth £25 from a woman in the same estate in Shankill. Despite his size, from an early age Moses proved time and time again that he was an angry and violent young man.

He also threatened his mother on more than one occasion. She was scared enough of him to change the locks at her home. But despite all this, she refused to wash her hands of her only child. Moses himself became a father in his early 20s, and Regina was extremely dedicated to her grandson. He named his son Andrew after his stepfather. Regina hoped the new arrival would inspire her son to turn his life around. "She really was an extraordinarily generous person. In her own family, she was too good to her son. He had a huge problem and was out of control. He threatened her before. We'd helped her change the locks," says Murphy. "We knew he was a problem. But when it comes to mothers and their sons, often logic plays no part. Gardaí knew of him. Some people can't be helped. Moses couldn't be helped. She'd been in fear of her life before because of him. You always think people are exaggerating when they say that, but she wasn't."

Regina's life since her husband's death was far from easy. Her son was a violent drug addict and her kidney problems left her seriously debilitated at times. One ray of light in her life was seeing her young grandson. Moses was no longer in a relationship with the child's mother, but Regina maintained contact with the young woman. "I knew Regina for five or six years. She was a very private person and a lovely woman," says Ann Rountree, who met Regina regularly as both women were undergoing dialysis treatment. "It took me a long time to figure out she had a grandson. Her face would light up when she spoke about him. She was besotted with her grandchild, a typical granny. She didn't talk much about Moses but she did tell me once that he was aggressive. Once she told me he was in jail. The nurse in the hospital always said, and I agreed with her, that Regina could have been an ambassador for her country. She was very private and kept her problems to herself. I used to go down to the amazing weekend flower sales she had for the Irish Kidney Association. There would be 800 to 1,000 plants. She had amazing green fingers."

Tending to her garden and seeing her grandson Andrew were Regina's main sources of happiness. "She had turned her front garden into a virtual forest of different plants. Other Africans living here tried to emulate it. That's what kept her going and she had a Chinese gardener who helped her," says Murphy. Regina's illness made coping with her difficult son even more challenging. But crucially, it also made her unable to defend herself from him. "She was a tiny person. She wouldn't have had the strength to fight back. Her health probably sometimes wasn't good enough to deal with him," adds Murphy.

The summer before she was murdered, Regina went to live in a nursing home in Kilcock, Co. Kildare. When her health improved over the summer and she moved home to Blackrock, she was keen to get back to her garden. She also tried never to let her illness get her down too much, always putting on a brave face. "Once, I met her at a barbecue. She had a line into her chest for her dialysis treatment. She refused to hide it, to try and cover it up. That was Regina," recalls Ann Rountree. "She wore her patch with pride. It was a fact of her life and she got on with it. She was really so gracious, such a dignified and lovely woman. She never complained about her illness. Some people moan and groan about it, but never Regina. It was such an awful thing that happened. I got the feeling her son was always looking for money. I know that he threatened her before. He opened the door to police when they called in because she missed her dialysis appointment. Why do people have to murder someone? It's so senseless. He obviously had some kind of psychological problem."

When Moses was released from prison in 2005, his mother decided to give him another chance. Despite the fact that she went to court to get a barring order out against him, she allowed her son to move back into the family home. It's likely he had nowhere else to go. Within months, he would express his gratitude for her kindness by taking her life. Over the years, he had occasionally lived in the shed in the back garden. But it seemed relations between mother and son had improved to an extent shortly before he murdered her and she felt comfortable enough to allow him back into their home.

On 12 November 2007, almost two years after Moses killed his mother, he appeared at Dublin Central Criminal Court to face trial. All along, he had denied responsibility for what happened, so gardaí were prepared for a murder trial. Because of his erratic behaviour when he was arrested, there was a question mark over his fitness to enter a plea. Before the trial, he was medically and psychologically assessed and found to be medically fit to enter a plea. To the surprise of gardaí, Moses O'Connor pleaded guilty to the murder of his mother.

It seemed that in the two years that had passed, Moses O'Connor was of sound mind. But in the immediate aftermath of the murder, he gave the impression of being mentally unhinged. Detective Inspector Martin Cummins told the court that O'Connor was "one of the most disturbed people" he had ever seen in garda custody. The inspector explained to Justice Paul

Carney how the young man's life went into freefall at a young age which culminated in the eventual murder of his mother. He said that Kenyan-born Moses was a talented sportsman but had developed problems in secondary school, getting involved in drugs and crime and spending time in foster care. In 2005, at the end of a prison term, he went to live with his mother despite the fact that she had taken out a barring order against him.

Inspector Cummins said that his relationship with his mother had "totally broken down" at the time of the killing. The inspector also told Justice Carney that the young man "didn't have life easy," a reference to how Moses struggled to come to terms with his identity growing up in Ireland as a black man. The court heard how Moses experimented with most types of drugs and he had lived rough on occasion. After his arrest for murder, Moses O'Connor was "very perturbed, confused and irrational," Inspector Cummins told Justice Carney. His early life had shown promise, the garda continued. He had played League of Ireland soccer at one point. "But somewhere between primary school and secondary school, his aggression began to show . . . Once he went into prison, he didn't come out any better."

As he entered a guilty plea for murder, Justice Carney handed down a mandatory life sentence. But an entirely different scenario could have unfolded at the Central Criminal Court. While O'Connor was deemed medically fit to enter a plea, it could have been argued that he was in an entirely different psychological state when he carried out his horrific crime. His ramblings to gardaí while in custody would have backed up this claim. His legal defence team could have queried his mental stability, given that he did not flee the house or try and hide his mother's body, even though gardaí visited the house and spoke to Moses two days in a row before finding her dead body on the third day. Instead of going on the run after the killing, the 24-year old stayed in the house with his mother that he had knifed to death. He even washed her bloodstained sheets. But Moses O'Connor's legal defence team could not query his state of mind without instruction from their client. And Moses never indicated to his solicitor that he was mentally unwell when he killed his mother.

It is equally plausible that the 24-year old knew exactly what he was doing when he committed the murder. Perhaps he had planned it for months. Maybe, by the time his trial came around, Moses deeply regretted the killing and wanted to be punished for his unspeakable crime. No one knows because Moses O'Connor never explained his actions. All he said in court was confirm that he was pleading guilty to murder. His mother's last will and testament found in his bedroom stating that he would receive most of her money upon his 25th birthday on condition that he was drug-free provided a clear motive for his actions. But if the sole reason he killed her was for money, Moses never saw a penny of it. Instead, the majority of Regina O'Connor's wealth was left to her young grandson Andrew upon her death.

Neighbours recall Regina O'Connor happiest sitting on the bench in her garden during the summer, chatting to people walking by who asked her questions about the flowers. Her garden has been described as a metaphor for her spirit, how she lived life, a place where beautiful things that died were later resurrected. Friends and neighbours left bouquets at the gate of her home in the days after her murder. Among them, one stood out. Its message read: "In heaven, one more angel. God bless."

16 | BAIBA SAULITE

She arrived in Ireland at just 20 years of age. Full of expectation, Baiba Saulite left her native Riga with her Latvian boyfriend to carve out a more prosperous life in Ireland. She didn't leave home out of necessity. She was simply in search of greener pastures and Ireland had earned the reputation in Eastern Europe as the land of opportunity. It was 1998. Eight years later, the mother-of-two would be returned to Latvia in a coffin. Four bullets fired into her body at close range shattered her immigrant's dream. Her murder also brought into focus the reality that gangland criminals were willing and able to kill innocent victims at will. Her murder sparked a unified sense of outrage in Irish society. But despite one of the most exhaustive garda investigations ever launched, no one has been brought to justice for the 28-year old's killing.

Baiba arrived in Ireland brimming with optimism and plans for her future. She wanted to study hotel management and improve her English. In Riga, both her parents were dentists and were well regarded in the community. The family were strict Lutherans. She immediately fell in love with Dublin, the hustle and bustle of the city and the friendliness of the people. But Baiba's relationship with her Latvian boyfriend did not survive

their move. She soon found herself alone in Dublin when her
boyfriend returned to Latvia in 1999. However, Baiba was
independent and strong willed and she decided to stay in Ireland
alone. It was a difficult time for her, but she wanted to stick it out
in Ireland, even though she only knew a handful of people. But
Baiba wasn't single for long. She met her future husband Hassan
Hassan over the Christmas period in 1999. He was from the
Lebanon and had been living in Ireland for several years. Within
six years of meeting him, Baiba would be shot dead by a hired
assassin as she stood smoking a cigarette while chatting to her
friend on the patio of her Swords home. Her two young sons slept
upstairs. Detectives believe that Hassan, who was by then
imprisoned, ordered his estranged wife's murder from behind
bars. Gardaí were convinced they had enough evidence against
Hassan for him to be charged with conspiracy to murder Baiba.
But in early 2010, the Director of Public Prosecutions (DPP)
directed that he should not face charges in relation to her death.
On Saturday 20 March, Hassan Hassan was released from
Portlaoise Prison. He had been serving a four year sentence for
his part in a stolen car ring and a consecutive two year sentence
for kidnapping his two sons in 2004. In a highly unusual move,
Hassan was taken straight from prison in an unmarked prison
van to Dublin Airport. The van was followed by gardaí. He flew
home to his native Lebanon and has since gone to neighbouring
Syria where he has been reunited with his two sons. The boys
were in the care of Hassan's family until his release from prison.
It is now extremely unlikely that anyone will face charges in
relation to the murder of Baiba Saulite.

When Baiba was introduced to Hassan at a Christmas party by
mutual friends, she was immediately drawn to him. Ten years her
senior, he was attractive, charismatic and wealthy. Like her, he had
left his homeland in search of opportunities. He had been in
Ireland for several years and was already an Irish citizen when
they met. She was suitably impressed by her new boyfriend's
lifestyle and didn't ask too many questions about the source of his
income. She was 22 years old and in love.

Hassan was a well-established criminal. His associations with various crime gangs is detailed in Paul Williams' book *Crime Wars*. He had links back in the Lebanon to organised crime gangs that specialised in the sale of illegal firearms. He was the unofficial leader of a group of middle-eastern criminals living in Ireland who at the time were involved in stealing high-powered cars to order. It was a sophisticated and lucrative operation. Gardaí also suspected the gang were also involved in the trade of firearms, but this was never proven. The criminals switched the chassis numbers and registration plates from cars written off in crashes to the stolen vehicles. The cars were then shipped out of Ireland to Eastern Europe while stolen cars were shipped in by the gang from the UK as part of the racket. Hassan had established links with organised criminals in Ireland and had a particularly strong working relationship with Martin 'Marlo' Hyland and his west Dublin associates. Hassan began to do business with Hyland on a regular basis. Hyland's gang, as well as other criminals, would steal the high-powered cars on behalf of Hassan and his associates. The two men began to work with each other around the turn of the century, the same time Hassan met Baiba.

Within months of meeting one another, Baiba and Hassan moved in together. It wasn't long before they decided to marry. But soon, Baiba started to wonder what kind of man she had chosen to spend her life with. He had told her he was a Christian when they wed. But when their first son Ali Alexsandra was born in 2001, he told his wife that he was in fact a Muslim and he wanted their son to be raised in this faith. Baiba herself was Lutheran. He also failed to mention that he had been previously married to an Irish woman, with whom he had a child. Two years later, Baiba gave birth to the couple's second boy, Mohammed Rami. At this stage, the family had moved to a house in Kinsealy in north Dublin. But the couple's relationship was faltering. Baiba felt that the person she had fallen in love with was completely different to the man she had married. Their entire relationship was based on lies. They fought constantly and she soon became terrified of her domineering husband, who began to try and control her every move. Whilst his marriage was deteriorating, gardaí were closing in on his gang's criminal activities. He was arrested in 2003 along with a number of his associates when detectives from west Dublin raided the car repair garage near Clane in Co. Kildare where the criminals were storing stolen cars. The investigation was led by Detective Inspector Brian Sherry, and two dozen luxury cars were recovered worth about €300,000. Some of them had already undergone modifications and were waiting to be exported. The gang had been exporting the cars from Dublin port. Detectives believe it was a multimillion euro operation. Hassan was charged for his role in the stolen car ring and was released on bail.

Within months, Baiba left her husband. Their relationship had completely broken down. At first he seemed to accept that it was over. Baiba was granted full custody of their two sons, but Hassan had regular access to his boys and the couple maintained an amiable relationship for the sake of their children. At least that's what Baiba thought. But on 6 December 2004, Hassan came and collected his two sons from their mother's home in Swords. He was supposed to have them for a couple of nights and then drop them back to their mother. But he did not return the children as arranged. Instead, he abducted his sons and sent them to live with his mother in Syria. Ali and Mohammed were Irish citizens, so gardaí immediately launched an investigation into the kidnapping when they were informed.

Baiba was inconsolable and at a loss about what to do. She decided she needed legal advice. She walked into the first solicitor's office she saw in Swords village. It was October 2004 and Hennessy & Perrozzi solicitors, in Forster Way in Swords, had only recently opened its doors to the public. She was introduced to solicitor John Hennessy and became one of his first clients. At their first meeting she told him about the disappearance of her sons and he began family law proceedings to try and force Hassan to bring the children back. She was at rock bottom and was utterly distraught. She had no idea if the boys were in Ireland or had been sent abroad. He didn't know it then, but John Hennessy's life would never be the same after his first encounter with the young Latvian woman. His life would be put under direct threat because of the legal battles he would later fight on behalf of his client against her estranged husband. Hennessy agreed to represent her and sought a court order compelling Hassan to return Ali and Mohammed to their mother. Over the next year, he explored every legal avenue to try and help his client get her children back.

Hassan was summoned to appear before Swords District Court to explain where the children were. He was ordered to return them to Ireland by Christmas Eve 2004. But instead, Hassan decided to show utter contempt and disregard for the court's direction. "He basically stuck two fingers up to the judicial system," says a senior garda involved in the investigation, who asked not to be named because of sensitivities around the case. Because Hassan failed to follow the judge's orders, he was jailed for three weeks for contempt of court. But he didn't seem to care. Senior gardaí involved in the kidnapping investigation and subsequent murder investigation say that Hassan is an unpredictable criminal who is willing to go to extreme lengths to get what he wants.

Baiba was only too aware of this. The once carefree young woman who had left Latvia at age 20 was gone. She was now a separated mother-of-two whose children had been kidnapped. She went on Joe Duffy's *Liveline* in January 2005 to explain her plight to the nation. She didn't have any idea where her sons were and thought it was possible they were still in Ireland. In an extensive interview, she spoke about her turbulent life with Hassan. "He told us [Baiba and their two sons] what we could eat, what we couldn't eat, what I have to wear, what I could do. He wouldn't let me go out to see my friends, nothing," she told radio listeners in an emotional 35 minute interview. "These children have always been with me, every day, every minute. These children must be very upset. The little baby [Mohammed Rami], he's a baby . . . But Ali, he's really a mammy's boy and he must be very upset about the situation because he doesn't know anybody. I never heard from them since the day I let them go. All that I want is just my babies back home safe with mummy. Just think how you would feel if it happened to your kids. I am the mummy and any kid needs a mother." The interview struck a chord with hundreds of thousands of listeners to Joe Duffy's show that afternoon. The pain and suffering in her voice spoke directly into people's hearts and minds.

In August 2005, Hassan was charged with kidnapping his two sons. He was remanded in custody. He was still on bail for his role in the stolen car racket. He applied for bail in the High Court on the kidnapping charges and it was granted on condition that he return his sons to their mother. Keen for his freedom, although he must have known he was facing jail time for the stolen car ring, he accepted defeat and returned the boys to Baiba. She had been without her children for ten long months. Elated and overjoyed, she hoped the nightmare was finally over. But it was only just beginning. With her sons safely home, she enrolled Mohammed in Montessori, while Ali started in junior infants at the Holy Family National School in River Valley in Swords. She also took a part-time job cleaning offices two days a week. But the stress of her children's abduction took its toll on the 28-year old. She suffered a nervous breakdown over fears for her young family and what her husband was capable of. She had fully recovered by the time of her death. Her dedication to her children helped her through her darkest days.

Not long after her two sons were returned to Ireland, concerns arose for the safety of solicitor John Hennessy. Hassan detested the solicitor because he fought so hard in the courts to get Baiba's sons back. When Hassan attempted to threaten Baiba in court at hearings before he had returned their children to Ireland, Hennessy was quick to warn him to keep his distance from his client or he would have him arrested. He refused to be bullied by a coward who would threaten women. It was just after 12.30 am on 27 February 2006 when the solicitor, who was drifting into sleep, was awoken by the fire alarm at his home. He quickly awoke his girlfriend who was asleep beside him and they ran downstairs, where a blaze had taken hold. The couple were lucky to escape unharmed. It was later established that a significant amount of petrol had been poured through the letterbox and set alight. The attack was taken very seriously by gardaí and possible motives for it were investigated. The solicitor was given security advice.

Meanwhile, the wheels of justice were continuing in motion against Hassan. In March 2006, he appeared at Naas Circuit Criminal Court for his role in the stolen car scam along with three other men from the Lebanon and Syria. Detectives believe cars and motorbikes totalling up to €3 million in value were stolen and exported before the ring was broken up. At the end of his trial, Hassan lied to the court. He said he was the sole custodian of his two sons and the children would be forced into care if he was jailed. Gardaí were appalled by Hassan's attempt to mislead the court. They contacted John Hennessy and asked if he would come down to the court and explain the truth to the judge. The solicitor was happy to do so, despite the arson attack on his home only a couple of weeks previously. He told Judge Alice Doyle that he represented Baiba Saulite and she was the sole guardian of the couple's two sons. His evidence was accepted by the judge, who was furious that Hassan had tried to manipulate the court. She jailed him for four years. Hennessy's appearance in court to give evidence contradicting Hassan's description of family life intensified the Lebanese criminal's hatred towards the solicitor. A senior detective present in court that day said the look on Hassan's face while the solicitor set the record straight went from shock to palpable anger. In Hassan's mind, the solicitor was responsible for all his problems. The criminal wanted him dead.

Seven months passed without incident. Hassan was serving his prison sentence and Baiba was trying to get back to a regular routine with her sons. Life went on as normal for John Hennessy too until gardaí from Swords called to see him on 11 October 2006. They had some disturbing news. A plot to murder the solicitor had been planned by Hassan in prison. He already had extensive links with criminals in Dublin before he was imprisoned and his ties with the McCarthy-Dundon crime gang in Limerick strengthened during his incarceration. Detectives from the Crime and Security branch received intelligence that Hassan, with the assistance of imprisoned Limerick criminal John Dundon, had enlisted a Moroccan asylum seeker to shoot John Hennessy dead. But the Moroccan man was arrested about an immigration matter, thwarting the planned attempt on the solicitor's life. This was a very serious development. The solicitor was kept under armed surveillance for the next two weeks until detectives were satisfied his life was no longer in immediate danger.

Things weren't much better for Baiba. Despite the fact that Hassan was behind bars, he continued to try and threaten and intimidate her. After she split from her husband, she soon became aware of the extent of criminality that he was involved in. A couple of weeks after gardaí became aware that Hassan had ordered the murder of John Hennessy, Baiba's car was set on fire outside her home in Swords. She told her friends she was scared of her estranged husband and asked their advice on what to do.

Gardaí believed John Hennessy was the object of Hassan's obsession for revenge, not the mother of his two sons. She was given security advice, but detectives did not uncover any threat to her life until it was too late. An internal garda inquiry is under way to establish whether there was any information that suggested the Latvian mother's life was under direct threat.

After her car was petrol bombed, Baiba's landlord asked her to move out. The landlord didn't want any trouble. She found a suitable two bedroomed townhouse in Holywell Square, Feltrim Road, Swords, for herself and her two sons. Just before 10 pm on Sunday 19 November 2006, Baiba was standing in the front porch of her home having a cigarette and chatting to a friend. Her two boys were asleep in bed upstairs. She may not have noticed the man in the baseball cap and wearing a scarf over his face walking briskly up her road. He turned into her driveway and pulled a 9 mm pistol from his jacket pocket. He quickly fired four shots into her upper body at almost point blank range, the sound of the bullets masked by a silencer. Her friend could do nothing but watch in disbelief as Baiba fell to the ground. She died almost instantly. The gunman jogged from the driveway to the end of the road where he was driven away in a waiting stolen BMW. It was later found burned out in the nearby Birchdale estate.

Within minutes, gardaí descended on the quiet Swords housing estate, their sirens wailing. It wasn't long before 5-year-old Ali and his 3-year-old brother Mohammed were woken up, confused by the commotion. They were prevented from seeing their mother lying dead outside their home. A murder investigation was immediately launched and Hassan became a major focus of garda enquiries.

Soon detectives learned that Hassan initially tried to engage two African men to carry out the assassination. They agreed at first, but eventually changed their minds when the reality of murdering a young mother in cold blood sank in. But this didn't put an end to Hassan's plans to kill the mother of his two sons. It was then that he asked his cellmate and friend John Dundon in Mountjoy if he could be of any assistance. Dundon suggested that Marlo Hyland could organise it. Hassan knew Marlo from their dealings with the stolen cars, but not particularly well. The Hyland and Dundon-McCarthy gangs had formed an alliance two years previously and Baiba's murder was carried out by the Finglas gang as a favour to their Limerick counterparts.

After accepting the contract to murder Baiba, the Dublin gang didn't waste any time making the necessary preparations. Eamon 'The Don' Dunne, one of Hyland's closest associates, arranged the murder. Dunne himself was shot dead in a gangland hit in April 2010. Within three days of Hyland being approached by the Dundons, Dunne arranged for a petty criminal from Finglas to steal a black BMW 520D from a house in Blackrock. He then passed it on to a member of Hyland's gang who fitted it with false registration plates so it could be used as the getaway car without attracting garda attention.

Baiba was placed under surveillance by the gang for about ten days before she was shot dead. The gunman was driven to Swords by a close associate who parked on the Feltrim Road and left the engine running. The gunman got out of the car but was back within two minutes, having completed the job efficiently and effectively. It was a professional gangland hit by criminals who had no qualms about executing a young mother in cold blood. Eamon Dunne and Marlo Hyland had little realisation of the backlash the murder would generate and the pressure it would put on their gang. It's a testament to the organisation and professionalism of the criminals involved that no one has ever been charged in relation to the murder of Baiba Saulite. The pressure on senior detectives to bring those responsible to justice has been immense. 2006 had been a particularly bloody one for gangland murder. Eight months earlier another innocent young woman had been shot dead. Twenty-two-year-old Donna Cleary was shot dead in Coolock at a party when a well-known criminal opened fire at the house when he wasn't allowed in. No one has ever been charged in relation to Donna Cleary's murder. The general public were appalled by the murder of the young Coolock mother and when Baiba's death followed a few months later, this added to a growing sense of discontent among society that criminals were acting with impunity to murder innocent people at will. One month after Baiba was shot dead, Marlo Hyland, who arranged her killing when approached by the McCarthy-Dundon gang, was himself shot dead. Twenty-year-old Anthony Campbell was working fixing a radiator when Marlo's own gang came to execute him. They also shot dead the innocent apprentice plumber. In a strange twist, the suspected gunman and getaway driver in Baiba's murder were also suspected of direct involvement in the murder of Marlo and young Anthony Campbell. Both men are in their forties. One is from Finglas while the other is originally from the north inner city.

Baiba's killing was condemned by then Taoiseach Bertie Ahern in the Dáil, who said that the murder required the government to do everything it could to find the culprits. In the days following her death, the Law Society came out and condemned death threats made against solicitor John Hennessy. In the immediate aftermath of Baiba's murder, Hennessy was put under immediate armed garda protection and it was recommended that he leave the country for a couple of weeks, which he did. To this day, he remains under 24 hour garda protection. There were several late night meetings between senior gardaí and the justice minister of the day, Michael McDowell. The media became captivated by the sensational story and it was Joe Duffy's *Liveline* that best captured the mood of the general public. People phoned in in their thousands in the weeks following Baiba's death to express their utter revulsion over the murder. Joe Duffy said he hadn't seen such public outrage since the assassination of journalist Veronica Guerin on 26 June 1996. It was as if Baiba was every child's mother and Anthony Campbell was every mother's son. Both were innocent victims executed by the same Finglas criminal gang within a month of each other.

No garda resource was spared in trying to track, arrest and convict those responsible for her killing. Leading the investigation was Detective Inspector Walter O'Sullivan, who has since been promoted to the rank of detective superintendent. He held a press conference three days after the murder and appealed directly to the Irish people to help in any way they could. "A young mother was gunned down in the prime of her life, the mother of two children," he told the large group of assembled journalists. "I would appeal to all persons who enjoy life, who love life and all that it has to offer, to come forward. There are no words left to describe this crime." Typically, garda press conferences are sombre affairs and the language used is quite formal. But the circumstances of this particular murder had struck a chord not just with the general public but also with the investigating detectives.

Within a week of Baiba's murder, Hassan made an application to Dublin Circuit Criminal Court for temporary release to attend her funeral and see his sons. Gardaí and the DPP strongly objected to his application and Det. Insp. O'Sullivan was forthright about the reasons why. "I do fear, from information received, that, if released on bail, he will commit further serious offences," he told the court gravely. "These are murder, assault, intimidation and interfering with witnesses."

The packed courtroom was also told that solicitor John Hennessy had been living in constant fear since the murder. "He has fear his life is in danger and that danger is in connection with Hassan Hassan," said Swords sergeant Liam Hughes. "He believes a contract has been put on his life and, in relation to Baiba Saulite, her car was subject to an arson attack. All these events have had a profound effect on Mr Hennessy."

Hassan's counsel insisted that he had maintained a cordial relation with Baiba before her death and she visited him in prison with their two boys. But Gardaí immediately contradicted this claim, much to Hassan's consternation. "Any visits she made to the prison she made under duress," Sgt Hughes responded. Immediately, Hassan jumped to his feet to respond. "He is lying," shouted the 38-year old. "He is giving evidence that is not true." Sgt Hughes added that he had spoken to Baiba the Tuesday before she was shot dead and she had expressed concern about her solicitor's safety as well as the safety of gardaí who pursued Hassan for abducting his children. As a result of what happened since then, Sgt Hughes said he believed John Hennessy and some gardaí were in grave danger. Judge Michael White denied bail. He said the court had a concern that there was a substantial risk that Hassan might leave the jurisdiction with his two children. As he was led back to prison after this court appearance, Hassan shouted to the waiting media that he was innocent of any involvement in Baiba's murder: "I, Hassan Hassan, am being blamed for my wife's murder. I am being framed. I did not kill my wife."

Four weeks later, on 18 December, Hassan was back before the court in front of the same judge to face sentencing for abducting his two sons and sending them to Syria to live with his mother. He had already pleaded guilty to this crime. He apologised for his actions but said he feared Baiba was going to return home to Latvia and he wouldn't see his sons again. The judge said there was no evidence that Baiba intended to leave Ireland with their children. The fact that the boys had clearly not been neglected or suffered cruelty was in Hassan's favour, the judge told him. But the court heard how he had attempted to intimidate his estranged wife to withdraw her complaint to gardaí about the disappearance of her children. These were all serious matters and the abduction was well planned, Judge Michael White told Hassan. He jailed him for a further two years for abducting his two boys.

Five-year-old Ali Alexsandra and 3-year-old Mohammed Rami were taken into the care of the HSE after their mother's murder. A foster family was found for the boys, who received intense psychological counselling to deal with the sudden loss of their mother in such violent circumstances. They stayed in care for several months while it was decided what would be best for them. As their mother was dead and their father in prison, deciding who should take care of the children until Hassan's release from prison was not a straightforward decision.

Thirteen days after she was shot dead, Baiba was laid to rest in an emotional ceremony at the Mesha Kapi Cemetery in Riga. The chief mourners were her parents Raitis and Ilze and her brother Karlis. Over 500 mourners attended in total, among them her solicitor John Hennessy, who came out of hiding to attend the funeral, accompanied by undercover armed gardaí. Baiba's two sons did not attend.

Twelve weeks after his sister's murder, Karlis Saulite travelled to Ireland to visit his two nephews and speak to gardaí about how the murder investigation was progressing. He wanted the boys to live with him and his partner Jurita in Latvia, at least until Hassan was released from prison. But Hassan's sister Rawaa, who was then living in Dublin, also wanted custody. While he was in Ireland, Karlis went to visit Hassan in prison. He journeyed to Ireland on behalf of his entire family. His mother Ilze fell into a deep depression after her daughter's death and could not travel. Her husband Raitis wanted to stay by his wife's side. So, on behalf of the family, Karlis came to Dublin to try and figure out what would become of his two nephews and try and learn more about why his sister was gunned down. "Every time I look at pictures of the children, I want to cry, I feel so sad," he told the *Sunday Tribune* in an extensive interview shortly after his return to Latvia after visiting Dublin. "They were the main reason for my visit to Ireland. I wanted to see them, and to find out what is happening to them." The children were old enough to understand that their lives had been thrown into utter chaos. They knew that their mother was dead and their father was in prison. Ali Alexsandra and Mohammed Rami had to deal with their grief in a house full of strangers rather than with their family.

Karlis and the rest of the Saulite family desperately wanted to take the boys back to Latvia. "The social workers in Ireland have helped as much as they can, and I think they really are doing their best to help the children," said Karlis. "But it's nearly three months and they're living with people who are not related to them and who cannot give them real love even if they tried. And at that age, the children really need love. Especially because Baiba was such a caring mother. Now they're just searching for something to remind them of her; they're searching for that love. It was such a tragic situation. Even though the children are very small, they know what has happened. We try to laugh and we try to smile all the time, but you can still see in their eyes that they are very sad."

During his visit, he took the boys out to lunch. There was a family sitting at the table next to them. "Baiba's children looked at that family with such eyes, as if it was a miracle to see a father and mother and children together," he said. "I have seen a lot of things in my life, but what the children are going through now, and what they are feeling, you can understand that only when you see them."

Karlis also visited Hassan in prison to discuss who should care for the boys. "We wanted to talk about the children, and I asked him if we could take them to Latvia until he is free. He told us he wouldn't like it," he said. "I don't understand the position of Hassan. We are connected by blood to these children. It has to be all about them now. They are small human beings who need love. Children are not animals. They need a family to live with."

Karlis also met with gardaí investigating his sister's murder. He said the family were frustrated by the lack of progress three months on from her murder but understood that it was a complicated investigation. He felt strongly that if she had been shot dead in Latvia those responsible for her murder would have been brought to justice within weeks. "You live in a democracy that gives more rights to criminals—it gives me pain just to think about it," he continued. "My father is doing all right, but my mother is very bad. She is on drugs for depression. She is weak now, and has big problems with her health. Baiba was her only daughter. They haven't been to Ireland yet to visit the children. My mother still cannot gather herself to make the trip."

Adding to the family's grief was the widescale speculation that

Hassan was involved in Baiba's murder. Karlis decided to ask Hassan directly if he arranged to have his only sister shot dead. "He said that he was not guilty. Do I believe him?" asked Karlis. "I may believe what I want. Right now the question is not about Baiba, because we cannot bring her back. Now we have to focus on the children. That is what she would have wanted." Only a couple of more months passed before the Saulites learned the fate of the two young boys. The decision was not in their favour and they were bitterly disappointed. As the children's father, Hassan had a say in what would be best for his sons. He told the authorities he wanted them to live with his sister in Dublin so that they could be brought to visit him regularly until his release. The boys were placed in the care of Rawaa and her husband Ahmed Elsayed.

Hassan's relationship with his sister was strained at times, to put it mildly. He was charged with threatening to kill her at her home in 2005. But the trial collapsed in April 2007, when Rawaa retracted much of her complaint against her brother, and her husband Ahmed Elsayed and teenage daughter failed to appear in court to give evidence against the criminal. Hassan struck fear into the hearts of everyone he came in contact with, including his own relatives.

His trial for threatening to kill his sister was heard on 26 April 2007 in front of Judge Frank O'Donnell at Dublin Circuit Criminal Court. The judge directed the jury to find him not guilty because the two key witnesses failed to show up. In his statement to gardaí, Rawaa's husband claimed that he heard Hassan tell his wife he would strangle her, while her 15-year-old daughter stated that she called gardaí after hearing her mother crying. In her garda statement after the row with her brother, she told gardaí Hassan said to her: "I kill you. You don't know what time I kill you." But at his trial, Rawaa changed her evidence, claiming what she had told officers about his threat to kill her was untrue. Clearly, something had changed in the two years since Rawaa told gardaí about her brother's threat. One major event was the murder of Baiba. Suddenly Hassan's sister was no longer willing to stand over her complaint against her criminal brother.

When questioned in court, she rejected a suggestion that she refused to give evidence against him because she had resolved her differences with him or was afraid of her brother. She admitted that he had pointed his finger at her and said: "I swear to God I will beat you," when she refused to give him a video of his children. But this was something that people in her country would often say but did not mean literally, she told the court.

But despite their obviously turbulent relationship, Rawaa agreed to take care of her brother's two sons. She loved the two little boys and they became part of her family until her brother was released from prison in March 2010. Ahead of her brother's release, Rawaa and her family moved back to the Lebanon to be closer to their extended family. After his release from prison, Hassan was reunited with his sons in neighbouring Syria, where he was living at the time of publication. Hassan is an Irish citizen, as are his sons, and they can all return to Ireland at any stage if they wish.

Hassan was interviewed in prison on several occasions by detectives investigating Baiba's murder. He repeatedly denied any involvement. Over 20 people were arrested in total during the wide-spanning investigation, but no one has been charged. Senior gardaí have questioned the suspected gunman, getaway driver, the man who is thought to have collected the stolen car and the young thief who stole it from Blackrock. They also arrested members of the Finglas gang that gardaí believe arranged the logistics of the murder as well as those they suspect disposed of the firearm. Many of those arrested are hardened criminals and did not co-operate in custody.

Detectives sent an extensive file to the DPP in late 2007 detailing the evidence gathered and were confident this would result in a charge against Hassan for conspiring to murder his estranged wife. Gardaí also sought charges against the suspected gunman and getaway driver from Marlo Hyland's gang, although the evidence against these two men was not as robust. The evidence against Hassan was largely circumstantial. Detectives interviewed the two North African men Hassan initially arranged to shoot Baiba. They admitted following the young woman and taking surveillance shots of her which were then sent to Hassan's camera phone in prison. Gardaí also had a statement from a foreign national who told detectives he overheard Hassan saying he wanted to kill his wife and her solicitor John Hennessy in a courtroom in 2006.

But the DPP decided in early 2010 that the evidence against the Lebanese national wasn't strong enough. To bring a charge of conspiracy to murder is an unusual and difficult one to prove and the evidence simply wasn't sufficient, gardaí were informed. Detectives were stunned. The DPP's office had approached them with minor queries in relation to the investigation and got them to recheck certain details several times over the previous two years. On a few occasions in 2009, gardaí were confident that the DPP would make the direction to charge Hassan. That the DPP considered the file for so long did not concern gardaí. If anything, it gave them optimism that he wanted to make sure the case against Hassan was airtight before making his direction.

The decision not to charge Hassan with ordering Baiba's murder devastated many of the officers involved in the extensive enquiry. Technically the case remains open as it is unsolved. But in reality, the investigation into one of the country's most callous murders has ended. One senior garda involved in the murder probe, who spoke on condition of anonymity, summed up best the frustration felt by the officers: "Hassan has got his wish. He now has their two children because he got her out of the way. That's what he wanted. He has got away with this."

In Latvia, Baiba's family feel utterly let down by the Irish system. But what has been most heartbreaking for them is that they have lost touch with Baiba's sons, Ali and Mohammed. Hassan and his family have not been forthcoming in maintaining contact with Baiba's family, despite efforts made by the Saulites. They have now resigned themselves to the fact that they may never see the boys again.

As Baiba's sons grow up, they will eventually become aware that gardaí investigating their mother's murder suspected their father of ordering her killing. How they deal with such devastating information remains to be seen. As Ali is two years older than his brother Mohammed, his memories of his mother will be more vivid. Yet memories fade. But the motherly and protective love Baiba felt for her two sons before her murder can never be taken away. The anger felt by the Saulites in Latvia over no one being brought to justice for her death also seems unlikely to dissipate. When contacted, Karlis Saulite no longer wanted to discuss in detail the tragedy that has befallen his family. His anger is palpable. "Gardaí and prosecutor's office know all particular details of what happened. If the prosecutor's office is to arbitrate in this way [decide not to prosecute], for sure make conclusions in what [type of] country are you living."

17 | MANUELA RIEDO

The young French student knows she had a lucky escape. But to describe her as fortunate seems wholly inappropriate. "I am surprised that I am still alive. Why was I let go? Why am I still breathing?" she asked in her victim impact statement. But there are no answers. In August 2007, the 21-year-old French woman was raped by Galway man Gerald Barry. Seven weeks later, he would strike again, this time sexually assaulting and murdering 17-year-old Swiss student Manuela Riedo.

Like Manuela, the French student was walking home alone in an isolated part of the outskirts of Galway city when 27-year-old Barry preyed upon her. "Do what I want and I won't kill you. I just want to shag you," he whispered in her ear after he crept up behind her, grabbed her by the hair and held a knife to her throat. He dragged her to St James's GAA pitch on Walter Macken Road. He continuously threatened to kill her if she turned to look at him. She told him she was a virgin and pleaded with him to let her go. But he had no intention of releasing her. Instead, he began to pull at her clothes and touch her body. "He asked me if I liked it. I said, 'No.' He said, 'You will like it.'" He forced her to her knees and then anally raped her. She felt like it would never end. He continued to threaten her, saying: "I know where you are living. If you go to the police I will kill you." As he raped her, he continued to talk to her. "You're a nice girl . . . I have the power over you."

Halfway through the ordeal, he told his victim that if she gave him oral sex one more time he would let her go. But afterwards, he refused. Instead he ordered her to take off her clothes and anally raped her twice more. After the final rape, he noticed that the woman was cut. This pleased him. "Hey," he exclaimed. "You are bleeding. Great!"

He eventually let her go, all the while threatening to kill her if she told anyone. The 21-year old was studying at NUI Galway and working as a part-time waitress at the time. She had been on the way home after enjoying a night out with friends listening to traditional music when her path crossed Barry's. She stumbled home, showered and tried to sleep. The next day, she went to the hospital but had to write down on a piece of paper that she was raped. She was too traumatised to speak the words. The memory of Barry still fresh in her mind, she was initially too terrified to speak to gardaí but eventually gave them a full statement. "He is not a human or a man. He is a liar, a rapist and a murderer. I beg you not to let him out because he will do it again," she told detectives. "How can he sleep at night, be living, breathing, walking, laughing, and listening to music?"

The woman did not return to Ireland for Gerald Barry's sentencing after he pleaded guilty to orally and anally raping her. She never wants to set foot in Ireland again. In March 2009, Barry, of Rosan Glas, Rahoon, was sentenced to life in prison after he was convicted of the murder of Manuela Riedo. Four months later in July 2009, Barry was handed down two more life sentences for orally and anally raping the French student, the maximum that could be imposed by Justice Paul Carney. He was in custody in Castlerea Prison awaiting his murder trial when DNA samples confirmed that semen found on the French victim's underwear matched his. "From the accused's previous records, I believe he is a person who has the propensity to kill and rape and is highly likely to do so again," the judge told the Central Criminal Court in Galway. There was no "tunnel of hope" for Barry, the judge added.

After he raped the French woman, Barry went to the home of

his ex-partner and physically attacked her. It was not the first time he had assaulted her. Gardaí were well aware that she was terrified of the father of her child; she had complained that he regularly beat her over the course of their tumultuous relationship and she had obtained a court protection order. In 2005, he broke into her home one night and sexually assaulted her. He was later convicted of sexual assault and received an 18 month sentence.

On the night he attacked her in 2007, his ex-partner immediately contacted gardaí and was able to provide a description of what he was wearing that night, a white hoodie and a baseball cap. This matched the description the French woman gave of the man who repeatedly raped her. Two days later, Gerald Barry was arrested. He was questioned about the rape, but refused to participate in an identity parade and also refused to give a blood sample. But he did allow gardaí to take a DNA sample from his mouth. He was held in custody and the following day appeared at the Galway District Court charged with the attack on his former partner. Gardaí objected strongly to bail. He was a suspect in the rape of the French woman although they didn't yet have forensic evidence linking him to the crime. But bail was granted despite the express concerns of gardaí. Detectives were still investigating the rape of the French student when Barry struck again seven weeks later, murdering Manuela Riedo. Had the court acted in accordance with garda recommendations and not granted Barry bail for the assault on his partner, the Swiss student would never have crossed paths with Gerald Barry.

The 17-year old arrived in Galway on 5 October 2007 from her native Switzerland. It was her first trip abroad without her parents, Hans-Peter and Arlette. She was an only child and the apple of their eye. She was part of a group of 43 pupils and two teachers taking part in an English language course in Galway. She was staying with the Tierney family in Renmore. Her trip was due to last two weeks and the course was to help improve her English ahead of going to college. She had applied for a hotel management course in San Diego. Two days after her body was found, the teenager received a letter from the US college informing her she had earned a place.

On Monday 8 October, she walked to class along an isolated pathway known as The Line, a shortcut along a railway line that links Renmore to the city centre. Her host Martin Tierney had warned her not to take this shortcut into town. It was badly lit and people walking this path had been victims of petty crime. But later that night, Manuela again took this route. She was probably encouraged by the fact that she had already walked along this pathway on a few occasions with friends. She probably felt safe because she knew the route. The 17-year old had no idea what she was about to encounter.

She had arranged to meet some friends at 9 pm in the King's Head in the city centre, one of Galway's most popular pubs. But she never arrived. Her friend Azaria Maurer sent her a text just before 9 pm. "Where are you—are you not coming to the King's Head?" it read. The next morning, she noticed her friend was not in class. She tried to phone her mobile, but the automated voice told her the phone was no longer in use. She thought this was very strange.

That morning, Manuela's partially clothed body was found on wasteground along the shortcut between Renmore and Galway city by local artist Sam Beardon, who was out walking his dog. She was naked from the waist down, partially covered by her coat, which was secured by a rock. Her clothes were scattered in the bushes. She had been strangled to death.

The brutal murder of the young tourist in Galway sent shockwaves through the local community. Given his criminal background including a conviction for sexual assault, Gerald Barry became an immediate suspect. It didn't take detectives long to establish through mobile phone records that he was in the vicinity where the teenager was murdered. Nine days after her body was found, Barry was arrested in relation to her murder. He denied having anything to do with her death. He said he had woken up at 3 pm on the day in question, had driven around with his brother and friend and went to Salthill. He insisted he hadn't gone into Galway city that day. "Neither did I walk along the railway line to Renmore," he told gardaí. "It's three weeks since I used it to get to my mother's house."

But gardaí had found a condom snagged in a bush at the scene of the killing. A DNA profile extracted from the contents of the condom matched Barry's. A mixed DNA profile was found on the outside of the condom, containing DNA from both Barry and Manuela. But still he denied being anywhere near where her body was found. In court, Barry would dramatically change his evidence and admit that he lied to gardaí. He would claim he killed Manuela accidentally after consensual sex. Her parents were forced to listen to Barry's fictitious account of what happened before it was rejected as further lies by the jury. On 19 October, the day after his arrest, 27-year-old Barry was charged with the murder of the Swiss student at a special sitting of Galway District Court.

As he was led into court, he displayed his aggression by lunging at photographers. Barry was jeered and booed by a large group of spectators who had gathered. It is rare, but not unheard of in Ireland, for groups of people to gather and taunt a person accused of a serious crime as they are led into court. These spur-of-the-moment expressions of mob anger are usually reserved for those accused of particularly heinous crimes. The people of Galway were appalled and disgusted by the murder of the young tourist in their midst. Barry was still innocent of the crime in the eyes of the law, but some locals seemed incapable of refraining themselves from directing their revulsion towards him.

Inside the courtroom, Barry remained agitated and was flanked by several gardaí. During the brief hearing, he listened with his head bowed as Det. Sgt Brendan Carroll gave evidence of arresting him and he shook his head after being charged with murder. He was remanded in custody. He could not apply for bail at the District Court and at later court sittings no applications for bail were made. Barry was then led out a side entrance to a waiting garda car and driven away under heavy escort. The crowd of about 100 spectators outside noticed he was being spirited away and some made a rush towards the unmarked car. But up to 30 gardaí surrounded the vehicle and held the people back as they tried to thump the car with their fists as it drove away. People then broke out into spontaneous applause for gardaí, pleased that the man detectives believed was responsible for the murder was in custody. Seventeen months later, Barry stood trial for the murder of Manuela Riedo. Physically, he cut a very different figure to the skinny man charged with her murder. He had gained considerable weight as a result of antipsychotic medications he was prescribed in custody.

While the murder of Manuela and the rape of the French woman were by far his most heinous crimes, Barry had long before accumulated an almost unbelievable criminal record. It took Detective Superintendent PJ Durkin 20 minutes to read his list of previous convictions after he was found guilty of Manuela's murder. He was just 16 when it became apparent he was developing into a serious criminal.

One of nine children born in Mervue, a suburb of Galway city, Barry came from a highly dysfunctional family. As a child he witnessed sexual abuse in the family home and was regularly beaten. His mother suffered from mental health problems and spent much of his childhood in institutional care. She was also an alcoholic. After years in an unhappy marriage, his parents eventually separated. The family were notorious in the area for causing trouble. His father, a trucker, ruled the house with an iron fist, but the children still ran wild. The family kept mice and gaping holes were made linking every room in the house so the pets could roam around the inner walls in the house. "They were a notorious family. People in the neighbourhood were terrified of them. Gerald was known to be vicious even as a young boy in school," says a local source that knows the family, who asked to remain anonymous. "Gardaí were in and out of the house. They knew about the problems, but in those days it wasn't *en vogue* to get social workers involved. That's changed now of course. When we heard he was arrested for the murder of Manuela, we weren't surprised one bit. His crimes are indicative of his upbringing. People have been blaming the courts for granting him bail. He shouldn't have got it. But he also probably should have been taken into care as a young child."

As a youngster, Barry got into continuous minor scuffles with the law. But in the summer of 1996, at just 16 years of age, he was part of a gang of four who set upon a stag party in Galway's Eyre Square, resulting in the death of 26-year-old Colm Phelan from

Tipperary, who died after being struck on the head with a bottle. Phelan was waiting for a taxi with friends in Eyre Square when Barry and his friends attacked them. The rest of the gang pleaded guilty to violent disorder, but Barry—in what would become his trademark fashion of denial—insisted that he was innocent. He was jailed for five years for his role in the killing. It was a random, senseless attack, the type of violence that Barry would soon become renowned for.

Spells in teenage remand centres such as Trinity House and St Patrick's Institution failed to rehabilitate his violent streak. Convictions for theft, public order and burglary, as well as a string of drug and road traffic offences followed. In 1998, he again showed what he was capable of when he was jailed for two years for viciously assaulting an elderly man during a break-in at his home. The pensioner was blinded by Barry in the ruthless assault. In between his prison stretches, Barry started a relationship with a local woman with whom he has a child. She lived in a state of terror because of the violence he inflicted on her, and their relationship soon deteriorated. He sexually assaulted her in 2005, leading to an 18 month prison sentence and he was also placed on the sex offenders' register. He also had a second child with another local woman. Long before his callous murder of the Swiss student, Gerald Barry had irrevocably damaged the lives of his many victims. He seemed hell-bent on a path of destruction.

In accordance with the law, the jury knew nothing of Barry's criminal past when he stood trial for the murder of Manuela Riedo. His trial lasted just seven days. The DNA evidence from the condom in itself was damning. The court was told that the chances of a person unrelated to Barry having the same profile would be one in a thousand million. Mobile phone evidence also put Barry close to the murder scene at the time of the killing—it was proven that a phone mast in the immediate vicinity of the murder scene routed his calls and texts. The evidence against him was insurmountable, so he changed his story. He admitted playing a part in her death but claimed he killed her accidentally. His claim that the sex he had with the 17-year old had been consensual deeply injured Manuela's parents, present for the entirety of the trial. Barry said he bumped into the teenager near a shop in Renmore at 7 pm on the night of her death. The pair got chatting and he offered to show her a shortcut into the city. After he showed her the way, he thought she left and he was alone, he said. He then sat on a telegraph pole and began skinning a joint. But she came back. "She sat down on the other side of the pole and asked me why I was smoking that. I told her cos I liked the buzz of it. It relaxes me. I asked her if she wanted to smoke it. She said no," he quietly told the hushed courtroom. They continued to chat easily, he said, and then he kissed her. "I told her I thought she was beautiful and I leaned in and kissed her. She kissed me back. We were kissing and fondling and a few minutes later I suggested we lie down on the grass. I put my jacket down and she put her jacket down," he said. "I suggested we have sex. She asked if I had a condom. I said I did." Afterwards, he said they lay together on the grass and then she tried to get up, saying she had to go and meet her friends. "I sat up behind her and grabbed her from behind. I told her not to go, to stay with me for a while longer. I made a joke. I told her she could even tell them about me," he said. But Barry said the teenager didn't respond. "I kind of sat up and took my arm away. She kind of slid . . . on to the ground. Her head kind of flopped. I shook her and got no response." In shock, he said he then pulled her body to where it was found the following day. Asked why he lied to gardaí in the days following the killing, he said: "Because I thought if I kept denying it, it'd go away."

His story sounded hollow to all who heard it in the courtroom that afternoon. It also didn't bear up to any scrutiny. Firstly, Manuela did not need to ask him for directions into town. She had taken the same shortcut earlier that day and on other occasions since her arrival. The idea that the 17-year-old teenager would agree to have sex with Gerald Barry on isolated wasteground just minutes after meeting him also sounded dubious.

Under cross-examination, Barry was asked about an unusual injury to the teenager's groin area. A piece of skin had been removed using a sharp object after she died, the post-mortem found. Barry insisted he did not inflict that injury. "I'm suggesting that you attacked and murdered her," prosecuting counsel Isobel Kennedy told him. "It was an accident. I didn't mean to cause her any harm," he replied. When her body was found, some of the buttons from Manuela's coat were missing and one was found on the walkway near by, behind a wall. The threads on the coat appeared to have been pulled. "Could it be explained that you met her on that walkway and dragged her in over that wall?" Kennedy asked. "No, that's not what happened," insisted Barry. He was then asked if he knew anything about a laceration to the back of Manuela's head. "I don't know, unless it happened when her head flopped."

Arlette and Hans-Peter sat and quietly listened to all the evidence, holding hands at particularly difficult moments. Hans-Peter broke down in tears as he heard details of the horrific injuries his daughter suffered. His wife hugged him close. Manuela had been strangled and a patch of skin two inches by three had been removed from her groin area. Markings around the wound indicated that she was cut with a knife. The state pathologist Marie Cassidy told the court that death was due to asphyxiation. Barry had pressed down so hard on her neck that the thin gold chain she wore with two small gold crosses had left a lasting imprint on her skin. Barry put pressure on her neck using his forearm, overpowering her. She had four separate injuries to her head, most likely the result of being punched. There were no injuries to suggest a struggle. It would have all been over very quickly. When he was sure she was dead, Barry rifled through her belongings, stealing her camera and mobile phone.

Photographs taken from the memory card of her camera show a smiling Manuela enjoying her holiday in Ireland. In one, she is standing beside her friend Azaria Maurer outside a traditional Irish pub. A photograph taken by Manuela on the day she died shows the Galway classroom she spent most of her time in. She did not usually walk the path where she was murdered alone. On most other mornings and evenings she met Azaria Maurer at the barracks in Renmore and the pair walked together. But on the evening of her murder she had arranged to meet her friend at the pub rather than at the barracks in Renmore, as she was having her evening meal at a different time to her friend.

When he was arrested by gardaí, Gerald Barry denied being near Galway city that evening. He said he had been driving around with his brother Kevin Barry and his brother-in-law Dennis Ward for most of the evening. They had gone back to Dennis Ward's house and watched 'Banged Up Abroad' on TV, he said. After eating some dinner he said he got a lift back to his sister's apartment, where he was living, and was in bed by around 11.30 pm.

His brother and brother-in-law gave evidence that they spent time with Barry on the night of the murder, but said they didn't meet until after 8 pm. Dennis Ward picked him up in his car outside Supermac's at the bottom of Shop Street after Barry rang him. At that stage, Manuela Riedo was already dead. Dennis Ward said his brother-in-law didn't seem worried or out of sorts that evening. His brother said he was wearing a red jacket and carrying a plastic bag when they met him outside Supermac's. CCTV footage showed a man walking from Mainguard St towards the junction of Cross St and Bridge St at 8.27 pm that night wearing a red jacket, a black cap and a black T-shirt, and was carrying a plastic bag. That man was Gerald Barry, walking to meet his brother and brother-in-law after he murdered Manuela Riedo. When asked in garda custody if it was him in the CCTV, he replied: "No, no, he's taller than me. I've never owned a red jacket or a baseball cap."

Gardaí searched the house where Barry was living with his sister at Rosan Glas in Rahoon and found Manuela's Olympus digital camera under his bed. She had received it as a gift from her uncle. Barry lied about it when he was arrested, saying he had no idea how it had ended up in his bedroom. "I never saw that camera in my life. It's the first time I've ever seen one of those cameras to be honest, only ones I've seen are disposable . . . I never seen a camera in the bedroom," he told detectives. But later, he admitted to stealing her camera and mobile phone. The day before he was arrested, he sold Manuela's Sony Ericsson phone to his sister's boyfriend, Mark Kealy, for €30. He deleted some numbers from the phone before handing it over, but there were still some text messages written in German in the memory.

Manuela had bought the phone a week before she came to Ireland.

In his charge to the jury of six men and six women before they were sent out to consider the verdict, Judge Barry White told them to use their common sense in assessing the evidence. Prosecution counsel pointed out that Barry had told various lies to gardaí about his involvement in her killing. "He lied because he killed Ms Riedo and that he intended to kill her," Isobel Kennedy told the court. "He says in his evidence that it was all an accident, that he didn't mean it, but I suggest to you that on the evidence of Professor Cassidy that Ms Riedo was held in an armlock from behind giving rise to neck compression and definite signs of asphyxiation." Barry's defence counsel urged the jury to find him guilty of manslaughter, not murder. He described his client as "an extremely incompetent person".

The jury took just two hours and 38 minutes to find Gerald Barry guilty of murder, having retired overnight. They also found him guilty of stealing Manuela Riedo's camera and her phone. He didn't flinch as the foreman of the jury announced the verdict. Along with handing down a mandatory life sentence, Justice Barry White gave Barry two five year sentences to run concurrently for the theft of the teenager's camera and mobile phone.

Neither did Barry show any emotion when a translation of Manuela's father Hans-Peter's victim impact statement was read out in court. The statement directly addressed their daughter's murderer. "You really can't put into words what the death of our beloved daughter Manuela has taken from us. You have robbed Manuela of 60 or 70 years of her life and taken the future away from us, her parents," he told Barry. "I will never lead my daughter as a bride to the altar, and my wife will never knit baby clothes for a grandchild, and we won't have anyone to look after us when we are old."

He told the court how the couple had always been very protective of their only child. "Manuela was the centre of our lives and our sunshine. We always looked out for Manuela very carefully. As her father, I often drove out with the car at night to pick her up so that she would arrive safely back home. No way was too long for me to bring her back. Her trip to Ireland was her first trip without us parents. Manuela would have soon turned 18 and we wanted to gradually let her discover the world on her own," he explained. "We had heard only good things about Ireland and thus we had no misgivings about sending her to this beautiful country. Before she left, she said that she hoped to get through the two weeks without feeling homesick and that the trip would be a test for future long trips."

While Ireland will forever be tainted in their minds because of the loss of their daughter, he ended by saying he did not hold the people of Ireland responsible for the actions of one man. "We have lost our angel but we have gotten to know many fine people now."

Manuela grew up in the village of Hinterkappelen about 10 km from the Swiss capital Berne. Her final resting place is marked by a brown cross on a hilltop overlooking Lake Wohlen. A headstone bearing a Claddagh ring emblem marks the spot. Her grave stands opposite where her parents were married. Every day, they go to her graveside to light a candle and say a prayer.

Arlette and Hans-Peter have been overwhelmed by the support and kindness from the people of Ireland since their daughter's murder. They have received hundreds of letters of support and condolence from people in Ireland, and the messages of solidarity continue to come. After Gerald Barry was found guilty, Justice Barry White asked the couple to find it in their hearts to forgive the Irish people. But the Riedos say there is nothing to forgive.

Instead, they have tried to channel their sense of loss into something positive. The Manuela Riedo Foundation aims to raise awareness among teenagers of the dangers of rape and sexual assault, while also providing support for the victims and their families across Europe. It was established by Irish publican Brendan McGuinness, who lives in Basel in Switzerland, shortly after the teenager's death and has the support of Arlette and Hans-Peter. The Riedos have since had a public row with McGuinness over money raised at his pub. He is no longer associated with the foundation.

At the launch of the Manuela Riedo Foundation in Basel, her

parents spoke about how they can never forgive their daughter's murderer and their hopes that he is never released from prison. Just because Barry was raised in a dysfunctional family, this does not excuse his behaviour, said Manuela's father. "My father also had a bad childhood, but he never became a criminal or a murderer. There is no excuse and there is no understanding," he told those gathered to launch the foundation in April 2009. "After 10 or 15 convictions, you cannot rehabilitate, you cannot make them better. When he [Barry] came out of jail he could have made a better life for himself, but he chose the bad way and it led to the death of Manuela."

Several fundraisers in Switzerland and Ireland have been held to raise money for the foundation. In October 2009, Manuela's parents returned to Galway to mark the second anniversary of their daughter's death and attend a fundraising concert. A few months later, the Manuela Riedo Foundation donated €50,000 to supporting rape victims and increasing safety awareness in Galway. They said it was their wish that the money would stay in the Galway area. They thanked the people of Galway in an emotional statement for the warmth and support they had shown them each time they returned. "On 2 October, while walking with our rose bouquet along the railway line towards Renmore, something wonderful happened," the couple recalled. "We met lots of people who wanted to accompany us to the church. Afterwards, we walked along Lough Atalia towards the place where the tragic event occurred. There were people at every crossroads who wanted to walk with us for support." Manuela's parents had initially wanted to make the journey alone but found it helped them when they realised that they were not alone. "At the same time it was very sad. Why was Manuela not so fortunate on 8 October 2007?" they asked. "We look forward every day to returning to Galway, to our new friends and to Manuela."

18 | MARIUSZ SZWAJKOS AND PAWEL KALITE

It was just after 6 pm and Pawel Kalite was hungry. The Polish man had put in a full day's work as a mechanic at Ace Autobody's and afterwards decided to walk the short distance from his home to the Drimnagh Takeaway. It was your typical Saturday in the busy south Dublin suburb that winter's evening in February 2008. Little did Pawel know but his innocuous excursion for food would end with the violent murder of both him and his housemate.

Within an hour of heading off to the chipper, 29-year-old Pawel and his friend and fellow countryman Mariusz Szwajkos (29) would be stabbed with a screwdriver through the head by 17-year-old David Curran. With lethal precision, the out-of-control teenager murdered the two Polish mechanics in a ruthless attack that astounded the country. The general public's sense of outrage over the killings intensified when it emerged that some of the group of teenagers involved in racially taunting the two men before their murder were children.

The Drimnagh Takeaway was doing its usual brisk trade as evening was setting in on Saturday 23 February 2008. A few cars were parked outside as people went in and out to order food. Outside the chipper, a 15-year-old boy in a grey tracksuit was hanging around. He cannot be named for legal reasons. The teenager was asking passers-by for cigarettes and some people would later remark that it seemed that he had some drink taken. Inside the takeaway, two 15-year-old girls, who also cannot be named for legal reasons, were queuing for food. They were carrying bottles of vodka and wine. Pawel arrived at the chipper just after six o'clock and joined the queue. He lived just up the road at 48 Benbulben Road with his best friend Mariusz and two other Polish friends. Both men worked as mechanics and panel-beaters for Ace Autobody's in the nearby Robin Hood Industrial Estate. Pawel and Mariusz both enjoyed the work and were highly regarded by their employer. Pawel was a well-built man. He had been living in Ireland for just over a year. Just a couple of hours before he was murdered, Pawel had been on the phone to his aunt in Poland. He told her how he planned to come home soon and wanted to rent an apartment with his girlfriend, who lived in Poland.

Pawel emerged from the takeaway at 6.25 pm carrying his bag of chips. The 15-year old who was hanging around outside walked towards him. The pair bumped into each other. After the minor collision, the Polish man continued walking, but then suddenly turned back towards the teenager.

There were three men sitting in a Mitsubishi Colt who saw what was beginning to unfold. One of them, Ciaran Poole, saw Pawel put down his chips, take off his hat and approach the teenager, who ran off. "The small man [Pawel] chased the other fella," Ciaran Poole told the Dublin Central Criminal Court during the double murder trial that opened in April 2010. "Then a jeep pulled up outside the butcher's. A man got out and looked like he tried to break up the scuffle." The man was Michael Curran, the 15-year old's uncle and David Curran's father. He grabbed Pawel by the throat and pushed him up against the shutters of the butcher's shop beside the takeaway. He told him he should leave the kid alone. The two 15-year-old girls who had been in the chipper also came outside and got involved in the unfolding row. They knew David Curran and his cousin. The Polish man was then knocked to the ground and was kicked and punched. Tracey Dillon also witnessed what happened. She was going into another shop on the street. "The lad in the grey tracksuit, the two young girls and this older chap were basically killing the bald chap on the ground. They were kicking him," she told the murder trial. It wasn't a serious beating and it soon ended when the landlord of the butcher's came out to see what the commotion was outside his shop. Rory O'Connor helped Pawel to his feet and told the group attacking him: "He's had enough."

That put an end to the matter for the time being. Pawel picked up the bag of chips he had left down when the trouble started, and began to walk home. As he passed by the two teenage girls, one of them hit him hard across the head. Pawel barely reacted. He just continued to walk away. "One of them [teenage girls] gave him a clatter across the face, across the neck. He done nothing," recalled Tracey Dillon. "He just crossed the road."

Michael Curran left in a car and that was the end of his involvement in the incident. But the teenagers remained outside the chipper. Their emotions were running high. One of the teenage girls was crying; the other was angry. David Curran's 15-year-old cousin was agitated and kept saying he wasn't going to let what happened go. While the fight had ended, some people who had witnessed what happened had a sense that that wasn't the end of the matter. There was a palpable sense of tension. Tracey Dillon was concerned enough to get into her car and phone gardaí. So too did butcher Darren Lee, who witnessed what had happened with his landlord Rory O'Connor. But Rory O'Connor couldn't shake the feeling that a dangerous situation was developing and he decided to get into his car and drive after the Polish man to offer him a lift home. "I sensed there was going to be trouble," he said. He was right. But no one could have imagined the extent of the violence that was about to unfold. By the time Rory O'Connor had reached Benbulben Road in his car, Pawel had already gone into his house.

Outside the chipper, one of the teenage girls got out her phone and rang David Curran to tell him what had just happened. Within a few minutes, he materialised along with his friend 19-

year-old Seán Keogh. In his hand, David, whose nickname was Schillaci, was carrying a screwdriver. He had stolen it earlier that day. It was obvious to anyone who saw him that he was totally out of control. He ran up to the Mitsubishi Colt parked outside the chipper and kicked the car. "Was it youse who did it?" he roared. Somebody else said, "It's not them."

Butcher Darren Lee went back inside his shop and rang gardaí again. At this stage, Rory O'Connor was arriving back outside the butcher's shop after failing to locate the Polish man. But when he noticed the group of angry teenagers had grown in number, he decided to park his car further up the road.

Pawel was hurt, angry and upset when he got home. He pushed past his housemate Kamila Szeremeta who was in the garden when he arrived back. She noticed he had a scratch on his forehead. When she asked him what had happened, he said he had been beaten up by some kids. When he got into the hall, Pawel took off his boots and told his housemates Radek Szeremeta, Kamila's brother, and Mariusz what had happened. "I'm almost 30 and those stupid little punks attacked me with a baseball bat," he told them. He felt like killing them, he told them, at this stage in a rage with tears streaming down his face. As he recounted what happened, it seemed to make him more irate. Suddenly, he started to put his boots back on to go back outside. His housemates warned him to stay inside. But they could not stop him. Kamila, who was still outside in the garden, grabbed his hand to try and stop him going any further.

David Curran and his friends' tempers were also rising. The 17-year old wanted to find out where the man who had clashed with his cousin had gone. "They were screaming: 'Where's the bastard? I'm going to kill him. Where's the cunt?'" recalled Tracey Dillon. "I rang the police on my mobile." She got through to an operator and warned that there was going to be a row. "I told them there was going to be killings on Benbulben Road and to get someone up there quick," she said.

But the group of teenagers were quicker than the gardaí, as the chipper was only a few hundred yards from Pawel's house. They began to wander up Benbulben Road, shouting and screaming, looking for Pawel. The group consisted of David Curran, his friend Seán Keogh, the two teenage girls and Curran's 15-year-old cousin. Curran had spent the entire day drinking and taking drugs. He was a young man whose life seemed entirely without direction. The eldest of five children, he had been expelled from school when he was 15 years old. He was already well acquainted with crime, having received two convictions for driving offences. Just three days before he murdered the two men, he was convicted of driving without insurance and a licence. The following day, 21 February 2008, he himself was stabbed in the back during a row. It wasn't a serious wound, but he had had to get stitches in the hospital.

Born on Bloomsday in 1990, David Curran grew up in Lissadel Green in Drimnagh. He came into contact with the law early in his life, ending up in the Children's Court on many occasions. He wasn't involved with the feuding gangs in Drimnagh or nearby Crumlin; he was mostly involved in stealing and break-ins. He often carried a screwdriver. He had also developed a worrying drug habit. In November 2006, he presented at the Ciall Youth Project seeking treatment for addiction. He was put on a 12 week counselling course, but just two months later he was back seeking help as he hadn't been able to kick his habit. In January 2008, he made a third attempt to get clean. While he had been abusing alcohol and cannabis for a long time, he had also started taking a lot of prescription drugs. He was developing an addiction to benzodiazepines, a class of relaxant drugs that included Valium and sleeping tablets. But in the week leading up to the double murder, he again lapsed. The day before he would commit double murder, Curran attended a scheduled appointment at the Ciall Drug Project. But because of his injuries over the stabbing he had sustained, the counsellors decided to reschedule his appointment. He was in no fit physical state and was sent home to rest.

The next morning David Curran got up early. Just after 10 am he went and bought a bottle of vodka. He said he had every intention of getting "off his head". He then went down to the Grand Canal with a group of friends, including Seán Keogh. They spent the day drinking, smoking joints and taking "yellows and blues" tablets, types of benzodiazepines. Despite the fact that it was February, Curran and some of his friends went swimming in the canal. "Just another day down at the canal" is how David Curran described the day of the double murder when he gave evidence at his trial. After spending several hours down at the canal, the group moved on and went to the fields near St Michael's estate in Inchicore. As the afternoon set in, they stole a moped from outside a pub. But when they couldn't get it started and noticed gardaí further up the road, they torched it. But the teenager first removed two bottles of wine and the murder weapon, a black and orange Phillips screwdriver from the moped. Curran was now armed. Not long after this, he got a phone call from one of the 15-year-old girls telling him that his cousin had been in a fight. He had been planning to break into a factory with Seán Keogh but when he heard what happened, the pair immediately set off in the direction of the Drimnagh Takeaway, running down across the Luas tracks at Goldenbridge to get there quicker.

Pawel Kalite and Mariusz Szwajkos had had an entirely different day to that of their young murderer, whose path they were about to cross with devastating consequences. Both had been working at Ace Autobody's on the day they died. Unlike their young killer, both men led full, happy lives working and making plans for the future.

Pawel's parents described their son as an honest, diligent and law-abiding man who lived a simple and peaceful life. All he wanted was to build a better future for himself. That's why he chose to temporarily move to Dublin.

He found a job he enjoyed and was working hard on improving his English, they explained in an emotional victim impact statement to the court, read out after David Curran was found guilty of murder. Though happy here, he was homesick and always planned to return to Poland. Pawel and his girlfriend, Marcela, whom he "dearly, deeply, truly loved", were beginning to talk about marriage and building a future together. He was talking of a move back home that June.

But now all his dreams will remain unrealised, his parents wrote, since a stranger had decided his future without considering him or his best friend Mariusz. "Pawel never hurt anybody in his life. This wasn't his nature. He didn't know how to fight," they said, and wondered, "How much cruelty and anger do you have to have in yourself to take someone else's life away?"

Their only small consolation now lies in knowing that his heart, given in organ donation, still beats on.

Mariusz Szwajkos's sister, Gosia, spoke in her victim impact statement how her brother's death had changed every aspect of her family's life for ever. Gosia has suffered from a fear of phone calls after receiving the terrible news over the phone. Mariusz usually rang his parents every single day from Ireland. "After the funeral I remember my father saying that he lost not only his son but also his very best friend," Gosia said. She wondered how she could explain to her two nephews, Jakub and Nicholas, what had happened to their beloved uncle, 'Mariusz the Mechanic'. "How can you explain such a tragic death without leaving kids with this trauma for the rest of their lives? But I know that despite how difficult it will be, one day I will tell a story of his life to my baby—how smiling, joyful and always willing to help people he was. And we will always love and remember him."

The direction the two Polish mechanics' lives were taking could not have been further removed from David Curran's existence. His seemed to be that of a young man hell-bent on destruction. But nothing could stop their worlds colliding that February evening in 2008.

As Pawel stood in the garden still visibly angry from the altercation at the chipper, David Curran and his friends came into view. They could be heard before they were seen. At this stage, Mariusz was standing at the front door and was trying to get his friend to come back inside. The teenagers were on the opposite side of the road. Kamila, who was still standing in the garden, remembered them shouting: "All Poles are fuckers." She called back to them: "Why?"

But Curran had decided the time for talking was over. He ran across the road towards Kamila and Pawel with the screwdriver gripped firmly in his hand. He lunged at Kamila, his weapon held high above his head. She ducked to avoid the first blow. "He had a tool in his hand and he was going for my head," she recalled. But the screwdriver had found another target. He drove the screwdriver through Pawel Kalite's temple, piercing his skull and damaging beyond repair his brain matter. The Polish man fell heavily to the ground. As he lay there, Seán Keogh, who had joined his friend, kicked him in the face, breaking his teeth. The young man, from Vincent Street West in Inchicore, would later be found not guilty of the double murder but admitted, and was convicted of, assaulting Pawel Kalite.

But David Curran's act of savagery was not finished. Mariusz jumped over the fence in the garden when he saw his friend fall to the ground. Curran swung the implement once more. Again, the screwdriver proved a capable murder weapon. He suffered an almost identical head wound as his friend. His brain and skull were deeply punctured. Kamila watched as her second friend fell to the ground. She cannot seem to expel from her mind the noise he made as he hit the ground: "You could feel it on the pavement."

Tracey Dillon, who had witnessed the first part of the row outside the chipper and called gardaí, was pulling into her driveway when she saw the outcome of what she had feared would happen. She lived just ten houses down from the Polish men. "I seen a body on the ground, on the footpath. I honestly thought to myself they were after getting him," she said. As she pulled into her driveway, she noticed that there was more than one person down. After she parked her car, she walked back. One man was lying on the footpath. The other was lying face down just inside the garden of number 48. "The chap I saw at the chipper was lying face down at the very last step of the garden with his face smashed into the step," she explained. "I thought they were dead." But both men were still clinically alive. Mariusz died two days later in St James's Hospital, Pawel two days later again. Gardaí were *en route* to the scene when David Curran committed his brutal crime. About 90 seconds after he stabbed both men, gardaí arrived at the scene. But Curran and his friends were already gone. "Come on Schillaci [David Curran's nickname], they're dead," a young boy shouted. With that, the group fled.

The 17-year old went home. He had a curry, which he said he threw up immediately after eating it. Then he went to his aunt's house to lie low for several days.

In the immediate aftermath of his crime, David Curran and one of the 15-year-old girls who was involved in the initial row at the chipper, tried to concoct an alibi. They sent each other several text messages that showed how utterly unremorseful they both were for what had happened. The 15-year old also exchanged several texts with Seán Keogh. The teenage girl gave evidence via video link at the murder trial.

The teenage girl texted Curran at about 10.10 pm on the night of the killings when news of the screwdriver deaths became widely known: "Ha I just reading what it says on the news. Ha. Shit xxxx."

He replied: "Ha ha. You're mad."

She wrote back: "Ha ha but like I can't believe it . . . Mad night xxxxx."

David Curran replied: "Fuck it. Delete message. Get a new number tomorrow xxx."

When she asked why, he texted: "If they ask you for your phone number xx."

He later texted her: "Ah fuck it xx."

But the messages took on a different tone after midnight. David Curran texted at 12.13 am: "Did you hear about that in Drimnagh? It's going around I done it cos I got stabbed the other night."

She replied: "No way, is it?"

Curran answered: "Yeah. Fuckin weirdos. Wasn't in Drimnagh all day."

She wrote back: "Yeah I know ha ha. I have a plan but not going to text it."

Gardaí found another text saved in the draft folder of the girl's phone, which she admitted she was going to send to David Curran. It said: "Do you know what I was thinking we could say, that you and me was only . . . babysitting cos you and me are the only ones who don't have an alibi."

She admitted when giving evidence at the murder trial that the texts were an attempt to cover their tracks. "He was just trying to get the two of us out of it." She also admitted that she was the one who had phoned David Curran to tell him his cousin was involved in a fight outside the chipper.

The girl also texted the other accused, Seán Keogh.

Seán Keogh texted her at 10.48 pm, saying: "Ring me." Later he texted again: "The man meant to be dead . . . Tell David Curran to ring me quick."

She replied: "He has no credit."

Later Seán Keogh texted her again: "That's on teletext about other thing. We're fucked."

It didn't take gardaí long to learn of Curran's involvement in the savage assault. When he was first questioned by gardaí four days after the screwdriver stabbings, he denied any involvement in the attack. Over the course of seven interviews with gardaí, Curran eventually tried to blame it entirely on Seán Keogh. He initially claimed he wasn't even with the 19-year old that night and denied they were friends. "No. More of an enemy," he said in his fourth garda interview. Then he changed his story, telling gardaí he was there that night and saw Keogh carry out the crime. "Did you actually see Seán Keogh stab them?" he was asked by gardaí. "Sure did," he replied. "I was standing right beside him. He stuck the screwdriver into his head around the temple area." He told gardaí that he had punched the second Polish man who came out of the house and that Seán Keogh also stabbed this man. "He went straight for Seán for hitting his friend," he added. "Seán stuck the screwdriver in his throat.

Detectives did not believe what Curran was telling them. But he tried to be as convincing as he could, even making up an excuse for why he did not immediately tell the truth. "One, there was a life sentence on my head and two I'd be put down as a rat," he said. "But I'd rather be put down as a rat than a murderer." David Curran's mother accompanied him during one of the interviews, while a youth worker attended all the others, as he was a juvenile

But detectives had enough eye-witness evidence to charge David Curran with the double murder. Seán Keogh was also charged with the same crime. The prosecution's case was that Seán Keogh was involved in the "joint enterprise" of the murders and was therefore equally responsible, even though he did not inflict the screwdriver injuries. By the time the court case came around two years and two months later, Curran had stopped trying to blame his friend and admitted the screwdriver attack on the two men. But he claimed he was provoked. His barrister Giolliaosa Ó Lidheadha said his client admitted causing the fatal injuries but was the subject of a sudden and total loss of control. He said the blows were inflicted in circumstances where he was incapable of restraining himself. But his plea of manslaughter was not accepted by the DPP. Both men stood trial in April 2010 at the Dublin Central Criminal Court. The trial lasted three and a half weeks. Seán Keogh admitted to kicking Pawel as he lay injured on the ground. The jury disagreed that he was responsible for the double murder on the basis of joint enterprise and found him not guilty of murder. During the trial, it became clear that the two young men were no longer friends. Keogh was extremely aggrieved that his young friend had lied to gardaí and tried to blame him for stabbing both men to death. Curran also tried to convince gardaí and the jury that he was told by one of the 15-year-old girls that his father had been stabbed during the row at the chipper. This was why he flew into such a rage, he claimed. But the two teenage girls both denied telling him his father had been stabbed. The jury ultimately did not accept that Curran believed his father had suffered stab wounds

It took the jury of eight women and four men almost six hours to reject David Curran's provocation defence and find him guilty of the double murder. The next day, 7 May 2010, the then 19-year-old Curran was jailed for life for the murder of the two mechanics by Justice Liam McKechnie.

The judge did not mince his words when passing two mandatory life sentences on Curran. "From an incident of almost meaningless consequence in which David Curran had no part, he ended up killing, murdering these two people," said the judge.

"There's something profoundly sinister in what he did and how he did it. There were no blows to the arms, legs or torso and there wasn't even an attempt to do so. With lethal accuracy, David Curran aimed at probably the most vulnerable part of the human body, the temple. Then by a single blow, which penetrated the skull, he caused his [Pawel Kalite's] death. There was no possibility of recovery," he said. "That blow wasn't enough. He removed the screwdriver and with the same lethal accuracy, aiming it at the same point and in the same way, he murdered Mariusz."

Justice McKechnie noted the pathologist's evidence that stated it required great force to penetrate a person's skull to such a depth and to remove the screwdriver and repeat the process. "It leaves a chilling and truly disturbing feeling as to what kind of person could do such a thing, brutal and savage, and one could well describe it as sadistic," he added.

The judge also looked unfavourably on David Curran's behaviour after murdering the men. "Within a few hours he set about scheming his way out of it. Phones had to be got rid of; alibis, concoctions abound. Then he tries to lay it off on [Seán] Keogh."

He noted that Curran's immediate reaction was to try and strategise a way to get away with his crime. "Without pause for thought, I unhesitatingly and without any reservation, wholly agreed with the verdict of the jury in relation to David Curran," he said before jailing him for life.

Speaking from Poland after Curran's conviction, Gosia says that her family did not take satisfaction from her brother Mariusz's murderer being jailed for life, because nothing can bring him back. But Gosia, who lived with her brother in Ennis before returning to live in Poland, has many memories of her brother to cherish. She feels lucky to have had her older brother in her life at all, even if it was only for 29 years. "He was not only my brother but also a friend," she explains. "I still have all the sweaters that he gave me. It happened several times. He was in the shop to buy something for himself but ended with the sweater for me and saying, "I saw it and I thought that it will be perfect for you.' He was always thinking about others—not himself. That is the first thing that comes to my mind as I think about him. He was always there for others."

19 | EUGENIA BRATIS

Eugenia Bratis travelled to Ireland from her native Romania in April 2008. The 50-year-old mother-of-two came to Ireland hoping to find a job. She had previously worked as a waitress in her hometown of Timisoara, the second biggest city in Romania. But Eugenia's timing was unfortunate. The Celtic Tiger went into terminal decline in the summer of 2008 and the recession began in earnest. Despite her best efforts, she couldn't secure a job. Fourteen months after she arrived in Dublin, Eugenia's body was discovered in a wooded area off Military Road in the Phoenix Park in August 2009. She had been stabbed to death. Not long before she was killed, the 50-year old fell on hard times and was living rough at the time of her death and begging for money to survive. No one has been charged in relation to her murder, but garda enquiries are now focusing on whether members of the Roma community could have targeted the mother-of-two. Her death has devastated her family in Romania. It was out of love for her children that Eugenia found herself in Ireland and ended up living in such precarious circumstances, which ultimately led to her murder.

Eugenia had two grown-up children in Romania. Her son Laviniu Abrihan was 25 at the time of his mother's death, while his sister Roxana Abrihan was aged 20. Eugenia and her husband divorced in 2007 and one of the reasons she moved to Ireland was possibly linked to the break-up of her marriage. Like many people who come out of a long-term relationship, she wanted a fresh start and new surroundings. Her daughter Roxana was studying and she needed financial support to continue with her college education. Eugenia couldn't find steady work in Timisoara, but she had heard there were plenty of job opportunities in Ireland. After considering her options, she decided to relocate to Dublin. Even though her son and daughter were adults, Eugenia still supported them financially as best she could, a testament to her dedication to her children.

She came to Ireland alone and knew no one living here. She had saved some money and had high hopes she would quickly get a job so that she could start sending money home to her children. Eugenia had been told that Ireland's economy was thriving and there was a lot of money to be made working in the restaurant trade. But the economic landscape of Dublin was changing in the summer of 2008. Tourism was plummeting and jobs in the food and beverage sector became scarce on the ground.

It didn't take long for the grim reality of her circumstances to sink in. Despite her best efforts, Eugenia couldn't find any work. She soon noticed that a lot of Romanians living in the capital were begging to support themselves. Most of her fellow countrymen begging were members of the Roma community. Roma people, also known as Roma gypsies, are travelling people and live in relative squalor and poverty in Ireland and across most of Europe. They mostly live in squats, run-down houses or on the streets and survive mainly on money earned begging. The Roma community have earned a reputation across Europe as skilled pickpockets as well as operating sophisticated begging gangs. Romas are a minority ethnic group and have experienced extreme discrimination in each country they relocate to, including Ireland. The Roma community are the most disadvantaged migrant community in Ireland. They are often unaware of their rights, entitlements and responsibilities and rely on informal information from within their own community which can lead to misinformation, confusion and exclusion.

Eugenia Bratis was not a member of the Roma community. She was one of seven children from a working-class background. She was completely alone in Ireland and was living in various hostels around the city centre. Soon, she began to get to know some of the Roma women begging on the streets of Dublin. It is traditional that Roma men do not beg; only the women and children. Still unable to secure a job, and with little else to do, Eugenia started begging too. She needed the money desperately. At this stage Eugenia had become quite friendly with a number of Roma women. But she did not beg with them. She was not a member of the Roma community so when she took to the streets seeking money from passers-by, she did so alone.

The money she earned begging she sent home to her daughter to help fund her education. In the 14 months she was in Ireland before she was murdered, Eugenia went home just once. In January 2008 she went back to visit her family for a couple weeks, returning to Dublin in February. Six months later, she would be stabbed to death in the Phoenix Park.

Those who beg for a living make in the region of between €10 and €70 each day in Ireland. It is unknown how much Eugenia was making, but it is believed she was not sleeping rough for very long when she was found stabbed to death in August 2009. Her body did not display any of the tell-tale signs that would indicate she had been homeless for a considerable amount of time. It seemed that she mostly stayed in hostels and was also earning enough to send some money home to her family. But sometimes, when she didn't make enough money, she ended up sleeping rough. The Phoenix Park has long been a popular location for homeless people.

At 3.30 pm on the afternoon of 5 August 2009, two women were out walking when they discovered her body. Her remains were in a wooded area off Military Road, between the Phoenix Park's Chapelizod and Islandbridge gates, near the playing fields known as the 15 acres. She had been stabbed eight times in the chest, through her jacket and top. Eugenia's remains were fully clothed and there were no signs of any sexual assault. Detectives believe she was stabbed to death in the spot where her remains were found, most likely in the 24 hour period before the discovery. A post-mortem examination revealed she had died as a result of internal trauma caused by multiple stab wounds to her upper body.

There was no identification on her person so the immediate issue for gardaí was trying to establish who this woman was. Two days after her body was discovered, gardaí took the unusual step of releasing a photograph of the dead woman in the hope that someone would recognise her. Gardaí at Blanchardstown are leading the murder probe, with Superintendent Dave Dowling and Detective Inspector Colm Fox heading the investigation. When no one came forward to report her missing, gardaí began to suspect the dead woman was a foreign national who was not yet missed by her friends and family. A medical examination of her teeth revealed that she had expensive dental work carried out, the type of dentistry that was widespread in south-eastern Europe. As well as a garda photo of the dead woman, detectives also released pictures of the clothes she was wearing when she was found. Eugenia was a small woman, standing at just 4' 10", of medium build, with short brown hair and light brown eyes. She was wearing a grey Marks and Spencer fleece zip-up jacket, a rugby-type top with pink and grey stripes and three-quarter length pink trousers. She was also wearing pink fleece socks and size five Karrimor runners. A white scarf and black zip-up jacket were found near her body, as was a ladies' black bicycle. Her toenails were painted with gold nail varnish. The fact that she was wearing nail polish, as well as the generally good condition of her remains, notwithstanding the stab wounds, suggested to detectives that she had not been homeless for long. She also wore a gold St Anthony-style religious medal tied with a piece of string, a silver Celtic cross necklace and gold Creole-type hooped earrings. All the national newspapers carried the photo of the dead woman. It was a stark image, impossible to ignore. But still no one came forward with information. Who was this mystery woman? A week after her body was found, Crimestoppers offered a €10,000 reward to anyone who could help identify her.

Gardaí also held a press conference the day after the TV appeal to keep the case in the public spotlight. "It could be that she is a non-Irish national living in Ireland for some time. Again this is speculation for the purpose of prompting people's memories. It could have been that she was living in a hostel," Superintendent John Gilligan, of the garda press office, told the assembled media. In relation to the religious and Celtic jewellery she was wearing, he added: "She may have met with nuns and priests and that she was given these items . . . There are people who live on the fringes of society, for whatever reason, and maybe they are not recognisable to someone who has known them in the past."

The nationwide media appeal had the desired effect. Julian Gillespie, an amateur photographer and part-time teacher and tour guide, recognised the woman from taking her photo a few months earlier. He snapped Eugenia Bratis as she sat begging on O'Connell Bridge three months before she was found murdered. Gillespie saw the photograph gardaí issued of the dead woman on television and it immediately reminded him of the photo he had taken three months earlier because of the two distinctive moles on her face. "I remember that she didn't look like a drunk or like she was on drugs. Her clothes were clean and she just looked down on her luck and miserable," he told the *Sunday Tribune*. "When I saw the garda picture of her after she died, I recognised the two moles on her face immediately, and it was the clincher. I didn't speak to her. I sometimes take pictures of people who are unaware they are being photographed."

Gillespie checked his photos and then contacted gardaí as he was sure it was the same woman. The officer took a note of what he said and his contact details and said someone would be in touch. Four days later, Gillespie went on holiday to France. A week into his trip, he received a call from gardaí at Cabra asking him to send them the photographs as soon as possible. "Luckily, I had the memory card with the photos on them and was able to email them. When I got back, I had to make a statement to gardaí about it. I wasn't aware there was a reward offered until I got back." He later received €500 out of the €10,000 reward offered by

Crimestoppers for providing gardaí with the last known photo of Eugenia when she was alive. Several other people also received money for assisting with her identification.

By the time gardaí had received Gillespie's pictures, a liaison officer with the Romanian community in Ireland had already seen the photographs gardaí released and recognised Eugenia. She had come into contact with her since her arrival in Ireland 14 months previously. She contacted the detectives, who then contacted the authorities in Romania. DNA samples were taken from her son and daughter and flown to Ireland to be cross-checked with DNA from the dead woman. Ten days after she was found dead, Eugenia Bratis's identity was finally confirmed.

Her family in Romania were devastated by the news. The garda investigation then began to gather pace and tracing her last movements became of paramount importance. Julian Gillespie's photos became significant in assisting gardaí in the second part of the investigation. The first phase of the garda probe was largely focused on identifying Eugenia. But a challenge to solving this case has been that as Eugenia was not identified for ten days, this time lapse has made it all the more difficult for gardaí to establish suspects and trace their movements. Gardaí were anxious to find out as much about Eugenia's life in Dublin as quickly as possible. Through enquiries and intelligence, they discovered that she largely kept to herself but that she did have some friends within the Roma community. With the help of interpreters, gardaí began to interview as many members of the Roma community as possible. Some of these people were helpful to gardaí, but others were not inclined to speak to investigating officers at all. Part of the reason for this was that some Romas had an inherent mistrust of gardaí because of their past experiences with police in Romania and other countries. But there was more to it than that. While investigating detectives stress that possible motives for her killing remain wide open, whether members of the Roma community may have murdered Eugenia following a botched robbery had become one main line of enquiry.

Gardaí learned that some of the Roma community were unhappy about where Eugenia chose to beg for money. She often